The Literature of Cinema

THE LITERATURE OF CINEMA presents
a comprehensive selection from the multitude
of writings about cinema, rediscovering ma-
terials on its origins, history, theoretical principles and techniques, aesthetics, economics,
and effects on societies and individuals. Included are works of inherent, lasting merit
and others of primarily historical significance.
These provide essential resources for serious
study and critical enjoyment of the "magic
shadows" that became one of the decisive cultural forces of modern times.

FILM *and* THEATRE

by

ALLARDYCE NICOLL

PROFESSOR OF THE HISTORY OF DRAMA
YALE UNIVERSITY

ARNO PRESS & THE NEW YORK TIMES

NEW YORK • 1972

Reprint Edition 1972 by Arno Press Inc.

Reprinted by permission of Allardyce Nicoll
Reprinted from a copy in The British Film
   Institute Library
LC# 77-169335
ISBN 0-405-03902-6

The Literature of Cinema - Series II
ISBN for complete set: 0-405-03887-9
See last pages of this volume for titles.

Manufactured in the United States of America

FILM AND THEATRE

FILM *and* THEATRE

by

ALLARDYCE NICOLL

GEORGE G. HARRAP & COMPANY, Ltd.

LONDON · BOMBAY · SIDNEY

To

MY WIFE,

WHO, THROUGH HER ADVICE AND ENCOURAGEMENT,

IS PART-AUTHOR OF THIS BOOK

PREFACE

This book has been written equally in the service of the theatre and in that of the film. Now that the first excitement attendant upon the cinema's growth has passed away, there seems to have come a time when we ought to pause and consider the position which the theatre must occupy during the years immediately to follow, in the midst of conditions essentially divergent from those prevailing three decades ago. During the course of those thirty years the film has slowly and with infinite labour been discovering its true field of expression. The more strenuous tasks completed, we have just arrived at a period when this field can be analysed calmly and its value assessed, when, too, it is possible, by comparison with cinematic aims, to clarify and determine the essentials, aims and methods which it seems the theatre's business to pursue.

The film library, as a glance at the bibliography to this volume will indicate, has grown of recent years to considerable dimensions, and among the hundreds of books published are several which have essayed to outline the aesthetics of the art of the film. In all of these much of genuine significance is to be discovered, but, while some among them are concerned with merely a single series of problems and so are limited in their scope, others are over-elaborated; nor has any great effort been made in either the former or the latter to discuss the theatre in its relation to the film. Much, therefore, remains to be done in this field, and, as in the field of theatre aesthetics, no doubt fresh aspects of the subject will constantly be discovered, even after the ground has been surveyed. In this book, I have sought to do merely two things—first, to present, in as simple and unelaborated a manner as possible, what appear to be the basic principles underlying artistic expression in the film, and, secondly, to relate that form of expression to the familiar art of the stage.

The attempt thus to establish basic principles is necessarily fraught with many difficulties, not least among which is the problem of how to exemplify the various arguments introduced. Mere descriptions culled from hundreds of films, many of which the reader will not have seen, are apt to prove but dull reading, and yet clearly it is necessary to point to specific instances when discussing any aspect of film craft. In preparing the following chapters, I have sought to avoid multiplication of such instances and to select such as proved absolutely essential from a limited number of recent films likely to be familiar to all. This procedure, it is hoped, will make the arguments clearer than they would have been had they been overloaded with verbal descriptions of diverse scenes and episodes culled from a larger variety of films.

The bibliography presented in the appendix, although not exhaustive, is, I believe, the first attempt made to survey in any fulness the entire scope of writings on the cinema. In several volumes, of course, have appeared brief reading lists, but hardly any of these have proceeded beyond the mentioning of a few dozen books. The present bibliography includes over a thousand titles; numerous omissions there must be, but I trust that this list will serve to provide a basis on which a completer and still more comprehensive survey may be built.

That, indeed, is the aim of the entire volume. The title

might have been "An Introduction to the Theory of the Cinema," theory being interpreted not as something separate from practice but that on which genuinely effective practice must be based. To determine that theory is no easy task, for even on the theory of the theatre, thousands of years after Aristotle, there is still much to be said. If, however, final judgments cannot yet be reached, at least an essay in their direction may be made.

Quotations from *A Tale of Two Cities* (screen-play by W. P. Lipscomb and S. N. Behrman) are given with the kind permission of Metro-Goldwyn-Mayer, from Rudolf Besier's *The Barretts of Wimpole Street* (screen-play by Ernest Vajda and Claudine West) by that of Little Brown & Co., and from Noel Coward's *Private Lives* (screen-play by Hans Kraly, Richard Schayer and Claudine West) by that of Doubleday, Doran & Co. All these screen-plays were produced by Metro-Goldwyn-Mayer. I wish to thank Mr. Brooks Atkinson, dramatic critic of *The New York Times,* for generously devoting time to the reading of the proofs.

Obviously, any writer on a subject of this kind must be indebted to the work of others. Rotha, Seldes, Pudovkin and others have contributed much of significance to cinematic theory; and a great deal of value is incorporated in the pages of such journals as *Intercine, Experimental Cinema* and *The Cinema Quarterly.* I regret that Spottiswoode's *A Grammar of the Film* came to my attention only after the proofs of this volume were in page form; to several of his conclusions I should have wished to make reference.

New Haven, Conn.
January, 1936.

CONTENTS

1

SHAKESPEARE AND THE CINEMA

THE cinema," remarks R. D. Charques in an essay on *The Future of Talking Films* contributed to *The Fortnightly Review,* "is designed to be popular, not to fathom new depths of artistic expression."

This judgment is a typical one and might easily find a hundred parallels. With wearisome reiteration we are informed that the cinema is an industry, not an art; and current denunciation of the weekly fare provided by the studios still forms a familiar theme in review and conversation. That that denunciation has ample justification no one may deny, nor is there the possibility of refuting the assertion that the whole sphere of film production is organised on a purely industrial basis. Yet the subject demands more thought and subtler attention than can be afforded by the mere repetition of catch-phrases. Were we to make a simple substitution of "theatre" for cinema in Mr. Charques' statement or declare that the theatre was an industry we should certainly be expressing a truth, but at once we should realise that that very truth created an erroneous impression precisely because it expressed but half of a required whole. The theatre is designed to be popular, no doubt, and no one constrains the playwright to fathom new depths of artistic expression, but the fact remains that out of its popularity grows strength and that the depths of artistic expression are constantly being plumbed by adventurous dramatists. Broadway's theatres are industries, certainly, yet a *Winterset,* a *Mary of Scotland,* a *Petrified Forest* emerges out of the efforts of commercialism.

But, it may be said, the film so far has not given us a *Winterset;* in vain we wait for something which shall be as vividly arresting and as profoundly searching as those things which the theatre has had to give us. This judgment too is eminently just, yet again the impression conveyed by it seems erroneous because it is not complete. The drama has lived now for nearly two thousand five hundred years. During that course of time traditions have been established and achievement has been built upon achievement; time there has been for the appearance of those masters who have given to the stage its eminence among the arts. Only a bare thirty years have elapsed since the first narrative film made its humble and hesitant bow to the public; only a few years have passed by since the introduction of speech created the typical film product of the present. What has been achieved in this form, therefore, has come within a period which is but a fraction of the theatre's scope of existence. Every pronouncement concerning the cinema ought clearly to be framed with full appreciation of this fact.

Nor is this all. Suppose for a moment that we were to pick up a book by a critic-historian and, opening it, cast our eyes over a passage containing a summary description of some form of entertainment popular at a certain time. "This form of entertainment," we might read,

was a thing of almost mushroom growth, having a valid tradition which extended over no more than a few decades. It delighted a motley audience in which the poorer and least educated classes predominated over the richer and more cultured. By many men with sincerely held critical beliefs and high literary aspirations it was utterly condemned—condemned because it sped from episode to episode, because it introduced a vast amount of farcical buffoonery, because it exploited freely the sensational, the trivially novel and the vicious, because it had an evil effect upon the youth of its time. In this form of entertainment the writers of the scripts were hampered and disturbed by many restrictions. Their work was not regarded seriously as an exercise in art; indeed, they themselves paid no attention to it after it had served its immediate purpose— the securing of some money. Having written, they might see their creations altered, torn apart, added to, and frequently, because of the necessity of providing material in clamorous haste, they were forced to call in the aid of coadjutors or else these coadjutors were thrust upon them from without. The necessity of haste, too, made them careless. Parasitically, they would snatch plot material from any source open to them— from earlier plays, from plays by their contemporaries, from novels, from biographies. Heedless of historical accuracy, they would travesty events narrated from the past, making a brave soldier into a poltroon and a wise monarch into a timorous fool, satisfied if only their efforts won popular esteem. From current crimes they would build their plots; but slender attention would they pay to the finer shadings of character or of theme, and inartistically would permit inconsistencies or absurdities to blot their best scenes. All this they would do with open eyes, for they knew that their audience was not subtly critical and that, in any case, a clownish comedian might insist on tumbling into any one of their serious scenes or a bombastically egotistic tragic actor compel them to insert additional material calculated to render the hero's role a trifle more adipose. Above all, they were aware that their created work, once paid for by the management, ceased to be their property, might be used in any way that that management saw fit and was not likely, save in exceptional circumstances, to view the light of day in printed form. As for the management itself, these writers of scripts realised that frequently it consisted of men who, starting their careers as costumiers or pawnbrokers or money-lenders, had taken up this form of entertainment from purely commercial motives and therefore were intent only on what the box-office receipts testified to be of immediate appeal.

This picture so painted by our critic-historian we may, perhaps, imagine that we instantly recognise. Nothing else, we may say, could have been intended by these words than the film. The writers of scripts are, of course, the authors of the screen-plays, the Hollywood magnates are the managers, and the clownish comedian is today's popular farceur.

First assumptions, however, are not always impeccable. Actually, the critic-historian was supposed to be delineating the conditions operative, not in a twentieth-century studio, but on the sixteenth-century stage; the form of entertainment in his mind was presumed to be, not the film, but the Elizabethan drama. Despised and condemned by cultured men who followed the lead of Sir Philip Sidney, dominated by those clowns to whom Shakespeare made slighting reference in *Hamlet,* dominated too by strutting tragedians, controlled often by illiterate money-lenders like Philip Henslowe, the dramatists forced (that they might earn the wherewithal to live) to turn out scores of plays and to watch these plays re-vamped by others—the Elizabethan theatre and its conditions of existence have been presented in this passage by no means in a distorted manner. Sidney said as severe things of "our Tragedies, and Comedies, (not without cause cried out against,) observing rules, neyther of honest civilitie, nor of skilfull Poetrie". Bitterly he attacked their violent change of scene and constant bustle, their fantastic plots and their extended action. Above all "these grosse absurdities," he marvelled

how all theyr Playes be neither right Tragedies, nor right
Comedies: mingling Kings and Clownes, not because the matter so carrieth it: but thrust in Clownes by head and shoulders,
to play a part in majesticall matters, with neither decencie, nor
discretion.

"Horn-pypes and Funeralls" he found here intermingled:

So falleth it out, that having indeed no right Comedy, in that
comicall part of our Tragedy, we have nothing but scurrility,
unworthy of any chaste eares: or some extreame shew of doltish-
ness, indeed fit to lift up a loude laughter, and nothing els. . . .

The sixteenth century public was a motley one and the
stage commercial, by its profits attracting to it many men
in no wise talented dramatically or otherwise eager to serve
the theatre's cause. Amid such conditions Shakespeare's
masterpieces were produced, in circumstances which would
have been likely to drive any modern playwright, distracted
and in protest, to some other sphere of literary activity.

For the late sixteenth century, the Elizabethan stage occupied a position by no means dissimilar to that taken in our
own times by the cinema.

OPPOSITION TO THE FILM

A realisation of this fact gives us to pause. So familiar
have we become with the complaint that the composite
authorship practised in the studios denies any possibility
of individual expression and of artistic growth; the film itself has become so common and so cheap a form of entertainment; and the records, true or false, of managerial
incompetence and illiteracy have been so bruited abroad
in current gossip, in newspaper paragraphs and in satirical
farces; that the cinema, where it has not been completely

condemned and despised, has been accepted merely as a thing which might make an hour pass easily, with no thought of its artistic possibilities. Lovers of the theatre are constantly seeing in it the cause of the drama's decline, and, noting the way in which the film has filched stage successes from every land, have denominated it fundamentally parasitic in its aims and in its methods. Horror of Hollywood and trembling at Elstree have possessed their beings, so that, while the film has been progressing rapidly and surely in popular esteem, it has remained outside the critical attention of many among those who have the good of the theatre at heart. At most a few individual films—*Little Women, David Copperfield* and *Les Miserables* among recent showings, *City Lights* and *The Gold Rush* among those of former years—have been, rather unwillingly, accepted and to these praise has been meted out sparingly, and often erroneously, for where the film accepted has been based on a novel, this praise has been given almost solely on the basis of faithfulness to the original work of fiction. That a filmic *David Copperfield* or *Little Women* could stand alone in the same way that an Elizabethan play stands apart from some Italian *novella* out of which its plot has been fashioned—that is a thought which hardly ever has come to such critics of the cinema. If *David Copperfield* has omitted one beloved character, the attack on that account far outweighs any mild approbation of clever renderings, and W. C. Fields is assessed, not as the impersonator of an independent filmic Micawber, but as the reproducer and animator of a set of Victorian illustrations.

Usually, however, the theatre lovers join forces with the moralists in belabouring and trouncing the entire cinematic machinery. Allowing for the disappearance of that stern religious enthusiasm which fired the hearts and made bitter the tongues of the Elizabethan sermonisers, we may perhaps see a fairly close connection between the opponents of the stage in the sixteenth century and the twentieth-century opponents of the film. Of hard words and of what is more galling than hard words—contempt, both have accorded much. Even if we neglect those who, for religious and moral reasons, seek to deflect their charges from doors that, in their opinion, open the way to the underworld (of gangsters or of devils), we realise that, although the film has become one of the most familiar and potent forces in modern life, comparatively little attention has been paid to its aims, its positive achievements and its potentialities by those more serious spectators from whose aid it might most have profited.

Nor, indeed, have there been wanting from within the ranks of the industry itself just such comments as Philip Henslowe, violently making hay in a Marlovian and Shakespearian sun, might have uttered in some Elizabethan tavern. Invited to lecture at New York University, Howard S. Cullman, director of the Roxy Theatre, recently took for his text "Why the motion pictures are not an art." Emphasising the fact that the films he chooses are selected, not on any aesthetic grounds but solely on account of their box-office values, he consequently deems that any "aesthetic" considerations are foolish and otiose. "As we sit in our projection room," he says, "we are more like shoe buyers looking over the Fall line than connoisseurs inspecting works of art. For the fact is that we, along with the shoe buyers, have only one thought uppermost—will the public pay its money for this article?" The ordinary commercial film he therefore assumes is to be regarded as if it were a mere object of merchandise. Interestingly, he seems to opine that the opposite of "aesthetic" is "democratic" and that by the former is signified solely the art of Greece:—

Certainly, the screen is a backward art—a super tabloid for young and old, moron and genius. Her sister Muses are the comic strips, the pulp magazines, the radio and all other forms of entertainment based on democratic rather than aesthetic principles. No one . . . wastes much time deploring the fact that Mickey Mouse is not patterned along classic Greek lines.

THE PURISTS

Unfortunately, a similar attitude has been adopted by a large number of genuine film lovers. Acting as Sir Philip Sidney did in the great days of the Elizabethan stage, they decry the popularly successful and plead for the esoteric. In 1595, when Shakespeare was reaching his maturity, there were two groups which attacked the public theatres—first, the religious enthusiasts and the civic authorities who would, had the power been granted them, have banished all the players and sternly closed their houses of entertainment, and second, the literary exquisites. The former, with their insistence upon the "corruption of youth with incontinence and lewdness" and upon the "great wasting both of the time and thrift of many poor people," sound a note familiar enough today; Shakespeare's Cleopatra, now become an examination question for school-children, once was regarded as more recent moralists regard the Cleopatra of De Mille. These, however, need not greatly concern us: more important are the littérateurs. For Sir Philip Sidney and those who thought with him, the drama was a fine thing and fit to be prized, but the contemporay play was not. In the grip of rude forces, the popular stage, they opined, was degrading the muses Thalia and Melpomene. Loving them in spite of their degradation, these men sought to encourage a purer form of artistic expression in dramatic terms. The chill, but regularly faultless and conventional, academic dramas, acted by students and gentlemen, not for hire but for their own amusement and edification, were their ideal. They esteemed the historically interesting but lifeless *Gorboduc* beyond any of the successful plays presented in the public theatres and ever aimed at stripping the stage of those meretricious ornaments which appealed to the idle and uncritical fancies of the crowd.

How closely allied were Sidney's views to those of some modern theorists becomes amply apparent when we turn from his strictures on the stage of his time to the writings of men belonging to the French "cinéma d'avant-garde". His contempt of the crowd is echoed there:—

Le film d'avant-garde ne s'adresse pas au simple plaisir de la foule. Il est à la fois, plus égoïste et plus altruiste. Égoïste, puisque manifestation personelle d'une pensée pure; altruiste, puisque dégagé de tout souci autre que le progrès.

There too resounds Sidney's objection to the stage's commercialism:

Le cinéma est un art et une industrie. Considéré sous l'angle artistique, il doit défendre jalousement la pureté de son expression, et ne jamais la travestir pour convaincre. Mais il est aussi industrie. Pour réaliser un film et le répandre, il faut de l'argent, beaucoup d'argent. La pellicule sur laquelle s'imprime l'image est chère, les traitements qu'elle subit, coûteux. En soi, chaque élément visuel ou sonore employé correspond à un chiffre et à des débours fixes. L'électricité nécessitée par un bel effet de lumière, ne s'obtient que contre monnaie, et aussi, l'objectif qui l'enregistre, par example. L'énumération se poursouivant risquerait d'être longue.

L'industrie du cinéma produit les films commerciaux, c'est-à-dire les films composés avec le souci de toucher la grande masse, et les films mercantiles. Il faut entendre par films mercantiles ceux qui, se soumettant à toutes les concessions, poursuivent un simple but financier et par films commerciaux ceux qui, s'emparant au mieux de l'expression et de la technique cinématographiques, produisent parfois des oeuvres intéressantes tout en visant des gains justifiés.

And as the result there comes the demand for a "purity" corresponding to Sidney's praise of the simple, conventionalised classic type of play, formal in its proportions and, by the use of chorus or other devices, far removed from the bustling adventure of life.

For consideration of their attitude nothing more is required than a realisation of the fact that the theatre has ever discovered its true strength in the addressing of large and representative audiences. Sophocles gained power from the vast body of Athenian citizens who filled the theatre of Dionysus for his *Œdipus Rex,* and to Shakespeare came vigor and vitality from the crowds of London citizens who flocked to the Globe playhouse, there to witness and to welcome a *Hamlet* and a *Twelfth Night.* The cinema in this may be regarded in a light no different from that in which we view the stage. The crowd's judgments, it is true, are often fickle and erratic; but that is a condition which all who practice these arts must accept. No doubt it is disturbing to find the same people hailing *Emperor Jones* and *Abie's Irish Rose* with kindred enthusiasm; no doubt we shudder and marvel to think that a profound

Hamlet and a dull *Mucedorus* tied for pride of place about the year 1600; but so the theatre is made and in such conditions we must rest content. After all, in every art form there are essential premises which must be agreed to before anything of creative value is produced. If you wish to be a dramatist you must be prepared to write for the established theatres of your day; and if you esteem the cinema and believe it to be an art you must be prepared to discover that art among the commercial films of Elstree and of Hollywood, calculated to appeal to the public at large.

THE COMMERCIAL FILM

Precisely here, of course, many men stumble, hesitate and retreat. No art exists, they cry, in Hollywood, nor may it ever be supposed by intelligent observers that any art can ever be dreamed to endure there. Let us but look impartially, they argue, at the fare provided in the picture-houses of today: unless we would be mistaken for insensible fools, how can we speak of art in connection with such things as the cinema industry presents?

Faced with such questions, we must be frank and honest. The truth is, of course, that these men are perfectly justified in their strictures. Only an infinitesimally small proportion of the films produced in any country contains anything of real value. Trivial themes, unimaginative direction, stupid voluptuousness, cheap vulgarity, incompetent performances are common, and excessively rare are the occasions when a vital thought and a moving interpretation stir us to an emotion of strength and vitality. At present, the organisation of the industry is such that the repetition of similar films is likely to continue for many years to come. That industry depends, like any other commercial undertaking, upon the public, and, while in this the cinema agrees with the theatre, the public for the film differs from a playhouse audience in that it is scattered over the whole world, numbering millions to the theatre's thousands. The stage may have one set of plays for London and New York, with another set for less sophisticated spectators in the provinces. A film, on the contrary, is supposed to be shown in Slumpton-on-the-Mud and Conger City as well as in the metropolitan "movie palaces." Unfortunately, too, more money in the end comes from the Slumpton-on-the-Muds and the Conger Cities than accrues from the larger centres. Necessarily, since profits are the immediate aim of the producing companies, there has been a determined working down to the limited intellectual capacities of the most obtuse of spectators. "Box office" has meant one thing for the stage and another for the screen.

Naturally, such an audience will be captured by novelty: and as a result many of the most significant cinematic innovations have been exploited, not in the interests of art, but in those of vulgar appeal. It was this which for so long retarded the development of the sound film; sound, having been invented, was exploited for its novelty and for nothing more. The noisier and the more blatant the performance, the better. And so, think many, it will ever be. A few fairly good films, perhaps; but for the rest little save vulgarity and nonsense—at most sufficient interest and laughter to provide a few hours' distracting entertainment, promptly to be forgotten. The film, they opine, must ever be compelled by its destiny to favor the worst. The crowd loves sensation, and accordingly the cinema will pass from sensationalism to sensationalism, running airmen till the public tires of airmen, sentimentalising gangsters till social conscience calls a halt, thereupon turning to extol the forces of the law in terms equally absurd.

A further complaint may be made. As a result of this many-headed public the star is made to occupy a wholly disproportionate position. That the mass of spectators adore a star cannot be questioned, and many a bad film has been saved by stellar attraction. To blame any producing company for catering to the public in this respect is difficult, but if we do not blame we may regret and at the same time despair. The exploitation of the star by clever advertising agents may be all to the good, commercially, but it seems to render the possibilities of artistic development hard, if not impossible. Seeing the force of these star-films and noting how much the public will accept if only a popular figure (in as much undress as may be) is placed before it, the producers, quite understandably, have had no occasion to summon to their aid many men of higher ideals for cinematic progress. The tendency, indeed, has been to make any such men who have mistakenly been given contracts to speak down to the levels of Slumpton-on-the-Mud and Conger City. "We speak another language here," was the overheard comment of one such man in a studio, "I've just had all my three-syllabled words removed." What need of art, when art, so far from encouraging success, is likely to antagonise the factory girls who feed on *Peg's Weekly* and the vacuous country bumpkins whose sixpences and dimes, carefully tended, make Hollywood's and Elstree's millions?

Other objections may readily be brought forward. In Russia, Pudovkin and Eisenstein insist on doing their own cutting; if that privilege were denied them, they would claim that, as artist-directors, the entire basis of their efforts would be reft away. Among commercial producing companies, however, the director who insists on cutting his own films is rare indeed. For this process a specially trained technician is employed. To him are sent the yards upon yards of celluloid which represent the work achieved in studio or on lot; his the duty to cut this down to manageable proportions. In the composition of any one film, therefore, many men take part. The original story is written by one; a scenario is prepared by another; a third adds dialogue and builds the screen play. From a dozen different quarters come suggestions, and these suggestions, often illogically and inartistically, are inserted in the text. This patchwork goes to the director, who starts to turn the verbally indicated stage business into visual images. Then comes the cutter, whose duty it is to reduce this material in accordance with his trained judgment concerning popular values. How, the opponents of the cinema enquire again, how can an art flourish under these conditions? The producer is nominally in control, and nominally there is one person (or several persons working in loose collaboration) in charge of the composition of the screen play; but in actual practice the author may see his work so transmogrified that it will bear no likeness to what he originally planned, while the director betrays a lack of appreciation regarding his own artistic mission, according to the Pudovkin theory, by delegating the most important part of his duties to another.

Maybe this delegation of duty is determined by other conditions, for, beyond the studio cutter, is a force more inimical still to the hope of artistic composition. The Censor, intangible presence, god-like in his majesty and yet immanent in a thousand human bodies, stands over each

completed studio film. Boards of judgment, sometimes composed of foolishly insensitive members, sit in conclave and,
with severe orders, slash and alter. What may proceed as
a unity from the producing company can well become a
maimed and bleeding victim when presented on the public
screen. Is there anything which can be said for this form
of entertainment, considered as an art, when all these
adverse conditions are present to operate against it?

The count is made and the decision seems inevitable.
The average film of the day is trivial in theme and often
vulgar in expression; that we cannot deny. Yet again a
doubt enters. Exactly in this way did Sidney speak a few
years before Shakespeare entered the service of the Lord
Chamberlain's players; and his error teaches us caution.
In Sidney's time a new theatre had barely been born. Dependent though the Elizabethan stage may be on medieval
achievements in the realm of the mystery play and the
comic interlude, fundamentally it started afresh and discovered its own life-force with the first regular comedies
and tragedies written shortly after the middle of the sixteenth century. Within thirty years Shakespeare had
arrived, but Sidney, penning his words immediately before
his advent, was impatient, expected too much and failed to
appreciate the signs already apparent in his time.

Nor was it that external conditions improved out of all
recognition within the intervening space of twenty or
thirty years. Shakespeare wrote for the same audience—a
general and many-headed audience—for the stinkards in
the yard as well as for the gentlemen in the sixpenny boxes.
The public was avid of novelty and sensationalism, de-
lighting mightily in the gory horrors of a *Titus Androni-
cus;* the theatrical managers exploited freely whatever

came uppermost at the moment, heaping ghosts upon the stage while the going of ghosts was good and mad ladies in white linen when ghosts began to pall; stars ruled the boards and a clownish Kemp or a bombastic Burbage demanded fat parts for the proper portrayal of his personality; considerations of art were left to the universities and little was aimed at on the public stage save immediate success; and over all stood the iron censor with his bowl of ink. Yet Shakespeare wrote.

Instead of recognising that the tradition of this dramatic form was short, instead of trying to enquire how the popular stage might be improved, Sidney condemned it utterly because of its apparent follies and inefficiencies; instead of endeavoring to encourage it by helpful prognostication, he attempted to kill it by means of immediate ridicule. Clearly, the caution we learn from an historical consideration of his failure correctly to assess the possibilities inherent in the theatre of his time demands that we, before judging the achievements of the film, should examine, briefly at least, the positive results so far brought forward, viewing these against the period of time during which the cinema has been free to develop.

THE FILM'S PROGRESS

Any elaborate historical analysis would obviously be out of place in a book of this kind, and in any case the story of the cinema's development has been narrated more than once; but at least the enumerating of a few landmarks is obligatory for making the ensuing arguments clear. The basis of a film is the photograph, and photography is an invention of the nineteenth century; nor was it until many decades had passed that the process of photography developed such technical resources as to make it serviceable for the, yet unborn, cinema. The old glass plate was useless for cinematic purposes, and, although we may hail Nicéphore Niepce for his epoch-making image of 1822 and laud Louis Jacques Daguerre for his elaboration of technical method, to George Eastman goes the credit of laying the material foundation of the film by substituting strips of emulsion-coated celluloid for the plates of glass hitherto employed.

While the photograph, of course, forms the basis, the idea of projection provides a second cardinal element in the creation of the cinematic image. This idea of projection has a certain respectable antiquity and even the seventeenth century knew of the "lucernam magicam et thaumaturgam," the "magic lantern" so dear to our childhood and still the delight of indolent lecturers; but it was not until fairly late in the development of photography that the images secured thereby were applied as objects suitable for being thrown on the screen. Once the combination of magic lantern and of photograph was secured, however, the cinema remained not far distant.

The third element in the cinema's structure is, obviously, the presence of an image which, in contradistinction to that in an ordinary photographic positive or that in a projection by means of a magic lantern, gives a semblance of movement. Some fantastically opine that the Egyptians possessed the secret when they painted a series of dancing figures on their walls, but only in the phenakistoscope of the nineteenth century can we trace an appreciation, crude though it may be, of the principles involved in the films of today. The phenakistoscope is that cylinder, once so familiar, with slots through which one looked at a strip of figures revolving and thus seemingly assuming movement.

These three elements, then—the photographic image on celluloid, the idea of photographic projection and the conception of simulated movement by means of a series of pictures in successive stages of motional development—although possibly adumbrated many centuries ago, are essentially less than a hundred years old; while the combination of the three in cinematic form cannot be dated back beyond a period about fifty years distant. To whom precisely the credit should go—for there are conflicting claims—the fact remains that the first fragmentary "motion pictures" did not appear till the year 1889, and only in 1895 did Lumière present his first short film-strip of workers leaving his factory. In 1895 and 1896, however, things really began to progress. Lumière added to his collection several films each from twenty four to fifty feet long; what was apparently the first "picture-house" opened in the basement of the Grand Café in the Boulevard des Capucines; and Edison showed, as a novelty at the close of a vaudeville program, a short section of experimental film.

Once discovered, however, the cinema had to wait for further development. Eight years elapsed before the first attempt was made to tell a story by this method. Fundamentally, then, the cinematic form as we know it is little more than thirty years old; and it must be observed that for at least another decade it remained nothing but a toy and a novelty in the hands of the curious. No doubt many important experiments were being made and many inventions introduced, but up to the year 1914 the cinema was hardly taken seriously by anyone save the technicians. These men, certainly, worked hard; improvement in the film itself, in the cinematic cameras, in the projectors came rapidly; although it is to be observed that only now are we beginning to feel that we have reached a certain stage of excellence. A film made even a few years ago seems to our eyes crude and imperfect; nowadays a certain assurance, at least, there is that our uncoloured films will not appear overcrude and harsh if they are revived in the year 1946. So far the cinema has been but feeling its way; until comparatively recently every year was bringing improvements which made the last year's films appear ridiculous.

A fresh step was taken by the Italian production of *Quo Vadis* in 1913 and by the American production of *The Birth of a Nation* the following year. From this time only did some men begin to take the cinema seriously and attempt an exploration of its potentialities. Such activity, however, was severely retarded by the outbreak of war, which served to prevent further European development and made Hollywood almost the sole centre of film-producing. In frantic and ever accelerating haste film after film was prepared to feed the growing demand. On the cessation of hostilities other countries started to organise or reorganise their studios, endeavouring to catch up with the American lead, and a new era began. The cinema had now fully captured the interested attention of the public; tentative essays started to appear on critical questions and a kind of theory concerning this cinematic art took gradual shape. Surveying the field from our vantage point in the thirties, we must agree that, both technically and artistically, the rate of progress from 1903 to 1914 or from 1914 to 1926 has hardly been equalled by any other manifestation of man's creative ability.

This rate of progress, however, remarkable though it was, proved as nothing to that with which the sound film developed from 1926 to 1935, a brief span of nine years.

Let anyone cast his mind back to the first experiments in this form, to Al Jolson's *The Singing Fool* and *The Jazz Singer,* and compare such films with any half dozen presented during the season 1935-1936 and he will realise what vast tracts of territory have been covered. This, too, in spite of the fact that almost all the young theorists of the silent film condemned the infant as bastard. Stalwartly entrenched in their opinions, they declared that, while the silent film had the fundamentals of a distinct and separate art, the sound film, ruining what with such travail had been so hardly won, was naught save an illegitimate and consequently worthless form. They ridiculed, and rightly, the extraordinarily bad vocal accompaniments, forgetting that this device was only in its infancy and that the silent film itself, not so many years distant, had been equally stupid and unruly. For the public, however, surer in its tastes though less articulate, the new form had come to stay. Hollywood was set ascrambling in its haste to convert old silents into new "talkies" and to find means of improving the reproduction of sound. Confusion, for a time, reigned predominant; indeed, only after a period of four or five years had elapsed—say from 1926 to 1931—did this atmosphere of stress and turmoil begin to subside. Barely five years thus far have been granted for the comparatively leisured production of adequate sound films.

Taking all these things into account, we must be forced to credit it truly extraordinary that in so brief a space of time, under commercial conditions which drew to Hollywood thousands in search of millions, with no traditions from which to draw strength and necessarily calling on the service of stage artists who, suspicious and contemptuous of this new device, were too indifferent carefully and honestly to study its technique, the film has succeeded in presenting us with such diverse examples as *The Private Life of Henry the Eighth, The House of Rothschild, Queen Christina, Catherine of Russia, Little Women, David Copperfield, The Story of Pasteur, The Informer, Man of Aran.* These are but a few titles from among several score of films which, even though all are manifestly but tentative in their approach, may honestly be regarded worthy of our esteem.

No end, no culmination, has so far been reached. The films mentioned above, and others such as *Chapayev* or *Thunder over Mexico,* only mark the beginnings of something vastly more powerful in the realm of the narrative film. Even technically the possibilities have not been fully explored. The new colour-process which, in full-length form, has been officially launched with *Becky Sharp.* may open up a field of breadth and excitement equivalent to that revealed by the introduction of sound. It is a brave world of technical invention we live in, and its bravery, even though at times it may become absurd and lead towards strange situations or foolish predicaments, deserves, not superior ridicule, but sincerest appreciation.

And appreciation means more than refraining from contempt or even than a mildly indifferent welcome extended to what seems better than most. True appreciation may be derived only from adequate knowledge; it is born of emotional acceptance and of intellectual analysis. Until we decide for ourselves what we want of an art we can never reach anything approaching this appreciation; at the best our judgments will be fumbling and insecure. Nor can we ever reach it if our basic assumptions are false; we cannot dream of appreciating any work of pictorial art if we believe that the painter's object should be merely to present a reproduction of reality. Still further, our appreciation will be limited unless we endeavor to gain some knowledge of the methods at the command of the artists and of the peculiar functions possessed by these methods; no true recognition of watercolour values is attainable until we know what watercolour, in contradistinction to oils, may hope to achieve. To assume, as many still seem to do, that the film is at its best merely a two-dimensional copy, with variations, of a stage performance or of a scene in life results in a prejudicing of appreciation; and a lack of questioning investigation into the means available to director and cameraman will leave unobserved many things out of which a film is built.

The cinema is even yet in a process of development, that is true; but at the stage it has now reached, some approximation at least may be made towards formulating a theory of its artistic aims and of its positive achievements. Placing ourselves there, in company with those who watched the early development of the Elizabethan drama, with all the predecessors of Shakespeare, each of whom in his own way and without any complete success was building a foundation for one greater than himself, we owe it to this new thing that is among us, this new thing concerning which so many hard words are still being said, that we should honestly consider its fundamental principles and endeavor to assess its potentialities.

THEATRE AND CINEMA

In this consideration, clearly it were useless to waste time upon filmic material which is manifestly trivial or worthless. No writer on dramatic theory would be expected to spend time with the thousands of ephemeral farces and of luridly sensational melodramas which once fretted an hour upon the stage; an historian might be called upon to deal with these, but for purposes of theoretical consideration only those plays which exhibited genuinely artistic qualities would be deemed serviceable. The dramatic critic, moreover, would not be asked to condemn these farces and melodramas, even in general terms; the theatre that produced *The Clouds, Œdipus Rex, King Lear* and *Twelfth Night* is not lessened in esteem because it also gave birth to *Içi on parle français* and *Bluebeard*.

The examination, then, of filmic aims and methods need take no account of the currently valueless; nor need this rejection of the worthless induce the supposition that therefore all connected with the cinema is praised. Concentration may be made upon the few significant films without in any wise misconceiving the quality of the average product. These few significant films bear to the entire cinematic output the relationship borne to the entire theatre of those hundred odd plays which we recognise as true dramatic masterpieces, or rather, since the cinema is but young and has had little time for the development of masterpieces, they may be regarded as forerunners of something more genuinely creative and harmoniously conceived to come.

To attempt an estimation of the potentially artistic value of the cinema, accordingly, should not confuse us into exaggerated glorification of what has hitherto been achieved, nor should it in any way create misapprehension concerning the proper functions of screen and stage. Belief in the future growth of an artistic, penetrating and emotionally arresting cinema is not antagonistic to an equally firm belief in the future development of the theatre.

The more we clarify our minds concerning the true objects of the film the greater likelihood there is that we shall thereby aid the stage into understanding its proper place in modern conditions.

And first of all, we ought to rid our minds of the fear that the cinema may kill the theatre. The theatre is not a thing easily to be destroyed. For these two thousand five hundred years it has endured, endured in ages of indifference and in ages of hostility, ever preserving latent vitality which it has always shown itself ready to display whenever the time arrived for a period of blossoming. Over many years when the delights of the arena attracted all men's eyes it retained its life-force; during periods when all thinking men condemned it utterly and sought its complete overthrow, it persisted in its clutch upon life. To assume that the mere advent of the cinema will prove its ruin and to weep anticipatory tears over its supposed corse is to overlook the lessons of history: far worse rivals than the cinema have confronted the theatre in the past, and the theatre has preserved its vitality still.

The truth is, of course, that, although the cinema and the theatre have many things in common, they represent distinct and separate means of expression and that, once we have passed by the period when the younger form has, imitatively, been forced to rely on the achievements of the elder, there will come a time when the two will settle down to pursuing their own independent paths. Novel and drama have similarly been confused in the past, and we can easily see that several of the Elizabethan dramatists were not sure whether they were engaged in creating a play or merely in providing immediate living embodiment for some current tale. These days, however, have passed;

narrative fiction has found its own characteristic methods and the play has ceased to be disturbed by too close identification with an art separate from its own. So it is almost certain to be with the cinema. The novelty of that form, no doubt, has attracted many away from the theatre's doors, and the drama, in a frantic endeavour to regain its lost adherents, has caught at cinematic devices of various kinds, even as the film, lacking courage, has filched many an idea from the stage. Future years will assuredly remedy these conditions. Already the cinema is beginning to realise its true functions; the theatre is losing its desire frenziedly to copy the novel devices; and audiences are coming to realise that what legitimately they may expect to gain from a stage performance they will not get from attendance at the picture-house.

While the more precise distinctions between cinematic and theatrical method may conveniently be left for later discussion, it is necessary here to determine the essential differences between the two forms. To say glibly that the presence of "flesh-and-blood" actors separates the stage from the screen is apt to prove both confusing and surface-skimming; that does not provide us with the material we seek. A more essential distinction lies in the fact that, whereas the film is an established creation which remains immutable as a painting or a piece of sculpture, the theatre presents an art-form which is never precisely to be determined in its outlines. Any theatrical performance is in the process of dying as it is born; and no two performances can ever be alike. The shape it assumes is determined by two variable forces:—the performers and the audience. An actor may feel "off-colour" one night; another may have a cold; a third may have just been handed a telegram of dreadful import—and inevitably the interpretation of the lines will change, not only the lines of that individual actor but those too of his fellows with whom he is collaborating. Apart from that, we must recognise that the audience in a playhouse contributes much towards building-up the general mood value experienced during the course of a performance. Those on stage are not the only persons who act; the spectators seated in orchestra and galleries perform too, and by their improvisation during the three-hour display of the spectacle comes a corresponding improvisation on the part of the actors. Every player knows that audiences vary from chill to warm. A joke early on in a comedy that fails to arouse its expected laugh, an inopportune titter at some seriously intended line in a drama, these may serve to discolour the entire show; even failure on the part of spectators to respond adequately to an emotional scene may disrupt and disturb all the later acts.

Never may we determine precisely what will be the exact impression created by any single evening's performance in the theatre. Minutely, but none the less significantly, one such performance will vary from that which immediately preceded it and from that which is to come after. No similar improvising reaction is possible in the cinema. Certainly the presence of a crowd audience is important here too, but only in so far as the presence of that crowd influences each individual spectator. So far as the actual performance is concerned, there can be, no matter what the audience's emotions, no change in the eternally fixed record presented by the film. Thus, then, the two forms are basically divided—one impermanent and in a constant state of flux, the other permanently established and unchangeable.

From this basic difference, other deviations in method

and aim are determinable. To assess aright what exactly these are and to appreciate the need of exploiting in each form the qualities and values peculiar to its own structure and inner life, becomes of increasing importance in days when cinema and theatre seem at times to be struggling for supremacy and when in that struggle each seizes the weapons its supposed opponent knows best how to wield. In the service of the theatre and in that of the cinema alike we need apply ourselves to these questions and analyse impartially, without praise or blame, the diverse new approaches and fundamental methods presented by the film.

THE OBSTACLES

In saying that the cinema is reaching towards recognition of its true position in the world of expression, we must, of necessity, bear in mind potentialities rather than positive achievement, noting at the same time that potentiality and promise are often more interesting and more exciting than duller realisation of lesser aims. A crudely youthful Shelley, the Shelley of *Queen Mab,* is vastly to be preferred to a mature Tupper. Unfortunately, the Tupperian achievements of this life are apt to catch more of the public attention, for good or for evil, than the aberrations of struggling talent. Talent has been displayed by the film, but we are much more easily led to condemn general conditions and general results than, from an appreciation of a few significant but less immediately arresting experiments, to pattern forth finer conditions for the future.

That there are many disadvantages and difficult obstacles in the way of more powerful film creation is obvious, but signs are not wanting that changes are imminent, likely to lead towards the preparing of a more fruitful soil. Freely we admit, for example, that the present public for the film is unmanageable and that it includes a larger percentage of less intelligent elements than a typical theatre audience does or did; but one tendency of recent years we must note—the tendency towards the making of more particularised appeal. The producing companies are becoming aware of the fact that, so long as their orientation is wholly in the direction of Slumpton-on-the-Mud or Conger City, an entire body of spectators will gradually fall away from attendance at the cinemas. This maybe would not cause them much concern; but another thing, too, is being observed. The vaster unintellectual public begins to grow up mentally. Where a few years ago it would have applauded some utterly stupid film and gaped in uncomprehending wonder at a more finished production, it starts to be bored by the one and genuinely moved by the other. These two things must be taken together. The second means that the general level of the films is rising and must continue to rise; the first explains the definite effort of certain commercial companies to turn out at least a few films of richer appeal. The success of *Little Women* meant much. It meant that the producers came to realise that a well-told story, efficiently directed, could draw a larger public than a vulgarly stupendous *Cleopatra* with multitudes of sex-appeals or a foolishly bizarre *Scarlet Empress* dominated by Dietrich and demons. *The Informer* and *The Scoundrel,* however much these may have failed artistically to achieve success, marked movements decidedly in the right direction; and the courage displayed in preparing *A Midsummer Night's Dream* is relatable to the courage which inspired the making of the first talking films. To prophesy

either that the entire level of audience appreciation is going
to rise in the course of the next few years or that the producing companies will endeavour to cater for a variety of
publics were temerarious; yet such indications as have been
referred to above seem to point in this direction. Already
in London and in New York there are houses that special-
ise in particular types of film, and maybe these will make
their influence so felt in the future that efforts will deliberately be made to cater for them along with the others.

Another thing is certain. While the introduction of sound
wrought immediate havoc and obscured the vices of many
bad films, the new form is now coming to be utilised for
legitimate ends. A fresh element, certainly, has recently
been brought forward in the use of colour; but that, hap-
pily, has made its official bow (in full-length form) under
the able hands of Kenneth Macgowan and Robert Edmond
Jones, and it seems as if the turmoil of the early sound film
were to be obviated. But even if we are deluged with a
mass of ruddy colour films directed less skilfully and sensi-
tively we may be sure that soon the element of colour too
will be incorporated harmoniously with the other elements
making up the cinematic world. Already, thought is being
paid to the emotional values securable by the use of tinted
light, and pictorial colour values are being eagerly experi-
mented with. The truth, of course, is that novelty soon
wears itself out and that yesterday's marvel becomes the
commonplace of today. The time has not yet come for a
complete settling down of various disruptive constituents
of the film; but that time seems now not far distant.

The summoning of men such as Macgowan and Edmond
Jones to Hollywood indicates, too, the beginning of a new
policy. In the studios the mere craftsman who boasted his

insensibility to aesthetic values still is present; but alongside of these men grows an increasing band of men who,
without being so aloof and superior as to aim at things
beyond the comprehension of all save a select few, are
intent on bringing into the cinema something of vigour,
beauty and significance. Even a cursory comparison of the
showings during the past two seasons with those of any two
years chosen from any previous period will demonstrate
what advance the cinema has made and what achievements
have been attained.

A particularly encouraging sign has been the recent departure from complete dependence on the stage for plot
material. Eminently understandable, this dependence was
bound to be at once distracting and fettering. Already
dialogue was there to hand, and, while changes were fundamentally imperative, the presence of that dialogue often
prevented the completely fresh approach towards language
more fitting to the requirements of the screen, prevented
also the free establishment of cinematic time and space
development. One may deplore the fact that, with the
habitual herd-like attitude displayed by some of the producing companies, too great use has lately been made of
material culled from narrative fiction. Dickens, Thackeray,
Barrie, Hugo are being ransacked in a frantic endeavour to
exploit this field, and no doubt Richardson, Fielding, Jane
Austen will follow. On the other hand, material from
novels really forms a better basis for a film than material
from plays. The scope of that material is more extended
and usually there is so much of it that choice may be made
of this section or of that. Restrictive, in that knowledge
of the original novel among the members of the public
must retard the freer movement of the creative imagina-

tion, the novel yet comes closer, in its narrative method, to the cinema than does the stage, for the novel, too, can create its own time and has liberty to range whithersoever its authors will.

The next and final step, towards which some hesitating advances have already been made, will naturally be that of free and independent creation especially calculated for cinematic use. This the cinema deserves no less than the theatre. Always, no doubt, there will be room for the cinematization of some popular stage success or of some particularly effective piece of prose narrative, just as the stage has room for dramatizations on the lines of *The Old Maid, Dodsworth* and *Tobacco Road.* When, however, we think of the theatre, not on these do our minds rest; they rest on *The Silver Tassie,* on *The Petrified Forest,* on *Mary of Scotland,* on *Winterset.* Similarly, before the cinema may account itself fully mature we must be able to bring to mind, without effort and spontaneously, a great body of characteristic film-material which has found no other form of artistic expression or which, if historical in theme, has been wholly worked out in terms of camera and of screen. On the threshold of that period of maturity we now stand.

One other thing, too, is essential, or perhaps two things bound into one. As has been seen, a theatrical performance, save for the reactions it has caused in the audience, is gone as soon as it is seen and heard. Two limitations there are in the path of repeating these reactions. The first is that, insensibly yet none the less surely, one performance differs from another. Strictly we never have seen any general production of *Hamlet* or *Romeo and Juliet* or *The Petrified Forest;* all we have seen is these plays presented on particular nights. The second limitation is that revivals are comparatively rare. A selected few plays from the world's repertory will be represented occasionally, but for more than ninety nine and ninety nine hundredths per cent of the total body of plays written and produced since the time of Æschylus we can have no actual theatre experience. Over against this we have to place the fact that thousands upon thousands of plays are readily accessible in print. This is the form in which, for the most part, we know our Greek dramatists, our Shakespeares, our Ibsens, our Strindbergs. There is a large play-reading public and a modern dramatist may count on at least a fair sale for any of his plays which have proved successful on the stage. We may, therefore, easily by this means refresh our memories of what we have seen and conjure up mental pictures of what we have not been privileged to watch in stage performance. By this means a certain continuity of tradition is established; to what is essentially ephemeral is granted a permanent form and substance; for what might readily be regarded slightingly as merely an evening's amusement is provided a lineage and a dignified assurance of worth.

With these conditions may be compared the conditions operative in the world of the cinema. A film is prepared and released. First it goes to some special high-priced cinemas in the larger towns and there runs for anything from a week to a month. Then it gets handed over to other houses and descends in the social scale until it finally reaches the lowest-priced houses where it briefly occupies part of a half-weekly bill. Thereafter it vanishes completely unless some worthy film society deems it suitable, on account of its artistic interest or of its historical value, for revival. Such revivals, however, are exceedingly rare, so that all save an infinitesimally small portion of the total cinematic output disappears into a Cimmerian darkness.

Nor do we possess, at present, adequate means for refreshing our memories of productions once seen. Screen plays are but rarely published; and almost the only means readily available lies in perusal of film reviews in the files of the more serious newspapers—at the best, an opportunity of releasing faintest recollections of the original. There can be no hope of turning to the text and to the stage directions as we turn to those of a *Hamlet* or *A Doll's House*.

Before the film becomes properly established in the realm of artistic creation, these conditions must be remedied. The printing of screen-plays no doubt will come immediately the cinema starts to build up its independent stock of plots. There would be, for example, but a small demand for the film version of *The Barretts of Wimpole Street* because the stage play is easier to read and in any case must take precedence. To examine several screen-plays in comparison with original dramas might prove entertaining to some and assuredly would be of considerable critical value, but it is not a procedure for which any extended popularity could be hoped. On the other hand, once the film begins to develop its own themes, then the time will have arrived for the presentation of those themes in screen-play versions. From them one thing will be demanded—a literary style in presentation apt to convey in words what the film so largely conveys in visual images. Poetry must enter into the cinema. The situation is not unlike that operative in England during the latter years of the nineteenth century when the lack of any adequate copyright laws persuaded the dramatists to withhold their plays from the printing press. As Henry Arthur Jones saw clearly, if the habit grew of having dramas issued in book form, the theatre inevitably would gain in prestige and the authors would take greater pains in the penning of their works. Precisely this came to pass, and, as years advanced, to Bernard Shaw came the further realisation that well-written dialogue was not enough: to render the plays acceptable to a reading public had to be added stage directions of a kind entirely different from those laconically technical commands hitherto employed. "Enter L." had to be substituted by a lengthy paragraph of description. In publishing his plays, therefore, he provided both readable matter to accompany the dialogue and prefaces intended to add to the impression made by perusal of the dramas themselves. It is not, perhaps, too much to dream of screen plays similarly published—not with technical directions calculated solely for the studio but with a re-rendering of these directions in terms of a general reading public. Let a new Shaw of the films arise and his wit need not fear lack of appreciation.

This alone is not enough; some means must be found for the reviving of older films. That the time has come for a kind of cinema repertory may well be argued, and in the larger centres there is need for the establishment of houses specifically devoted to the revival of outstanding films which have been driven from the ordinary theatres by later rivals. Assuredly the great public would still flock to the new things; but sufficient numbers might still make such ventures commercially self-supporting. At the same time, and maybe in association with these, film libraries must be established. One such has found a home in The Museum of Modern Art at New York; others spread throughout the country are clearly needed. In these the reels of old film would find a security and from them reproductions could be made as desired. Technical developments during recent years have made possible such organisations, for now it is an easy matter to have the expensive full-size reels reduced to a "sub-standard" form, while the introduction of moderately priced light-and-sound projectors permits of the wider dissemination of the filmic "library." The Museum of Modern Art has made a beginning; out of its effort much may come and hence those interested in the art of the film may be granted an opportunity of seeing almost any notable production which they may call for.

If this were done, and there seems to be no reason for doubting its achievement, one thing is immediately real-ised:—the cinematic art, supposedly impermanent, would be rendered truly more permanent than that of the stage. One projection on the screen is fundamentally the same as another; there is no variation due to the physical limita-tions of the actors and to the influence upon them of audience reactions. What many have regarded as a weak-ness in the cinema, its lack of life, would then turn itself into an asset. By means of printed screen plays and of such "revivals" we should be able to hold before us, intact, all the achievements in this kind. Perhaps it were too much to hope for the immediate bringing of this about; but there can be no question that towards such an organisation of its material the cinema is tending.

So far as the actual production is concerned, it will clearly be necessary to determine more precisely the func-tions of those concerned in the various branches of activity involved in cinematic work. Perhaps we may agree that director and cutter should be identical; but, in formulating this decision, we must not overlook practical considerations and misunderstand the basis of cinematic and of theatrical art alike. A particularly talented and versatile director may on occasion assume almost entire responsibility and be equally aware of literary, directional and photographic values; yet it would appear that in the studio the same conditions hold good as prevail on the stage—co-operation of effort and mutual appreciation of varied talents will be the sought-for ideal. An Übermanndirektor, combining in himself the functions of playwright, director and scene-designer, is an ideal impossible of realisation, and the stage must continue to subsist on the combination of diverse talents. Excellent results have been achieved in the theatre by such a combination of talents; none less may be expected on the screen. The alliance of F. W. Murnau, Karl Mayer and Karl Freund on *The Last Laugh, Tartuffe* and *Faust* or that of F. A. Wagner and G. W. Pabst on *Die Dreigroschenoper* has produced unified results, intangibly harmonised so that separation of the diverse elements becomes virtually impossible. At present many of the studios are far from realising this ideal harmony, and the script-writers in particular grumble under the burdens laid upon them; but again we must recognise that passing of time is demanded for the formulation of method and for organised effort, and that, as the public comes more and more to demand better things from the film, the film will react and provide a suitable basis for their creation.

The extraordinary thing is that, in so short a time, with so many disadvantages, catering for a public wholly un-tutored to criticise this new form of expression, the cinema has succeeded in giving us so much already that is valuable and aesthetically stimulating. The Hollywood studios may introduce absurdities compared with which the hilarious episodes of *Once in a Lifetime* seem like understatements, yet Hollywood has produced many things which may be worthily esteemed. These are its apology and defence, and if improvements in organisation, firmer ideals in artistic expression and definite establishment of basic aims are desirable, these are things which may readily come when the first fervors of excitement give way to consolidation and to less frantic, more self-assured achievement.

2

THE BASIS

AFTER a ruthless stripping of inessentials and of incidental material, the basic element in theatre and in
cinema alike may be defined as movement. Drama demands words, and it is by the glory of words that the
masterpieces of dramatic literature have been passed down
over the generations; but the theatre embraces more within
itself than may be frontiered by the dramatists alone. By
wordless mime and by ballet theatrical impressions, no less
sure and potent in their appeal, may be aroused and so take
their place alongside comedy and tragedy within the hege-
mony of the playhouse. Even when attention is confined to
the spoken play, we realise that two things are necessary
for certainty of success—physical movement accompanying,
and inextricably bound up with, the dialogue given to the
various characters and a dialogue which itself provides
a maximum sense of movement. The one thing fatal to a
drama is an even flow, monotonous and unvarying in its
intensity. Any thoroughly vital performance must introduce words that move, words that suggest ideas instinct
with mental mobility, and physically the actors must be
provided with action that is dynamic. Aristotle's insistence
on περιπέτεια, the peripeteia or turn of the plot, may be
over-emphasised because of the peculiar conditions of the
Greek theatre, but in varying and diverse forms just such
a measure of peripeteia is to be discovered in every play in
which is recognisable the essentially dramatic quality.

Obviously, if this is true of the theatre, it is equally true of the cinema. The films themselves are popularly known as "movies" and by this current term the people on whose support the entire cinematic world depends have signalised that element which to them seems of greatest import. It is the motion of the shapes cast upon the screen, not the shapes themselves, which capture and hold the attention of spectators. This quality of movement in the cinema will demand further examination and analysis; for the moment we must confine ourselves to the basic elements. In the theatre the movement usually is brought upon the stage by living performers. Occasionally light is made to play its part, but for all practical purposes it may be said that on the stage movement of human actors is what we expect and demand. The scenic effects are almost always of a static kind and the light may be, and usually is, either unchanged throughout a scene or else so graduated as to exhibit little sign of alteration. At first, perhaps, we might be tempted to assert that the cinema provides us with a similar set of conditions, the only difference being in the fact that, while there are living actors on the stage, nothing save the two-dimensional images of these actors are shown to us when we look upon the screen. Here, however, is a question which demands further examination, for precisely at this point enters in a cleavage in opinion, determination concerning which must be made before we pass on further.

INDIVIDUAL IMAGES

To consider adequately the problems involved, we must first fix definitely in our minds the typical, and indeed necessary, make-up of any ordinary film. That film primarily consists in a certain number of individual pictures or images. Each one of these images, technically called "frames," is a separate unit and may, if desired, be considered independently of its companions. Considered so, however, it will be merely a photograph; it can assume cinematic quality only when, in combination with its companions, it is passed through the projector in such a manner that its separate individuality is lost or rendered indistinct. While we watch the progress of a film we are expected completely to forget that that film is created out of thousands of distinct images; in our consciousness must remain only the result fashioned by the rapid throwing of one image on the track of another.

Nevertheless, behind the moving patterns projected on the screen, these separate images retain their existence and at any moment they may be extracted and assessed for their artistic quality precisely as any ordinary photograph may be assessed. A "still" reproduced in a theatre magazine is no more than a representation, in two-dimensional form and in masses of light and shade, of a single moment in a stage production, yet it has a value and significance of its own. Unless each stage grouping, even down to those which are held but for a brief fraction of a second, has a certain grace and compositional value, the scene in which it occurs will exhibit a blemish—infinitesimal maybe and almost unnoticeable, yet a blemish still. One might employ the analogy of a dancer, saying that unless a dancer trains his or her body movements in such a way that there is a constant graceful and rhythmic gradation from one position to the next, the resultant dance can never be wholly satisfying; an ugly and awkward photograph of Pavlova or of Nijinsky would be impossible since the very perfection of their art arose from an innate sense of and technical striving for rhythmic gradations of this kind. The truly fine and aesthetically appealing stage production will display just such a sense of harmonious and rhythmic movement, and no instantaneous action photograph taken at any single moment in the course of the performance should be without its inherent grace and beauty.

In a precisely similar manner, unless the separate pictures or images making up a strip of film possess their own compositional strength, significance and loveliness, the resultant film will be lacking by so much the artistic unity at which it strives. The ordinary photograph today, in the hands of modern experts gifted with sensibility and technical skill, has become a thing capable of great artistic expressiveness; the creators of a truly important and beautiful film need to have at their command all the resources and all the artistic sensibility required for the making of such effective photographic pictures. Here it is to be observed that basically the photograph, even when not treated by the hands of an expert, contains within itself the elements of artistry. As André Levinson has demonstrated, the fact that it reduces nature to a plane surface, sets this nature in a frame and provides an exaggerated perspective at once renders it more than a mere imitation of reality. Within these conditions the operation of man to which we give the name of art can progress and out of that in turn may proceed a value incorporable in the cinematic form.

No really good film will present separate images or frames which are lacking independent worth.

THE SHOTS

That this worth, except when the images are printed off as "stills," is not perceived by us consciously is self-evident: in any "shot" or episode in a film numbers of such images are passed so rapidly through the projector that they become combined visually into one single "moving picture." A shot may be long or short, but, whatever its length, it forms the first unit we can appreciate formally in the witnessing of a film. We may summarily define a shot as a single filmic episode, as the picture of any piece of action taken in one complete whole by the camera. Thus the presentation for a brief two seconds of a door-knocker might be given by itself and be consequently regarded as a shot; while, on the other hand, a single shot might show us a man walking towards the entrance to a house, follow his movements continuously while he raised his hand towards the knocker, continue following them until the door was opened and he vanished within.

Each shot Pudovkin, the Russian director and theorist, likens to a word in the hands of a poet; but in reality any shot in a film is so much more than a word as the individual image is less than a word. However brief any episode may be, yet in it something definitely is told or said; that something possibly does not find completion within the scope of the shot itself but sufficient is brought forward to suggest the complete whole of which it forms a greater or a lesser part. Considered in terms of language, the shot always expresses an action with subject and predicate, or else, by its symbolic content, excites the mind to an energy which indirectly introduces these two elements. Rather than to a word, the cinematic shot may be likened to a complete sentence or at least to a clause. Exact parallelism between language and filmic expression cannot, of course, be established but, as will be seen later, there may be some value in suggesting at least an approximate correspondence.

How many shots go to make up the entire length of a film is determined only by the nature and scope of the film itself. Lengthy shots and brief shots possess their separate functions and the most careful consideration and innate appreciation of filmic values is demanded for their composition and binding together. This subject, however, is one that may for the moment be left for later consideration; here it is important to note that in addition to the individual image and to the separate episode, we may recognise the shot-combination as an appreciable unit of larger proportions. If the analogy of poetry be pursued, one might suggest that the former represented sentences and the latter stanzas, each taking shape and achieving form only when related to the whole of which they form parts.

By a shot-combination is intended a grouping of separate episodes connected together by their subject-matter or by their orientation towards the building up of a situation or of an emotional theme. We might, for example, imagine, preceding the shot which shows the man at the doorway, one in which this man receives a letter bidding him to go to the house we later see him enter and another subsequent shot in which we watch him confronting the sender of this letter. The three episodes, while distinct, would be bound together by a common idea or action, and clearly we should be justified in treating them together, as a formal unit within the complete film. A useful example of such shot-combinations occurs in *David Copperfield*. On leaving the Micawbers little David walks along a London street and is cheated of his trunk by a rascally scoundrel—one sequence; followed by a second, considerably more complex, in which a series of episodes displays the progressive stages of the boy's long and weary tramp to Dover.

THE PHOTOGRAPHIC MATERIAL

Precisely here enters in a set of important questions. The first is this. Behind the separate images, shots and sequences obviously must exist an original from which each of these has been derived. The camera may not invent its own material; all it is permitted to do is to reproduce (often, of course, with modifications and in artistically altered tones) objects which come within the range of its lens. Of such objects or original forms there may, clearly, be several distinct kinds.

At one extreme may be placed those originals which, static in themselves, are given apparent motion by being photographed in a series of altered positions. We may take, for example a dozen three-dimensional geometric objects —a cube, a globe and what not—and by taking first one combination and then another we shall be able to present pictures which seem to set these things into movement. A clever advertising film prepared for a certain tooth-paste showed thus a number of sticks which appeared to travel back and forth over the screen in a sort of musical military formation. This may serve as a current example; although those familiar with the showings of intellectual film societies will be able to recall several others presented with more self-consciously "artistic" aims.

The same principle underlies the animated cartoon. Walt Disney and his assistants prepare thousands of individual drawings, each in itself motionless; when these are photographed in rotation by the camera and the resultant frames passed through the projector the forms take motion and seem to acquire the functions of life. The only essential difference lies in the fact that, although both are manufactured objects, the former possesses only an interest dependent upon aesthetic appreciation of mass and line while the latter introduces in addition the interest of narrative and "plot." Of the same kind are the plastic figures used in the Russian film, *The New Gulliver*. If ten or a dozen such figures are made with slightly differing attitudes or facial expressions and each is separately photographed on several frames, movement and hence the impression of life will be given to objects which, static in themselves, combine to present a picture apparently dynamic.

Keeping within the sphere of the manufactured object, we next pass to the realm of the marionette. The marionette, too, is a creation of man and, like a Walt Disney drawing, may in itself be assessed for its own independent artistic qualities, but whereas the drawing could never suggest movement without being linked to other drawings, a marionette of Podrecca's, through human ingenuity, is endowed with the power of reproducing or of approaching human mobility and consequently the camera may catch that movement directly.

Generally, however, when we speak of the cinema, this is not the kind of thing we have in mind. The films of pure form are rare, and, while puppets have been familiarised on the screen (*I am Suzanne* forms a good example) and Walt Disney's cartoons are universally known, these do not at once come to the mind when we contemplate a visit to the "picture-house"; the pictures we anticipate seeing there are those typical, representative films which use for their material animate and inanimate nature, particularly the movements of living men and women.

This typical film, however, is again not one and indivisible; within its scope two main forms at least immediately separate themselves. Commonly, we expect, when the screen announces the showing of this or that film, to see presented before us a story told by means of moving pictures which, we are aware, have been taken in some studio with groups of trained professional players supervised by a director and performing against specially constructed sets. Regularly we go to "see" Greta Garbo or Marlene Dietrich or Clark Gable in parts specially created for these artists, just as, when we enter the theatre, we expect to see on the stage men and women who, talented histrionically, are engaged in interpreting fictional roles. Against this commonly accepted filmic method, on the other hand, there has come recently a violent reaction from the left. Pudovkin, following the lead of Lev Kuleshov, thus proceeds to examine wherein lies the essential nature of cinematic art and develops an argumentation opposed to the employment of professional performers. If, he reasons, this essential nature lies in the artistry displayed by actors and actresses, then the cinema must be judged truly a pale reflection of the stage. The director who controls their movements might as well be rehearsing his characters for an ordinary theatrical show, and the resultant filmic reproduction of the original action is to be regarded in a light precisely similar to that in which we look at a photographic copy of an oil painting. No doubt an Alinari reproduction of some canvas by Botticelli or Raphael proves useful to us; but in that reproduction there can be no art, only technical competence, while no one could be so foolish as to suppose that contemplation of this copy might convey an impression that in any respect rose to the height of the impression created by contemplation of the original. All the art, the compositional value, the massing of the forms, resides in that from which this copy was made; even so, the photograph can never hope to capture the subtler elements in the design or the delicate shading of the colours.

Reacting thus, these film theorists and practitioners—Pudovkin and Eisenstein with reservations, Dziga-Vertov and his Cine-Eye group wholeheartedly—propose to substitute "nature" for the simulated nature of the professional performers. Leaving aside the most extreme experiments of Dziga-Vertov, we may note how Eisenstein in *Thunder over Mexico* purposely avoids the employment of studio artists and of studio shots, preferring to scenes elaborately prepared and rehearsed for the occasion, scenes and types observable every day in a typical Mexican village. One famous example of this is Pudovkin's treatment of a crowd in *The Heir of Jenghis Khan*. Deliberately putting aside the use of professional artists, he chose instead an ordinary group of peasants. These in one shot were expected to display astonishment and admiring wonder. No amount of directing could have produced such a result, and in any case that result would have involved a certain falsity. Pudovkin solved his problem by introducing a juggler. Carefully keeping this performer out of camera range, he photographed the crowd while they remained intent upon the tricks being shown to them. The shot thus secured produced the filmic effect desired out of untutored and unrehearsed human material. In such ways, Pudovkin argues, ought the cinematic director to carry out most of his work.

NARRATIVE AND FORM

The basic questions, however, are by no means fully exhausted. One in particular must now be given attention. When we go to see any film, we usually expect to be provided with a story. Many film themes are based on novels, many others are derived from plays, and it is the action of novel or play which is presented visually before us. Yet, "if some miraculous power," wrote J. G. Fletcher, "could give . . . audiences the idea that what the screen was to give them was not a story at all, but only pictures—that is to say, pictorial art—the whole motion-picture industry would take a great stride forward," and his plea receives emphasis in different terms from no less important a man than Pirandello. Uncompromisingly, Pirandello declares that

the cinema must free itself of literature, leaving narrative to novels and the theatre. It should steep itself in music, but it should leave melodrama (opera) to the opera-house and jazz to the music-hall. I refer to that kind of music which can speak to everyone without the addition of any words and for which cinematography can become the visual medium. Thus, I would say, pure music and pure image. The eye and the ear are the most aesthetic of the senses, and they should become united in a single artistic delight, the beauty of which is felt by the heart so that the subconscious mind is moved and influenced by novel images that may be either as terrible as nightmares or mysterious as dreams; sometimes soothing and sometimes alarming according to the rhythm of the music.
Cinemelography: there is the new word for the true art revolution, the visible language of sound.

Between the two extremes—that of the commercial film with its strong narrational emphasis and the "pure cinema" wherein form alone is deemed of account—are infinite gradations. No doubt most of those who oppose the telling of a story belong to the intelligentzia and despise the crowd. The supporters of the French "cinéma pur," like Germaine Dulac, thus look to a preciously refined art-form which could have but little popular appeal. "Ces films," writes one, "ne pouvant guère être appréciés que par des initiés, de petites salles spécialisées vont ouvrir leurs portes." Specialised efforts of the kind sponsored by Armand Tallier and L. Myrga at the Studio des Ursulines, by Jean Tédesco at the Vieux-Colombier, by Jean Mauclair at Le Studio 28, by Jean Vallée at L'Oeil de Paris—Abel Gance's *La roue* or Germaine Dulac's *La coquille*—confessedly have an exceedingly limited appeal; and therefore, although we may recognise in them elements of worth, we may be prepared to set them on one side. Whatever of artistic value they may present, the cardinal assumption of their makers, that the applause of the crowd is vicious and so to be avoided, that a true and "pure" filmic art can develop only among small and cultured societies of initiates, is firmly to be refuted.

What, however, are we to say of Dziga-Vertov, who, equally an opponent of the narrational film, aims at interesting, if not the whole world, Russia's millions at least? Maybe it is true that the endeavours of his group, The Cine-Eye, have been due largely to the lack of film-shortage in Moscow and Leningrad, but that explanation does not take away from the fact that his methods embody a thoroughly reasonable approach to the cinema. In 1919, Dziga-Vertov being unable to secure unexposed film for the making of a new picture, created *A Year of Revolution* out of existing newsreels. Such success attended its showing that its director prepared two manifestos in which he outlined his theories succinctly and argued that the public should be given but one quarter of specially prepared "acted" material and three-quarters of "documentary" matter, composed harmoniously in accordance with his method. The eye of the camera, he argued, has a special function; through its means men are taught to see, by its means things which would pass unnoticed or which are virtually invisible are brought to common attention. Pursuing these theories, he produced *The Film-Eye* (1923), *The Man with the Camera* (1928) and *Three Songs about Lenin* (1933).

What decision we arrive at on this problem will depend upon our attitude towards still a further element in the creation of any film, that which the Russians have styled "montage." In approaching it, we must bear in mind, first, the compositional parts of a material kind (frame, shot, sequence) making up any film, second, the varieties of photographic original extending from the one extreme of static "manufactured" objects to the other of professional performances, and, third, the diverse purposes of those who aim at telling a story and of those who leave the moving pictures to conjure forth, by symbolic appeal and pictorial pattern, emotions independent of any plot.

MONTAGE

The theory of montage as developed by Pudovkin assumes that the principal foundation of cinematic art rests in the arrangement by the director of individual shots. In itself this theory, like Dziga-Vertov's use of newsreels, grew largely out of economic and external conditions, for, forced by the scarcity of film in Russia to enquire more carefully and with greater precision into the essential aims of the cinema, the Soviet directors stand almost alone in their close and painstaking analysis of aesthetic principles and of practical methods. When you have unlimited supplies of film you may well essay a hit-or-miss policy, correcting your mistakes by scrapping unsuccessful material; but when barely a few hundred feet are at your disposal you will be careful, before ever the camera is set in motion, to consider well exactly what you want to do and how best you will secure the desired result.

With logical directness, therefore, Lev Kuleshov went back to basic essentials. Every art, he argued, must have a material through which its expression is conveyed and a characteristic method. In the art of the cinema, he decided, the former was represented by the separate images or shots (not by the artistry of the performers) and the latter by the arrangement of these images or shots on the part of the artist director. Whereas, therefore, in the preparation of the average commercial film greatest pains are taken to get an adequate reproduction of some action already rehearsed, the Russian directors decided to devote most attention to the arrangement, the editing, of the material. For Kuleshov and Pudovkin the shots became words and phrases; art could not be said to begin until these words and phrases were combined, by the imaginative work of the director, into a poetic whole. In this sense, accordingly, montage implies much more than mere cutting or assembling; it assumes prime importance artistically in the creation of the final film.

How far this work in montage differs from common studio practice is realised at once when we consider even

more briefly the usual methods employed in film production. For most of the early commercial films and quite an
appreciable number of those still being produced, a story
is selected and a full scenario prepared; this scenario outlines the story more or less directly and in sequence of
incident so that shot follows shot in intellectually logical
order. Two recent films provide examples of this. Cinematically the technique of Noel Coward's *The Scoundrel*
and of Mae West's *Goin' to Town* was antiquated. In the
latter we start with the galloping ride of some cowboys;
hear three men remark that their leader is a "bad man";
see them enter the saloon; hear them ask for Cleo; watch
the camera pick up Cleo in a private room—and so on to
the end. The plot of *The Scoundrel* was presented in a
kindred manner. One episode after another was shown to
us, and these were arranged with little deviation from a
normal time sequence and without the introduction of any
shots not strictly of a narrational kind. Thus in these two
films (selected here solely for their characteristic values)
each shot represents a fundamental piece of the action and
itself involves action which may rationally be appreciated.
The method, as indicated above, is rapidly becoming old-
fashioned, and, although plentiful examples of it abound,
it is easy to see that the prominent directors of future years
will make comparatively sparing use of it or at least will
modify its employment by the introduction of other elements and other methods.

Cutting or assembling implies merely the gathering
together of the filmic material and its arrangement in logical order. Montage, on the contrary, implies an emotional,
creative and imaginative approach, and its aim is, not to
lead a story forward by intellectually appreciable stages,

but to stimulate and arouse the minds of the spectators into feeling and hence into emotionally accepting the purport of a particular scene. It frequently departs from the use of straight shots logically connected in favour of oblique shots emotionally bound together. The first film fully utilising this method of approach was *The Battleship Potemkin,* directed by Eisenstein; Pudovkin has adopted the same means of securing his effects, as, for example, in *Mother.* At one part of this film, the director's business was to display a prisoner's reactions upon receiving a letter of pardon. For the direct method this would have been done by concentrating on the actor; we should have been shown a shot of the prisoner, despairing, in his lonely cell, another of the warder entering with the letter, another of the reading of the letter, another (perhaps an enormous close-up) in which the performer strove to make his features express his joy. Instead of following this direct approach, Eisenstein utilised here the oblique method, introducing several shots which, although unrelated intellectually and logically, took shape and meaning when linked together in emotional sequence-shots of the prisoner's hands, of a bird flying outside the barred window, of a rippling stream. Two things are to be observed here:— first, the deliberate avoidance of concentration upon the actor, and, secondly, the equally deliberate endeavour, by the utilisation of indirect methods, to conjure up an emotional image of a subjective state of mind.

Montage, of course, may be either simple or complex, but, whether the one or the other, it always implies a breaking away from "straight" photography and usually introduces something of a symbolic content. If cutting is prose, montage is poetry. The simplest possible example would be, say, that of a shot showing the head of a ferocious panther, dissolving into that of a villain's head. Rather obvious, perhaps, but still montage. A more complex example occurs in the long walk from London to Dover in *David Copperfield;* there, instead of showing merely the tramping figure of the boy, use was made of a series of exceedingly short shots each with a symbolic and imaginative colouring, punctuated by shots of milestones recording the stages of the lonely journey.

From this theory of montage, it is easy to see how various styles and filmic aims have been evolved. These we must aim at assessing, for, until we formulate for ourselves our own demands of filmic art, adequate appreciation either of commercial work or of conscious experimentation along particular lines becomes virtually impossible.

CINEMATIC AIMS

Image, shot, sequence and montage we may accept as being definitely basic forces in the cinema's structure; the question to decide is the use to which these ought to be put. While recognising that in cinema and in theatre alike there are many mansions, it would seem that we are permitted to rule out of account two forms, one because it is too "artistic" and the other because it is not "artistic" enough. We are concerned with the cinema as a popular art-form, akin to the theatre in that it achieves its fullest expression when its appeal is widest, and therefore are forced to decide that the "pure" patterns beloved of the avant-garde should be neglected. These may serve a purpose in emphasising the pictorial values of mass and line, but clearly they can never become popular entertainment. Their function will be similar to that of the early neoclassic plays or to that of certain modern poetic dramas. We welcome experiments in the poetic drama; the significance of these experiments is great in that they provide suggestions which may serve a purpose in other plays; but in themselves they may stand so clearly apart from what the theatre essentially requires that they must be considered separately and appreciated for the emphasis they throw on certain neglected elements rather than for their direct relationship to current dramatic forms. In precisely the same way are the experiments in purely pictorial cinema to be regarded. The poetic playwrights have emphasised the need of poetic values on our stage and through their efforts something at least of those values begins to shatter the framework of the illusionistic theatre. Similarly, while the contemplation of moving forms by themselves will meet with no popular appeal, the emphasis thus thrown on pictorial elements is having its effect on the commercial films. The sequences in silver and grey which formed part of *Broadway Melody of 1936* owed much of their effect to a conscious appreciation of tonal values.

At the opposite extreme is the ordinary newsreel. The newsreel will always be popular and at times it may even be pictorially satisfying; but its relation to the larger cinema can be nothing more than that of the reporter's news paragraph to the poems of Shelley or to Hardy's novels. Technically, it may be brilliant; for its content it may be interesting; but of true artistic expression it is ever innocent. This, too, we therefore put aside.

Having placed the experimental "art" film and the newsreel apart, we are left with the narrational film of commercial manufacture, the emotional mood-film of Eisenstein, the elaborate Cine-Eye productions and the travelogue. For each of these there is likely to be a constant public, although the first will almost certainly remain the chief in esteem.

First, perhaps, it will be convenient to consider the scope of the Dziga-Vertov activities, together with several films so closely associated with these that they demand simultaneous attention. In the former the separate shots are of the newsreel type. Some will have been taken solely for the purpose of recording current events; others the director will have taken with the object of fitting them into his completed whole. To create the entire film, no attempt is made to work out a narrational scenario; at the most there is an effort to bind the various shots together by emphasis upon a chosen theme. Thus, without the aid of any formal "story," unity was provided for *Three Songs about Lenin* through the emphasis continually placed upon the spirit of Leninism, and the technique employed was not that of logical development from one achievement to another but rather, by means of careful and imaginative montage, the creation of a mood evoked both by the pictures themselves and by their combinations. Unquestionably, a peculiar impression can be aroused by this means; a kind of *Cavalcade* effect results from the skilful handling of the material. On the other hand, it is seriously to be questioned whether the claims put forward for his chosen method by Dziga-Vertov are to be seriously considered. When we compare his typical work with similar films, such as *The Battleship Potemkin* and *Chapayev,* wherein the newsreel type of film has been wrought into the framework of a story, we are inevitably forced to believe that the latter are likely always to maintain their priority in appeal. Similar convictions are forced upon us when we note how, in *Thunder over*

Mexico, Eisenstein has emphasised his general abstract theme by concentration upon concrete instances, weaving a story of direct narrational value into a filmic structure essentially thematic. The answer to the previously posed question becomes apparent: cinema like theatre normally anticipates something along the lines of narrational action and the public to which it appeals finds greater interest in work which has a regularly developed plot, no matter how slight, to unfold. Living Chapayev possesses more force, in the cinema's world, than Lenin dead.

Another question may also be answered here. The theory that only material of the "natural" kind may be used without destroying the fundamental artistic basis of the film cannot be maintained. Logically the argument seems to possess considerable justification; but with similar logic one might strip the theatre of nearly all the elements commonly associated with it. Because the *commedia dell' arte* players, with a peculiarly brilliant technique, improvised their performances, we might logically deny to the stage the service of its playwrights; because some skilful mimes have created a powerful theatrical impression—an impression equivalent or even superior to that effected by actors using words—we might assume that the basic element in a stage performance is the actor's silent impersonation; because the imagination can conjure up rich and effective settings on a bare, unadorned platform, we might deny the theatre any right to the fancies of the scene-designer. The truth, naturally, is obvious. The theatre presents to us an art-form in which movement of living actors is the first and necessary attribute, and any theatre which refuses to make use of this element is clearly falsifying its essential purpose; but if greater beauty and greater effectiveness can be secured by summoning to its aid the services of other arts—the dialogue of the playwright, the line and colour values of the scene-designer, the compositions, too, of the musician—then the theatre would be equally false to its aims in rejecting such assistance.

Precisely the same is true of the cinema. Undoubtedly, the essential filmic art does not start with the original from which the photographic images are created—so much is to be granted at once. A shot of mountain, sea or sky may be more impressive and emotionally effective than one of a man-made object with claims to artistic excellence. On the other hand, where a preliminary use of such art will add to the value of the resultant film, there can be no justification for not employing its services. The present prevailing emphasis on the "star" may be unfortunate, but if a star is able to give an impersonation which will be more convincing and more appealing than that of another person, trained or untrained, then unquestionably he or she will contribute materially to the finished cinematic expression. The same is true of the sets. Nature may provide what is demanded, but to assume that no artificial properties or manufactured sets should be made use of seems merely a logical error.

The truth is that anything may prove suitable as the foundation or original for a film shot—a real object in nature, a model, a drawing, a built-up set; that which is to be judged is the shot itself and no methods employed in obtaining the result are to be condemned. A trick shot may be deemed false in the sense that it does not reproduce reality, but it may be essentially true to the conditions of the cinematic form. We need no more despise it than we should despise an actor who, having to impersonate a suicide on the stage, refuses to use a loaded revolver or to plunge a real dagger into his quivering flesh.

Closely associated with the Cine-Eye film is such a work as Eisenstein's *Romance Sentimentale*. The basis here is music, and the attempt is made to present visual pictures corresponding to the movements of the musical rhythm. No two shots have any logical connection; from seascape the pictures move to woodland, from woodland to a studio interior, from studio interior to a flower. That Eisenstein's effort was not successful artistically should not, of course, lead us to condemn his aim; and perhaps we may be prepared to recognise that there are many as yet undeveloped possibilities in this direction. It would seem, however, that, brilliantly though a director might accomplish his purpose, the resultant achievement would always be a trifle recherché and strange to the common desires of a general public. Again, the truth of this statement is realised when we compare Eisenstein's film with others in which a kindred technique has been inserted in a narrational framework. The story of *Man of Aran* is slight—a barest suggestion only, but at least there is no flitting about from symbolic image to symbolic image. The island itself and its inhabitants taken collectively seize hold on us and are permanently fixed in our memory. For that reason *Man of Aran* has a more general appeal, and its combination of exquisite pictorial shots and of dramatic conflict has given it an important place in the cinema's history. To be observed also is the fact that it approaches, in some respects at least, the territory of the ordinary travelogue.

Only one stage removed is *Sequoia*. Although the producing company saw fit to introduce there two directly told stories—that of the puma and the deer, and that of a limited number of human characters—still story value was clearly not its chief element; its interest, like that of *Man of Aran,* depended fundamentally upon the clever and artistically conceived photographing of nature in movement. One further stage yet is marked by *The Blue Light,* where a stronger tale was narrated against the rich background of the Tyrol mountains. For plot alone *The Blue Light* would certainly not be remembered; but for the exquisite rendering of mountain and cloud it lingers fondly in the memory, and, recalling it, we realise how much of an atmosphere and emotional content was provided by purely pictorial values ably handled.

Within the region indicated by these films much may yet be achieved, always providing, perhaps, more of a *succès d'estime* than a genuinely popular triumph, but nevertheless with just sufficient of that triumphing to make their production worthwhile commercially. The balance, however, will no doubt swing more towards *The Blue Light* than towards the plotless *Romance Sentimentale* or the only faintly narrational *Man of Aran.*

The argument seems to tend steadily in one direction: our main conclusion must be that the current "commercial" and narrational type of film is that to which we must devote most attention, just as, if we are concerned with the theatre, our minds must go, not to the "closet dramas" and untheatrical poetic experiments, but to the regular fare offered by the Broadway producers. The first requirement in film and in play is that it should be suited for public appreciation. There is no need to introduce perplexing difficulties and confusions here. The commercial cinema obviously has often failed utterly to exploit the possibilities offered so generously to it or, if such exploitation is attempted, the path has frequently been pursued only half-heartedly and meretriciously; but this fact is not one that must lead inevitably towards a general condemnation. The theatre, too, possesses much that is unworthy, yet, when we speak of drama, not of these lesser forms of play-production do we think; we think in terms of Shakespeare and Ibsen, Strindberg and Shaw, Chechov and O'Neill. A play of Shakespeare's soars far beyond a cheaply popular melodrama, but both have the same essential basis in that each has adapted itself to the requirements of the current theatre of its time.

In saying, therefore, that it is towards the commercial film we should look implies no more than a statement that a true drama must be calculated for theatrical representation. A truly fine film will introduce things undreamt of in some vulgarly trivial production, but the two will agree in the possession of certain elements basically necessary if either is to make a general appeal. Each will have a clearly told, significant and arresting story or a theme of major import; human characters will be there and a pictorially beautiful setting; and, in the narrative, the director will employ a montage which makes use of the specific attributes of the cinematic form. The commercial film of this type, therefore, like the commercial play, is our objective; there is no call to condemn either or to attempt the discovery of a fresh foundation.

3

THE METHODS OF THE CINEMA

AN examination of the basic elements in the cinema
has convinced us that the narrational film deserves most
of our attention. The cinema, like the theatre, is realised to
be an art of entertainment which depends for its very being
upon a wide popular appeal. On the stage the public has
always demanded good strong stories, and the cinema is
sufficiently akin to the theatre to require, normally, stories
of a cognate sort. While, therefore, we may be prepared to
recognise that the cinema can produce interesting forms
in which a plot is almost entirely or even wholly absent, we
shall concern ourselves mainly with those manifestations of
filmic art which, boldly plotted and narrational in scope, are
likely to capture the esteem of the greater mass of spectators.

Since the film in this respect bears such a close relationship to the theatrical production, no surprise need be
felt in observing that, with a few exceptions, the efforts of
those concerned with the cinema have, until recent years,
been heavily influenced by stage practice. The theatre has
had a tradition stretching back thousands of years; experience in that art has brought knowledge and wisdom; generations of workers have contributed towards establishing
methods and determining possibilities. Amid the turmoil
attending the birth of this new form of expression, it was
but natural that men should turn for assistance to the com-
fortable security of the stage, adapting to the two-dimen-

sional sphere what had already been proved in the three-dimensional. Even although at a very early date the primitive cowboy films had provided suggestions concerning what the cinema might do in the way of depicting rapid movement and massed effects, the great proportion of films most familiar to us has been within the scope of those culled from past or present stage successes. So much so, indeed, that the term "parasitic" came with some show of justice to be applied to the new method, and that theatrical managers started confidently to count on Hollywood's millions to recoup themselves for Broadway's losses.

Under these conditions there inevitably arose a confusion between the long established aims and devices of the stage play and those of the screen drama. Vaguely everyone knew that these were not the same, but this realisation was frequently so faint that, in the rush of producing activity and in the face of the strongly felt kinship between the two forms of entertainment, it became obscured and forgotten. Some studios, even, went so far as to present films, like *Arms and the Man,* almost unaltered from their original stage shapes, and others, even when they introduced necessary variations, continued introducing basic material rehearsed in theatrical manner. Obvious though it may seem, the fact that there was a specific and appropriate filmic manner of expression distinct from a dramatic manner of expression was largely neglected, and all too often stage directors, without any knowledge of or aptitude for cinematic work, were called in to handle material which already had been tried on the boards of the theatre. Even now, many producers show that they have failed to recognise the distinctive qualities of the art in which they work. Numerous films of the present day, like *A Feather in Her*

Hat or *Scrooge,* create an impression of boredom because they do not acknowledge the all-importance of the visual element in the screen-play, because they are dominated by purely theatrical conceptions (witness the stagey empty chair to indicate Marley's ghost) and because, as a result, they neglect most of the essential features in cinematic production.

An investigation of this film manner of expression, clearly, even although it may be forced to cover much ground already traversed, becomes positively essential; and first we must apply ourselves to the elements which originally formed part of the silent film. This does not imply that there is no difference between the methods rightfully to be employed in sound and in silent films respectively. To assert this were to overlook many important aspects in each; but the fact remains that the mere introduction of sound has not caused a complete cleavage between the typical cinema work of today and the filmic masterpieces produced during the era of the "silent screen." The assumption that the bringing in of sound has separated these two and made the modern film a kind of substitute for the theatrical performance is entirely false. In spite of changes necessarily introduced, the basis of the cinema has remained unaltered by recent innovations; most of the judgments we may pass on the old "movie" are equally applicable to the presently popular "talkie." No particular excuse, therefore, need be offered for the immediate directing of attention to the purely visual aspects of film craft.

DRAMATIC AND CINEMATIC TECHNIQUE

For the purpose of determining the essential features in the cinema's proper and individual manner of expression, it may be convenient to start with a concrete example; the first few shots of a recently successful film may be taken for comparison with the stage-play from which it was derived. Most theatre-goers know of Rudolph Besier's *The Barretts of Wimpole Street* and recall its opening scene; here is the equivalent section of the screen play as adapted by Ernest Vajda and Claudine West:

1. FADE IN

   EXT. WIMPOLE STREET—LONG SHOT—

   It is dusk of a damp, winter's day. The street is wet from the afternoon's moisture, although no rain is falling now. A lamp post in the foreground bears the name "WIMPOLE STREET." In front of number "50" stands the carriage of Dr. Chambers. The house itself is gloomy and forbidding with all shades drawn. Iron rails surround the basement and cast exaggerated shadows upon the wall, giving the impression of a prison.

   Carriages and other vehicles are moving down the street, and it is to be noticed that as they pass number "50", the rumbling and rattling of their iron wheels becomes silenced by a heavy layer of straw, which has been spread across the street, in front of this residence.

   After HOLDING on this picture long enough to get over the idea that the house is the residence of an invalid, we move to:

2. CLOSE SHOT SIDEWALK IN FRONT OF THE HOUSE—

   where we pick up Flush, the cocker spaniel belonging to Elizabeth Barrett. Flush has completed whatever business he may have been sent from the house for and is trotting dutifully back to his domicile. WE MOVE WITH HIM as he climbs the steps leading to the front door and scratches, accompanying this by a short bark. After a moment, the door is opened and Flush enters.

3. HALL OF BARRETT HOME—

gloomy—imposing. A dignified butler is closing the door after having admitted the dog. He makes the sign to Flush that he is to keep quiet and as he does so, the voice of Edward Barrett is heard from the adjoining room off scene.

Voice of Barrett

Almighty Father, Giver of all good gifts, Who of Thy divine providence hath provided Thine unworthy servants with all things necessary to their bodily sustenance, we thank Thee for this food which Thou hast given us, and beseech Thy spiritual grace that we may enjoy in quietness of spirit the fruits of Thy bounty. Amen.

During this saying of Grace, Flush glances momentarily towards the dining room, and then, at the sound of that voice, his spirit seems to droop. He puts his tail between his legs and slinks up the stairs, in the direction of the room of his beloved mistress. THE CAMERA PANS WITH HIM as he ascends the staircase, and as he reaches the landing,

CUT TO:

4. LANDING—MEDIUM CLOSE SHOT—

Flush crosses the landing to the doorway of Elizabeth's room and scratches the door in his accustomed manner. It is opened by Wilson, Elizabeth's maid, and as Flush enters, Wilson comes out and closes the door after him. She is about to move toward the stairs when something apparently very shocking engages her attention. She stares, frowningly, off scene, raises a hand.

Wilson

(worriedly)

Tch! Tch! Tch!

She advances. CAMERA PANS WITH HER toward a window on the opposite side of the landing. It is open about an inch only, but enough to flutter the lace curtain. Wilson shuts and bolts it with a business-like snap and starts out of scene.

CUT TO:

5-8. LANDING AT DOOR TO ELIZABETH'S ROOM— CLOSE SHOT—

Wilson comes briskly in, looks off sternly in the direction of the window, holding up a hand to feel any possible draft. Apparently everything is satisfactory, for she goes out of scene in the direction of the stairs. WE STAY ON THE empty door for a moment, then,

DISSOLVE TO:

BEDROOM OF ELIZABETH   COMPOSITION SHOT

With this composition shot we are introduced to the dialogue between Dr. Chambers and Elizabeth, the dialogue which forms the opening episode of the stage play.

As will be immediately observed, certain things at once claim our attention in this short series of shots:— 1) the establishment of locale and the exciting of expectation by purely visual means, 2) the arousing of interest and mood by the employment of symbolic images, 3) the movement which imaginatively we ourselves make in harmony with the moving camera, 4) the utilisation of such things as the dog for the purpose of emphasising indirectly human character, 5) the ease with which certain objects—the window, for example—may be singled out for our particular notice, and 6) the tremendous expectancy created by a few special devices, for example the showing of the closed door to Elizabeth's room.

Only a few cinematic methods are here illustrated, yet already sufficient has been provided to indicate immediately the fundamental difference between dramatic and filmic aims. We feel instinctively, and can support the dictates of instinct and emotional appreciation by logical arguments, that the way in which Besier began his stage play was entirely right; with equal conviction do we feel that the opening of the screen play is just and appropriate. At once we realise that verbal exposition can largely be abandoned in the cinema and that, as a consequence, the business of planning treatment and action becomes a task of an entirely different kind. A certain amount, truly, a dramatist can tell to the eyes by means of his setting. A poverty-stricken kitchen presented visually before us saves an amount of description, establishes the fictional locality of a drama and maybe even sets the mood in which it is to be accepted; a richly-furnished boudoir may be made silently to convey a vast deal of information to an audience. Even so, however, the dramatist is strictly limited in the use he may legitimately make of these devices, nor can he dispense with the necessary words of preliminary exposition. In the screen version of *The Barretts of Wimpole Street,* before having met either Elizabeth or her father, we are enabled, with utmost simplicity, to grasp certain things relating to their characters and apt to set our mood for the drama about to be unfolded. We know that this is 50 Wimpole Street; we learn from the carriages that the period is mid-nineteenth century; we guess that someone is ill and at the same time have it suggested that the gloomily shuttered house is a prison; we realise that, in spite of the overheard words of prayer, a man whom as yet we have not seen possesses a temper capable of making a dog shrink from his presence. The whole business of preliminary exposition, incorporating the setting of mood, the presentation of facts and the suggestion of character, has been provided by a series of images almost entirely visual in their appeal. Though both film and play have the same plot, their methods of treatment are completely divergent—as divergent as are the methods employed by the dramatist and the writer of novels.

To discuss these methods exhaustively or even in considerable detail would prove a lengthy task. Here be it our business to pass under our consideration merely the more important among the cinema's many attributes and means of expression, comparing these, where advisable, with the more commonly understood and more fully discussed methods suitable for a stage performance and referring back to the brief passage chosen from this selected film, *The Barretts of Wimpole Street.*

MOVEMENT

The all-essential element in any film is movement. Kirk Bond's definition of the silent film may be accepted as a true one—"the observed motion of light and shade on a limited plane surface." From this definition it follows that the cinema "supplies the one missing order" of art endeavour. "Of the two higher senses—sight and hearing," Kirk Bond explains, "the latter is served by music both statically, as in the East, and dynamically, as in our own age, while there has been developed a plethora of arts based on visual form or design. It only remained to discover an art appealing to the eye through motion—motion, that is, conventionalized in a definite medium."

Continuing, he observes that

the single fact of motion definitely removes cinema from competition with the various graphic arts. Few people realise the vast difference caused by the simple incident of motion. The photograph is still to be judged by the canons of painting, composition, light, tonality, and because so much is determined by external conditions, photography can scarcely hope to do better than a romantic impressionism. Let the same photograph be put in motion and it is subject to a wholly new set of values. For the line of the artist is substituted the moving light of the artist. It is the distinction between a landscape with clouds, and the actual clouds shifting against the sky. A more pointed illustration is an ordinary fire. Painters, with rare exceptions, have passed it by for the obvious reason that there is nothing to paint, it is all motion. Yet there must have been some who wished to catch the bright, fluid colors of the flames, whose fascination is the very opposite of that of the pictures we are told to see there. Somewhat as color has come to be used in painting, as a functional equivalent for line, so on a larger scale the brush-made line gives way in cinema to the rhythmic ordering of less precise masses of light and shade.

Cinema possesses affinity with music. Even here, however, the relation is more useful in philosophical than in technical discussion. Music—Western music, that is—employs likewise temporal continuity, and the two are thus what might be called fourth-dimensional homologues, but they are not so similar in actual detail as to merit the many comparisons made, and the conclusions that have been drawn. . . .

If cinema is an aesthetic expression in time, it is still true that it is also a visual, and so a plastic art. Except in the purest abstract work, it is necessarily concerned, to some degree, with a representation of the physical world. It is, therefore, although closely related to neither the fine arts nor music, a sort of hybrid of the two, and cuts across the established distinction between them.

These remarks may require some qualification and several additions. Compositional value is inherent in the film, even although movement establishes a fresh set of values; and in the theatre we have an art wherein visual movement plays a large part in creating the aesthetic impression.

Between theatrical movement and cinematic, however, there is this essential distinction—that whereas the stage is limited (save for a very few exceptions in "experimental" productions) to one single kind of movement, the movement of the actors upon the boards, the cinema introduces to us a whole series of moving forms undreamt of and unrealisable in the theatre.

Movement in the cinema is, in reality, four-fold. First comes the movement of the actors (or of natural objects, or of abstract forms) depicted upon the screen—the movement we are familiar with in the theatre, save that, although only two-dimensional, it is considerably extended in scope. While the theatre can display at one time only a very limited number of persons, and generally prefers to introduce a bare half-dozen at most, the cinema can sweep a whole army within its range. Crowd scenes in the theatre may sometimes prove effective, but usually it is difficult or even impossible to create there the illusion of space so necessary an accompaniment and, resultant from that, there is commonly experienced an impression of artificiality in the various groupings and regroupings. In the cinema, on the other hand, many of the most memorable scenes have been those in which vast crowds of actors appeared in one series of shots, and many of the dullest have been those wherein attention was concentrated upon a limited number of persons. The close-ups in *The Covered Wagon* had little value; but no one who has seen that film will forget the panoramic view showing the long train of caravans moving over the plains and, in the middle distance, forking to right and left, one party making for the farm-lands of Oregon and the other for the excitements and perils of the Californian gold-fields. In the opportunities offered for the introduction of vast massed effects the film is granted the power of doing something quantitatively greater than it is in the command of the theatre to achieve; but beyond that the cinema can go towards the bringing in of things which, because original and unique, are qualitatively distinct. Obviously in a stage performance it is impossible to animate static objects; on the screen such animation may be effected at any desired moment. A Walt Disney cartoon or a film of the type represented by *The New Gulliver* shows this process in an extreme form, but the process itself, with infinite modifications and gradations, may readily be introduced in any kind of film, either for the purpose of exciting laughter in a comedy or for that of suggesting subjective approach. This and associated devices have a legitimate place in the cinematic world, even if in general we must agree that the basic element in an ordinary narrative film is likely to remain the movement of massed or separate human actors.

Closely connected with this is the power possessed by the camera both of varying the settings and of depicting any movement inherent in the natural objects which form backgrounds for the actors. On the stage the scenery normally remains static except in those instances where a palpably fan-made wind rustles artificial leaves or a Schwabe-Hasait projector sweeps clouds over an unreal sky; normally, too, the theatre restricts itself in the number of localities actually represented upon the stage. On the unadorned Elizabethan platform, certainly, some forty scenes might be included in the course of a single play, and in the modern theatre we have periodical appearances of dramas which, like *Dodsworth,* run to a dozen separate sets; but in general we feel—quite apart from physical difficulties involved in the preparation of these many scenes—that the typical and appropriate stage method is to find means for telling a story within a restricted number of settings. When Besier chooses the Robert Browning-Elizabeth Barrett theme, he shows his skill as a playwright by putting the entire action within one room which remains, save for such changes as may be obtained by the use of light, unaltered from the curtain rise to the conclusion of the drama. That the stage has in its possession a tremendous power through the bold acceptance and exploitation of the conventionalism imposed by such limitation is sure. Here we are considering, however, not merits and defects, but simply matters of difference, and, taking this approach, we are bound to acknowledge that much more is thus brought within the range of the cinema than ever could find adequate realisation in the theatre. In the former we expect to have variety in the scenes presented, we expect to see such movement in the scenes as would be associated with these scenes in reality, and, still further, we expect to see another form of movement conditioned by the shifting of the camera's range of vision.

The shifting of the camera's range of vision amounts practically to a sense of movement in the observer. In the theatre we sit still in one spot and view the stage pictures from left, right or centre; our orientation never changes and, if we are seated at the side, we entirely miss any action placed at the extreme edges of the set. Only once perhaps in the history of the theatre has movement of the spectator been permitted—in the peripatetic mystery stages where a group of "mansions," spread over a considerable tract of land, were placed in front of a crowd who, being furnished with no special seats, could wander around as they willed. Even so, however, the point of view was limited almost entirely to a horizontal range of vision with objects relatively at the same fixed distance from the eye, nor could there be any possibility of compelling a spectator's vision to some one desired spot. This peripatetic mystery stage was an exception and bears no relationship to modern conditions where the audience, seated in appointed places, watch the stage action each from his or her particular point of view. The early film-makers, tutored in the ways of the theatre, never thought of doing anything save shoot scenes in this direct manner, with the camera fixed immovably for each independent scene; but, once technical experimentation demonstrated that the camera itself could move, a whole new means was opened up for the director. Fundamentally, the camera serves as the eye of the observer, with the result that, although we remain seated in our chairs, we truly seem to move while the film displays to us, now a direct shot, now one taken from above, now one from below.

By this movement of the camera's eye, we, spectators, become precisely what the director at any given moment desires. Through the cinema we are magically released from the physical fetters chaining us in life and are granted the power of moving where we will. All things become possible; we may gallop madly over a plain, we may soar high in the heavens, we may delve leagues under the sea. Allied to this is the fact that, having watched the participants in the action being unfolded before us, we very easily identify ourselves with some one individual among these participants and look at the others from his supposed point of view. By this means, the director is enabled to single out any one part of the background he wishes, either for the purpose of drawing our attention to it objectively or else for that of emphasising what is, at a particular moment, being seen by one of his actors. On the stage we may, certainly, by skilful use of lights, properly motivated or expressionistically employed, have the power of blacking out part of the set, but clearly a device of this kind seems almost primitively crude when compared with the fluid ease whereby in those first few minutes of *The Barretts* the camera singles out street, street-door, lamppost, stairs, hall, landing and window. The last-mentioned, the window, occupies a special position. The other objects we have seen as detached spectators would view them, but this window, we realise, is being regarded by us in a fresh light, for we are looking at it, not simply as spectators, but through the eyes of Wilson. Nothing is inachievable in this way; we may even become God if the director commands. During the final set of shots in *The Scoundrel* a character begins to pray; almost immediately the camera sweeps upward and we find ourselves gazing down on his upturned face. Not very successfully carried out because the shot was too close and because we felt slightly embarrassed at becoming

Deity in an attic, the device yet indicated clearly the extent to which the camera can go in this direction.

This camera movement need not, of course, be confined to the presentation simply of a variety of separate shots each static in nature. The mobility of the camera and of the camera eye is infinite. By the use of "panning" the director can make us turn our eyes over a great tract of land or over a vaster crowd than may be brought within the ordinary camera vision; by the employment of a "travelling shot" he can make us approach or retreat from a particular object. With Flush we moved when he ran home along the street and up the stairs to his mistress's room—indeed, we varied our positions here, for on one occasion we actually moved in company with him and on another we stood still at the foot of the stairs, turning our gaze upwards to watch his ascent. In *Broadway Melody of 1936*, an amusing series of shots indicated a further use of the same device. These shots were designed to show an angry producer striding hurriedly through a great newspaper building, intent only on reaching the office of a columnist who had published some scandal concerning him. On the stage this episode would have been impossible of realisation, but in cinematic form it took on life and interest. The camera simply followed the producer's figure as room after room flashed rapidly by, the impetuosity of his haste causing papers to rise and flutter from the desks.

Because it is so closely associated with the essentials of the cinematic art and forms so distinctive a feature of that art, camera movement of this kind demands the greatest possible attention and analysis. One might, for example, question whether the familiar and frequently employed backward action whereby the field of vision is widened from a relatively close shot to a medium shot or a long is advisable except for special effects. If the camera lens corresponds to our eye, there is a certain strain in adjusting ourselves to a rearward motion—a motion we rarely employ in ordinary life—while at the same time we are abandoning the opportunity, by this too frequent use, of utilising the device effectively and legitimately to express fear in one of the characters. Perhaps, too, consideration ought to be given to Paul Rotha's argument that overuse of the moving camera tends to bring the film back to theatre standards, for the director, taking the easiest way, may be inclined to sacrifice the essentially cinematic montage and attempt to secure his effects by means of camera manipulation. That there is truth in these observations is certain, although we must remember that the moving camera also is fundamentally cinematic. Another example of the problems involved may be chosen from the usage associated with a panning camera or one moving in a straight line parallel to a field of action. The impression created by camera and figures proceeding in the same direction will differ materially from that produced by a combination of moving camera and static objects or from a combination of a camera travelling in one direction and figures coming against its path. These examples are mentioned here because, in spite of the fact that many excellent sequences have resulted from the careful employment of the mobile camera, insufficient attention seems to have been paid to the resultant audience reactions, and, since this provides one of the basic attributes of the cinema, clearly every endeavour ought to be made to determine precisely the various impressions and moods produced by such means. Perhaps, in order to demonstrate something of the minutiae connected with these

problems, one might refer to the fresh significance given
to the question of the familiar theatrical "left" or "right"
cross. It is fairly well known that stage directors commonly
use the expedient of bringing important characters on
from stage left and of using a left to right cross for a
specially significant action. The reason is that normally we
are accustomed (probably because of early training in
writing) to carry our gaze from our left to our right and
therefore are more arrested by movements proceeding in
an opposite direction. Now, the cinema director not only
has the same means as are possessed by the stage director,
permitting him to make use of left and right entrances in
this manner, he also is given the opportunity, through the
panning shot, of carrying our gaze in whichever way he
wills. A camera movement from left to right must inevitably produce an impression diverse from that occasioned
by a movement in the contrary direction; these, combined
with the directions which may be taken by the actors, introduce a complexity which goes considerably beyond the
complexity of the theatre.

Besides these, the cinema has still another means of
presenting movement. Basically, a film consists of an in-
determinate number of individual pictures (frames); these,
placed in the projector, are run off and the seemingly
moving images cast on to the screen. At first, no one
thought of passing these individual pictures through the
camera at any rate other than one conventionally determined; but, with increasing experimentation in cinematic
possibilities, it was soon found that, by increasing or de-
creasing the number of frames used for a single shot
effects of slow motion and of increased rapidity could
be produced, that the pictures might be run backward so

as to show reverse action and that at any given moment the whole movement of the film through the projector might be arrested and the eye of the spectator held by a "still" allowed to remain statically on the screen.

Many of such devices, of course, have been misapplied and many are of little use for ordinary cinematic purposes. Exaggerated slow and rapid motion belong largely to the realm of trick photography. It may be instructive and even aesthetically pleasing to see slow-motion pictures of horses leaping over hurdles and of waves dashing up against the rocks; but such shots can only rarely be of service in the presentation of filmic narrative. When unexaggerated, however, and carefully subdued, immense possibilities open themselves up in this field. Quite apart from the fact that the camera, by the trick use of such devices, may lead us into believing action to be swifter or slower than it could be in reality, a subtler employment may provide another kind of movement, not appreciated consciously but nevertheless of strong potential emotional appeal. An impression of haste or one of indolence may readily be achieved by these means and occasionally symbolic shots (say, the unfolding of a flower's petals) are thus rendered possible of execution. Even the use of an occasional "still" in the midst of a narrational film can prove of value, although most of the experiments made in this direction seem to indicate that the violent contrast between the moving images and the static picture is too disturbing to act as more than a very minor tool in the hands of the director.

Finally, there is a fourth sort of movement attainable by the cinematic method. The various shots out of which an entire film is created must obviously vary considerably in their duration; by the utilisation of several brief shots presented in sequence a very different impression of speed is conveyed from that which is aroused by the employment of longer shots. The combination of shot-lengths of differing duration, however, carries us over to the question of filmic rhythm and may at present be left aside for later consideration.

LINKAGE

The sense of movement in the cinema is added to even by methods which do not strictly apply to the shots themselves. Already it has been observed that a film differs structurally from a play in that whereas the latter has only a limited number of divisions, the former has many. The units in a film are the individual shots, which are short; the units in a play are the scenes, and it has been found that the theatre is in general best served by scenes which have a fair amplitude and present a major portion of the plot development. This is largely the explanation of the fact that, in general, dramas which concentrate on a rather limited period of time are more effective than those which cast their action over numbers of years. A certain following of the famous "unities" has distinguished many of the world's dramatic masterpieces. Even during the period of greatest dramatic freedom, the period of Elizabeth, there is evident a tendency, as in *Othello,* to restrict the scope of the action, or, where that proved impossible, a corresponding tendency to suggest such a restriction. Thus may be explained Shakespeare's "double clock," by means of which an impression is given that a narrative demanding the passing of months has been carried through in a brief passing of days. Outside of the Elizabethan theatre, this tendency is even more marked. Plays of the kind represented by Arnold Bennett's *Milestones* or James Bridie's *The Sleeping Clergyman* are comparatively rare.

Opposed to all these tendencies are the ways of the cinema. Long-drawn-out scenes there have been found lacking in appeal; the only legitimate way of telling a story filmically is to split it up into a variety of separate episodes. Because of this splitting up, the cinema almost demands extension in time-limit. One might in this connection compare Shakespeare's dramatic "double clock" with a similar, but inverted, device used in *The Informer*. In that film all the action was supposed to take place in a bare twelve hours, a strict "unity," but hardly a single spectator would have been prepared to say aught else than that this action really covered a longer period. Not, of course, that *The Informer* is by any means typical; generally we prefer a film to carry its story over months and years, finding no difficulty, rather delight, in accepting the aid of the cinematic time machine.

This leads to a consideration of the breaks which necessarily must come between scene and scene or between shot and shot. In general, the theatre possesses only a limited range in the means of separating the several portions of a drama. Very definite emotional effects, certainly, can be called forth by the use of a slow or a quick curtain and by short or long intermissions; but, since the director is given only a few opportunities for these and for the variety in treatment, they form only a minor element in his summoning of mood values. He may have a long intermission when the audience is permitted to troop into the foyer; he may have a scene-change within an act which lasts anything from a minute to four minutes; he may have a swift rise and fall of the curtain without a scene-change (to mark

the passing of time); he may have a scene-change effected
in full view of the audience. Beyond these he cannot go.
Between scene and scene, moreover, there is little possibility of linkage. An orchestra occasionally may play appropriate music; very occasionally there may be a structural
uniting of the two parts by sound or light. In the original
Belasco version of *Madam Butterfly,* for example, the little
Japanese bride and her children sat watching for the hus-
band's return; gradually the afternoon sun faded into twilight, the twilight gave way to darkness and that in turn
was pierced by the first rays of dawn, which revealed the
children asleep and the mother still waiting for her lover.
Shakespeare used a "chorus" in *Henry V* to bind sections
of his play together, a device followed by John Drinkwater
in *Abraham Lincoln;* a few dramatists have introduced
linkage material in the form of dialogue, drum-beats or
trumpet-calls, continuing through a change of setting. Such
devices, however, are rare, and we recognise their feeble-
ness when we turn to the innumerable opportunities offered in the cinema for linkage both by means of sound
and by visual means. The ordinary direct break is there,
corresponding to the pause or wait during a scene-change
or to the longer intermission. But this is merely one among
many others. By a fade-out the scene being shown may
be caused gradually to disappear—an exaggerated and more
suggestive version of the theatre's slow curtain. By a fade-
in a new scene may gradually take shape before our eyes.
A mix makes one shot imperceptibly intertwine itself with
that which is to follow. The fade-in, the fade-out and the
mix are to be regarded as normal means in the hands of the
director and we expect their use in almost every film. Further variation is securable by devices of the kind introduced

into *Broadway Melody of 1936,* where, instead of a fade-in, the whole image on the screen, as though set on a horizontal or vertical pivot, turned over, from right to left, from left to right or from top to bottom, revealing another picture at the rear. A similar linkage device is that whereby an image starts to split in ever lengthening wedges, these wedges, extending across the screen, gradually bringing into view the beginning of the next shot. Another was exemplified in *Thunder over Mexico* where a distinct variation in mood appreciation was produced by a kind of washing or rubbing-out effect linking the Aztec shots contrasted with the sharp breaks between the shots showing the Maya monuments. It is obvious that every one of these has its own significance and that the cinema director has opportunities offered to him in this respect of which the theatre director can make no avail.

Associated with these linking devices are the time-indicating shots which join two main portions of the filmic narrative. To suggest a passage of years there is, for example, the trick of showing the leaves of a calendar turning over rapidly—in its simple form a hackneyed trick, certainly, but one the scope of which is restricted by nothing save the imaginative power of the author and director. A shot of a full bottle fading into the bare remains of a banquet will demonstrate clearly, though silently, the passing of evening into morning. With added symbolic value, the flickering down of a candle will produce a similar impression. A modification of this device occurred in *The Age of Innocence* wherein we were shown, first, the revolving wheels of a buggy and then, without a break (by means of a mix or dissolve), the revolving wheels of an automobile. The simple change did all that was needed to bring us imaginatively from one generation's world into that of another. Longer and fuller time values may be combined with narrative elements in this way. In *Diamond Jim* we had to be informed that Jim Brady had started manufacturing in a small way, had proved successful and had consequently become the owner of a large factory. The method employed was strictly in accord with proper cinematic technique. A single shot showed us Brady speculating on his plan; the next revealed a small blacksmith's shop, this faded into a small factory while that in turn dissolved into a vaster expanse of factory buildings. Without a word story was told and time indicated.

Typical of what may be done in this direction is the journey from London to Dover in *David Copperfield*, already referred to. The story-teller's business here was to suggest, without dwelling upon, the long tramp which joined the earlier episodes to the later. At the most the theatre could have given us either narrative description in retrospect or else a vision of David setting off well-clad at the end of one scene and of his arrival, dust-covered, torn and weary at the beginning of the next. Filmically, the impression was secured by a series of disjointed shots: periodically and rhythmically the progressive milestones indicated the stages; these were inset with a few long shots showing David trudging along; with those went one or two close shots of his trousers and shoes, gradually becoming torn and worn; in one we saw only his hands passing over a coat into the fat hands of a pawnbroker; in another a coach rattled far into the distant roadway amid a storm of dust; still another introduced the eerie noises and fearsome shadows of the night; while one shot displayed the eating of a hunk of stale bread which had been rudely wrapped in newspaper. Altogether, and as a combination, hardly anything could have been conceived more strongly to evoke the mood desired and to provide the proper linking of sequence to sequence.

Such methods, too, must be considered, not only for their time-indicating and mood-creating values, but also for their significance in providing a sense of movement and for the technical requirements they demand in the preparation of a cinematic scenario. Obviously a series of separate shots, each sharply concluded and begun, will affect us far differently from the same series of shots blended and fluidly streaming from one action to another. Of this the stage knows little. A dramatist has to seek always for a "good curtain" to each scene; the film author, owing to the particular conditions of the art in which he is working, generally has to avoid these "good curtains" of a dramatic kind. In the cinema an imaginative power has to be called into play different from that required in the theatre, and particularly in this matter of linking the various shots a vigilance and an alertness are demanded separate from that care which the theatrical director will take in the timing of his curtain or from the painstaking thought the dramatist will devote to the final words of his scene.

FILMIC MAGNITUDE AND CONCENTRATION

Several of the cinematic devices mentioned above contribute to providing the film with another quality unpossessed by the stage. Already, in the short example from *The Barretts of Wimpole Street,* it has been observed that the camera may single out some one object so that, without the least chance of any spectator's failing to grasp the director's intention, all else in a scene is for the moment eliminated. The close-up, which more than any other device, contributes to securing this concentration, may, of course, be abused. We have become tired of watching a grossly magnified head of the heroine, followed by a similarly grossly magnified head of the hero; although it is quite understandable why, in the early days, directors conceived the close-up only in terms of the stars. The close-up, however, has a service and a function far removed from that of merely giving intimate pictures of popular features multiplied some forty fold; its function is to provide typically filmic magnitude and concentration. The first demands a word or two of explanation. On the stage an actor is an actor and a hornet is a hornet. That is to say, the spectators can see the actor as nothing but a man, six feet tall, standing from ten to a hundred paces from them; he can be no smaller and no larger than the playhouse conditions and the laws of optics permit. If a hornet buzzes unbidden onto the scene it will be invisible to practically everyone in the audience. But in the cinema, the actor may be made to appear any size the director wishes; and a hornet may be made to fill the entire screen. Real magnitude, like real time, is, on the screen, completely banished; and the director is empowered, if he so desires, to utilise this opportunity for adding to the effectiveness of his story.

To secure this impression, of course, other devices besides that of the close-up may be employed. In casting on the screen an enlarged image of a hornet the shape of this insect is truly made hundreds of times greater than it is in reality: but relative magnitude may be employed, without the aid of actual enlargement, to secure similar effects. If, for example, we are shown a picture of a house, mentally we give to that house the height it would be likely to have in real life and normally we should expect to see a man taking proportionate size by standing just underneath the lintel of the door. An easy cinematic device, however, could readily show us a human figure apparently towering over the roof, and, this presented to us, our minds would immediately credit this creature with superhuman stature. To create the seemingly enormous or the seemingly small in this way, to transform completely the familiar proportions of life, is a task of no difficulty in the cinema, and, although there may not often be opportunity for employing the device, the means is there, another tool at the service of the cinematic director. At least in films introducing the supernatural the method might prove of excellent service. In a cinematic rendering of *A Midsummer Night's Dream,* for instance, an interesting effect could be secured by showing the fairies at one time so small that they can truly rest in cowslip bells and at another assuming the stature of humans. The idea is explicit in Shakespeare's words although manifestly its physical expression on the stage would be utterly impossible; and one may suggest that Max Reinhardt missed a chance when, in his filmic version, he failed to differentiate his fairies and his humans in size. A little thought will demonstrate that his fairyland might easily, by this means, have been made much more thrilling, delicate and, because bound up with Shakespeare's poetic conceptions, inherently affecting.

Intimately associated with filmic magnitude and, indeed, in many instances, hardly to be separated from that, is the power of concentration which the cinema possesses. By the use of the close-up and in other ways the director can, as it were, take the whole audience by the hand and make them see what he wishes them to see. On the stage, "point-

ing" is a familiar device. By words, by actions, by placement of properties, by groupings, attention is drawn to
some one thing which the plot demands the spectators to
notice. With what labour and with what wearisome toil
this effect is secured, however, is proved by the witnessing
of any one good film. Here the director simply looks with
his camera at what he chooses and the audience is compelled to do the same. In *The Informer* the police notice of
reward is photographed in its entirety—no tedious reading
of its contents aloud as would happen on the stage; it is
photographed all crumpled up as it flutters along the murky
street and as the wind makes it cling to Gypo's legs; finally
it is photographed while the flames curl with caressing evil
around it and distort the face of the man who has been
betrayed. Control over its material is complete in the
film; the possibilities of selection are infinite and at
every moment attention may be concentrated on just those
things which are of essential import. "Guided by the mind
of the scenarist and director," rightly remarks Paul Rotha,
"the camera eliminates from the screen everything but
material absolutely significant to the exposition of the
dramatic content of the theme." What this implies a few
examples will demonstrate.

On the stage, an actor's whole body no doubt must play
its impersonation, but, unless we are among those who use
opera glasses, we must inevitably fail to notice many of
these body movements. A Moissi and a Hardwicke may
convey much by the use of their hands—the flashing flame-
like hands of the former in Franz Moor or the window-tap-
ping fingers of the latter in Barrett; but the possibility of
producing effect thereby is limited. All the camera has to
do to tell a story is to focus on a pair of hands clutched in

grief, clasped in agony, hypocritically expanded. A pair of boots will present a character, and a tragic tale may be shown in a silk hat. That Griffith was the first to realise the opportunities offered by the close-up is generally recognised, and one shot in *Intolerance* has become classical; to him we owe the discovery of what is perhaps the greatest of the film's assets. For we ought to note that this close-up provides not merely for intensification of something already shown in the large; it has the power of giving the film a fine selectiveness. On the stage—unless in a mystery thriller we decide to stimulate horror by showing the clutching hand of an unknown villain stealing from behind a curtain—any character called for by the plot, no matter how insignificant his part may be, must be displayed in the flesh. The character perhaps is given only one line, but there he must stand before us to say it. By means of the close-up the cinema is provided with the opportunity of revealing only the significant and, by selecting, of suggesting the whole. In *David Copperfield* the person of the pawnbroker to whom the boy pledged his coat did not need to be brought before our view; all the situation was clearly outlined by showing the man's hands as they took the coat and passed a piece of money to the trembling young hands stretched out to his.

The presence of these attributes—the power to alter size at will and to concentrate on just those elements which are regarded as significant—alters the entire scope of the cinema from that of the theatre, both in directional method and in that of scenario composition. The theatre, too, has the ability to concentrate in its effects, but the means of attaining this end are mostly different and, even when they are akin, are calculated to produce divergent reactions in an audience. The moving camera may introduce points of view which, aiding the concentration desired, utterly change by their orientation our vision of the objects presented. In a film we can look at an object from any angle, no matter how strange; we may be under a horse's hooves, we may suffer an automobile to pass right over us, we may see a man not only from front, back or side but also slanting-ways, from above, from beneath. In a hundred different respects the point of view can be altered. An interesting example occurred in the film version of *Children in Uniform*. The stage play necessarily confined the action to rooms within the school and each of these was viewed from the angle normal to anyone who might have entered such a room; in the film one of the most arresting shots showed a picture of the central stairway in the school, taken from the head of the shaft, and the peculiar placement of the camera did much toward building up the mood quality of that particular scene. In the theatre point of view is fixed and immutable; in the film it is free and varied.

Because of this the film director has other and different problems than those confronting his stage colleague. A theatre presents to the eyes of the audience a proscenium arch which forms a rectangular "picture-frame," and the director, in manipulating his cast, has in general just one major question to answer:—how best and most effectively to bring his characters into the view of the spectators. His frame at least remains static. On the screen, of course, is projected a similar static frame, for the screen itself is stationary; but the background revealed by the open frame is constantly changing, or rather may be made to change in accordance with the director's or author's wishes. In one scene the camera may remain motionless and the characters enter the field of vision much as they would do were they actors in a theatre; in another the actors may remain relatively motionless while the camera swings or retreats so as to draw more into the field of vision. Effects of surprise and suspense find ready and varied realisation in these ways.

Although it were out of place further to examine the innumerable technical devices of a purely filmic kind or to explore in detail the consequences resultant upon the utilisation of each, a conclusion in general terms may be reached to the effect that, whereas in drama a plot ought usually to be unfolded directly, indirect treatment is the true medium of the cinema. Two of the examples already given will serve to support this statement. A comparison of *The Barretts of Wimpole Street* in play and screen version, besides indicating now much in the latter is achieved by visual image, convinces us that, while for the one a straightforward development of narrational elements is essential, for the other the oblique shots of street, Flush, door, hall, staircase and window are clearly right and just. *The Informer* may similarly be considered. Were that a stage play, we should demand a logical moving forward, an explanation of the relation between the betrayer and the betrayed, an elaboration, in words, of the offered reward and of Gypo's temptations. All of these things are secured, and secured effectively, by the oblique filmic method, with the utilisation of concentrated images to make the facts and the psychological reactions intelligible.

The ability of the camera to control space and magnitude obviously gives it a kind of magical power. By its means we are enabled to do things impossible in our ordinary terrestrial existence and to see things which could never be in actuality. To transform the size of human beings is witchcraft and to set lifeless objects into animate motion is dark with the wizard's spell. The greater part of this magic no doubt is confined to the sphere of the cartoon which, in Walt Disney's hands, will display animals acting as humans amid the surroundings of man-made civilisation, will make furniture behave like sensible beings, will personify an abstract conception and give thought and emotion to a musical note. Here all the laws of our material lives are defied. That such magic, however, is not confined entirely to Disney's fantasies has already become clear. The simple operation of slow motion or of accelerated motion causes common phenomena to assume new and surprising appearances; by means of similar simple camera tricks a man may be shown walking upside-down over a ceiling, striding serenely across a cloud, rising wingless into the air. Reinhardt's fairies soared aloft like aeroplanes after a little run for a take-off; René Clair's spirit in *The Ghost goes West* was at will seemingly solid or transparent.

This camera magic was seized upon at a very early date in the history of the film. By 1902 George Méliès had produced *A Trip to the Moon,* a production which introduced many trick shots aiming at the creation of the absurdly impossible. His professors reach the lunar realms and watch their umbrellas (stuck in the soil) grow up to giant toadstools, or surprisingly find the moon's inhabitants, on receiving a blow, vanish in a puff of smoke. Méliès was wrong cinematically in the particular orientation he adopted, with his frankly painted backdrops and general vaudeville lay-out, but the principles involved in this film were such as may be put to service more legitimately in half a hundred ways.

His tricks we could not accept because they were so obvious, but a vast realm of invention stretches out in the combination of the seemingly actual and the patently impossible. For reasons which will be discussed later, film spectators can readily accept the obviously artificial (exemplified in the Disney cartoon) or the apparently real; they refuse to accept the theatrical. Within the scope of the apparently real, however, is included much more than that which is either familiar or possible. By easy gradations, an audience may be induced to treat the frankly impossible as if it were not only possible but positively realised. "The film," says a writer in *Intercine*, "can give us documentary fidelity even in the representation of the impossible and the marvellous. By the aid of its tricks, it shows us, with complete exactitude, the aspect that would be assumed by the impossible, if it were possible." To gain appreciation for this, all the cinema has to do is to introduce its material in a kind of matter-of-fact way.

A brief comparison between the basic approaches of *A Trip to the Moon* and of some shots in *Strike Me Pink* will illustrate this clearly. In the former the entire orientation was "theatrical." The latter set forth a story which, although containing elements of an exaggerated kind, was based on actuality. Having set this atmosphere of slightly fantastic realism, the director could then easily present "documentary fidelity" in the completely impossible. At one moment we were shown a dancer performing on a highly polished floor which mirrored his movements; suddenly his reflected image started to dance away to one side, and, even when he himself paused, it continued its tripping steps. If images and shadows could separate themselves from their creators, this is the way they would behave; no trip to the moon could ever be like that presented by Méliès. The same procedure was followed in another shot of *Strike Me Pink* where a dancer, leaping in the air, slowly descends and remains delicately balanced upon the outstretched hand of another figure. Were we able to make our bodies light as air, thus would we act. Kindred examples might be taken from a variety of recent films. The events, for example, presented in *The Invisible Man* were impossible, but the thought of their impossibility was dissipated by the apparent veracity of their documentary quality. To watch a real skull gradually turning into a human head would, we know, be something which life has no power to grant us; but seeing this on the screen brought a wondering thrill of acceptance. In things of this kind, so long as all is kept within the field of the imaginatively actual and out of that of the theatrical, everything goes well. Whenever the theatrical intrudes, the spell is destroyed and the illusion vanishes. Some shots in Reinhardt's *Midsummer Night's Dream* demonstrated this clearly. The actual transforming of Bottom's head was well done. Thus, we felt, could a head alter its shape almost imperceptibly. But when the transition process was completed and we looked upon the new Bottom we realised with a shock that he was wearing just such an ass-mask as we might have seen in any theatrical production of the play, and consequently the illusion which we had before been prepared to accept utterly left us. Not thus would a real ass-head appear in a world where such things had become possible.

Combination of screen-pictures and of sound effects obviously increases the film's control over magical effects of this kind. It is cinematically an easy task to show an animal—a dog or a horse, say—apparently speaking like a human being or to display a man who utters no words but expresses himself by means of a dog's growl or a horse's neigh. We are in a world here where anything may happen, and part of the delight we take in the cinema arises from the fact that we are in this way enabled, not only to see more clearly and with greater vividness the things which, because of their very commonness and easy familiarity, we are not accustomed to examine closely, but also to have presented before us objects and events which could never find realisation in this world. The Indian juggler's (seemingly mythical) rope-trick offers on the screen no difficulty in accomplishment and his mango-growing sleight-of-hand is achievable in thoroughly "realistic" terms. Within a space of three minutes we may watch a rose-tree rise from a cutting to a flowering plant or observe the three second's of a horse's jumping extended to cover a period of time multiplied a hundred-fold.

FILMIC TIME

Clearly, in a play the dramatist has the power of creating, within certain limits, his own time. A full-length comedy or tragedy contains, let us say, three acts, the first supposed to occur in January, the second in April, the third in November. These three acts, however, take only two and a half hours to present on the stage. License is given the author to imagine, within the intermission periods, the passing by of the requisite months; but within the acts he must bow to severe restrictions. A theatrical director, to secure an impression desired by himself or by the playwright, may cause a particular scene to be performed inordinately fast or considerably slower than might normally be expected, but rarely are we willing to accept in the theatre more than a slight increasing or diminishing of speed. So, too, we permit the author to "steal" time only when this "stealing" is not carried so far as to become obtrusive; a fictional half-hour's action can be lengthened to make forty minutes' playing or reduced to an actual performance of twenty. Occasionally, of course, this may be brought slightly further; thus the Greek tragic writers, during a choral chant, sometimes assumed a passage of time far in excess of the time actually spent by the chorus in the orchestra; but in general devices of this kind have now been incorporated in the act-intermissions or breaks between the scenes when time is permitted to slip by, unseen and unnoticed, between one section of a drama and another.

Normally, too, in a play, this fictional time, whether corresponding exactly to real time or not, has to flow onwards straight-forwardly. There are, of course, a few dramas in which deviations have been made, in which the action moves consistently backward, in which there is a sudden return to a period already passed, in which, even, two scenes, supposed to occur simultaneously, are given one after the other. Such experimental forms, however, are rare and, popular though they may be for a time, we feel that they are somewhat freakish and that the theatre is not likely to exploit their methods freely. This being so, it will be realised that usually the playwright, having to start in the midst of an action which must possess (no matter how self-inclusive the stage action seems) a past and a future, is compelled to pursue a direct and rectilinear path. His exposition must take the form either of bold conventional description of the kind used by Shakespeare in *The Tempest* or else of the provision, carefully concealed, of information inherent in the speeches given to his characters.

Direct narrative and description of this kind is by no means necessary in the films and consequently there enter in expository devices of an entirely different quality. Once more the credit of displaying the full possibilities of the cinema in this direction goes to D. W. Griffith. Ever an innovator, and with a true sense of filmic values, to him came the realisation that the cinema need not keep to a strictly natural time-sequence—that the flash-back was not only a legitimate cinematic device but one that was peculiarly suited to its purposes. Already has been demonstrated how much of antecedent material the film may present by means of visual images; but, in addition to this, the film possesses in the flash-back an opportunity of conveying information which normally could be conveyed in a drama only by the introduction of retrospective narrative. The device, as we have seen, has been employed in plays by Elmer Rice and a few other modern dramatists, but its sphere is properly cinematic and not theatrical. Of the flash-back there are two principal forms. In the first, the flash-back, by presenting a picture of events supposed to have taken place in the past, merely corresponds to the playwright's expository explanations. We are introduced, say, to a couple of characters; up to a certain point their story is unfolded and then an episode occurs which creates a very definite and marked reaction in one of them. To explain that reaction it is necessary to indicate that the episode shown is in some manner linked up with another which had taken place before the beginning of the selected action. On the stage only rarely can aught else save narrative be used for this purpose; in the film it is easy—because the film obeys solely the dictates of its own time-scheme—to break the chronological continuity and to summon from the past whatever may be desired. Watching a film, we entirely lose sight of the time-progression familiar to us in our daily lives, and without effort we are prepared to accept anything the director or author may choose to cull from that past which, cinematically, at any moment can be transmogrified into the present.

Separate from this simpler function of the flash-back, there is the second, where the flash-back is used to resummon that which we have already seen. Thus, towards the end of a plot we may desire to emphasise some episode which has occurred, and which we have seen occurring, at the beginning of the film. Nothing is simpler than to re-introduce these earlier shots and make them run their course a second time. No doubt over-use of this device, too, may become monotonous and distracting; but, carefully employed by the director for selected situations, it provides the film with opportunities barely realisable on the stage.

In the flash-back, the camera makes the past relive itself; but it can do more still, it may make the present live a double existence. The cinema, by thus destroying ordinary time and space, leads us into a kind of fourth dimensional world where our imaginations are released and where the spiritual takes control of the physical. Our eyes being in one place, it is, of course, impossible in reality to see two concurrent events at once; if we watch the happenings in one room we cannot watch those in another. But in the film this may readily be achieved. Several writers on the film have pointed out the use of this concurrent presentation of two simultaneous events in the early "Westerns." A familiar situation there was the plight of hero or heroine, threatened with death, while his or her friends galloped madly to the rescue. At one moment we saw the heroine; the next shot showed us the foam-flecked steeds; that following brought us back to the heroine; again the galloping horses succeeded—and so on, through a series rising crescendo until at the last moment the forces of virtue arrived to triumph over those of vice. We have become rather tired of such crude attempts nowadays, although the situation is still to be seen—was seen recently indeed in *Les Miserables* with considerable effectiveness; but once more we realise that the device is one capable of exceedingly subtle and artistic employment. Of it the stage had no conception until the cinema came to indicate this new approach; and clearly, even when the device is imitated there, we can hope for no great flexibility in its use. True, Bruckner experiments in this way with concurrent events in *Elizabeth and Essex* when he shows on one side of the stage Elizabeth and her courtiers praying for victory, on the other Philip and his nobles similarly engaged; but the sheer limitations of stage space forbid its further elaboration.

The methods by which concurrent events may be presented or suggested in the film are various. By pursuing a continuity in space instead of in time conceptions based on the familiar passing of moment to moment are dissipated. One might, for instance, have three or four shots of diverse localities, separated by it matters not how many leagues, and demonstrate to an audience their appearance at any chosen identical minute; actually, of course, these follow a time continuity in their running through the projector but that time progression will be forgotten in the emotional impression created. Or else two separate events may be shown at the same time, through the means of double exposure; each shot reveals a distinct action but because of the superimposition of one upon the other we are given the power of being in two places at once, of releasing ourselves for the nonce from the fettering restrictions laid upon us in actual life. Neither of these two devices could find a place in the theatre; both are thoroughly characteristic of the film. The most that the theatre might accomplish in this way would be the representation of, say, several rooms in a single house, all revealed to the audience simultaneously, but, even if in each of these rooms action proceeds concurrently, the proscenium frame is too large to permit our watching what occurs in every room; our gaze will stray from one to another without that concentration securable in the film. Associated with such cinematic devices are others wherein the idea of time enters in only indirectly. Imagine, for example, a scene of magic where a witch waves her wand and causes certain objects to vanish utterly or, waving her wand again, makes them assume their former shapes. The procedure is impossible in nature and could be represented in nothing but a clumsy manner on the stage, but by filmic method it is rendered easy of achievement. Time and space, in every respect, are controlled by the scenarist and director.

THE SUBJECTIVE APPROACH

The cinema's methods in these directions, involving the power to present not merely the actual or the imaginatively actual but also the purely imaginative, both in time and space continuity, necessitate the discussion of a further quality which sharply distinguishes the cinematic approach from the theatrical. In the theatre we are bound essentially to accept a wholly objective treatment of whatsoever is shown to us. In making this statement, one must, of course, indicate clearly what is implied in the use of the word "objective." Every work of art is subjective in the sense that into it the artist has thrown his own being; Shakespeare may not positively reveal himself in his plays, may not draw himself in his Romeo or his Hamlet, but the very spirit of Shakespeare is wrought within the fabric of his tragedies and his comedies. This is true not only of poetic plays; even in realistic dramas, if they are genuinely artistic, the presence of the creating author is to be felt, informing the course of the action, determining the positions and the words of his characters. Not in this way, however, are the terms "objective" and "subjective" employed here. Their present significance is determined by the necessary approach towards and means of presenting the action or the characters. Thus in the theatre normally we are confronted by a set of persons, viewed objectively as we view our friends and our neighbors in our common daily life; they may be set in a pattern, they may be made to reveal their motives more clearly than is common to men and women in daily existence but there is nothing qualitatively different in their fundamental appearance and behaviour. We are simply catching them, as it were, at significant moments in their lives even as, on occasion, we may catch real persons who, through a sudden shock or overwhelming emotion, cast off for a time their social masks and give us glimpses of their inner spirit. There are, of course, exceptions to this on the stage. O'Neill has sought in *Strange Interlude* to suggest deeper, secret thoughts and commonly concealed emotions, emotions and thoughts which ordinarily are hidden behind politely smiling exterior words and gestures; Pirandello has, in several plays, endeavoured to mix the world of outer "reality" and that of creative vision, going so far as to mingle "real" persons and the figures born of a playwright's mind; occasionally, too, we find dramas wherein one act is a fantastic one, the embodiment of some character's day-dreaming. In all such plays, however, we experience an impression of strain. Commenting recently on Elmer Rice's *Not for Children,* Charles Morgan declared that, "as a piece for the theatre—that is to say, for a place to which men and women come that their imagination may be impregnated by esthetic illusion," this drama suffered from the serious defect, "namely, that it obtrusively juggles with the planes of illusion, a process which, though often a necessary point of view of philosophic criticism, is the very devil of dullness when the stage itself engages in it." This judgment is fundamentally just. The normal stage procedure is being rudely stretched and we feel that, interesting though such experiments may be, too much is being pressed into a form essentially suited to contain matter less subtle. It seems certain, moreover, that the theatre will not suddenly abandon its old ways and whole-heartedly follow this new path; Pirandello's dramas are interesting but he will not be the master of a great new school. The theatre has ever found its strength in objective treatment and to that objective treatment it will continue to cling.

When, on the other hand, we turn to the cinema we discover something essentially different. *Broadway Melody of 1936* was an ordinary spectacular "musical" which sought in no wise to satisfy the "artistic" aims of intellectual purists. It was a typical Hollywood studio production. Were we to tell an ordinary spectator that in that film he had witnessed an example of subjective treatment of material, he would no doubt simply stare at us uncomprehendingly or incredulously; yet the example was there. In one shot we see a young girl with stage aspirations seated in the orchestra of an empty theatre, waiting for the producer to call her. Suddenly, without losing sight of the girl herself, we watch the bare stage miraculously become set with a rich scene, and there in the centre of the stage is this same girl dancing. Without any effort or strain we have entered into the girl's mind, we have passed easily and without recognition of the fact from an objective to a subjective approach. A similar device was used in *The Informer,* in the sequence when Gypo Nolan stands outside a tourist office window gazing at the advertisements there. From these advertisements his eyes descend to the model of a liner set out on display. Gradually the picture of the model dissolves into another showing the deck of a real ship on which stand Gypo himself and his "girl," Kate, dressed as bride and bridegroom, he holding the rail while the sea-winds blow her fluttering finery in the air. The shot is one of an event which never had been, and never could be, save in the mind of the character.

Perhaps the difference between the theatrically objective and the cinematically subjective approaches may be realised if we imagine a possible filmic treatment of a Shake-spearian play, say *Macbeth*. Were *Macbeth* to be rendered in terms of the screen, part of Macbeth's dreaming in regard to the glories attainable after Duncan's death might well be displayed visually as purely fantastic images conjured from the depths of his own mind; and so, too, many of his fears at the close, many of his sorrowful regrets, might effectively be shown us in actual shots. "The hosts of friends" and honours which he had for ever lost might take immediate form before our eyes. Another instance is suggested by *Hamlet*. For modern audiences there must always be difficulty in accepting the famous queen's closet scene. There Hamlet confronts his mother, only to be interrupted by the appearance of the ghost. This ghost is not merely a figment of the prince's mind, since it is given words to speak, yet the queen fails to see it. The fact that we watch this ghost moving across the stage makes us incredulous of Gertrude's inability to trace its form, and consequently a certain tenseness in the scene is destroyed. In the cinema such an episode would present no difficulty. When Hamlet looks the ghost is there; when the queen looks it is absent. The task would be easy, for in the film we are granted the power of seeing through many different eyes when we look upon the screen.

The subjective approach, naturally, may assume a variety of diverse forms. Again turning to *The Informer*, we recall the direct presentation of the reward notice with its photographic reproduction of Frankie MacPhillip's features; after the betrayal, Gypo comes to the bare wall from which he has torn down this notice and almost imperceptibly the paper once more takes shape in front of his eyes, only this time the photographed face bears an angry and accusing scowl. Perhaps most effective are those shots in which the imaginative, subjective image is mixed into the "real" one, as when the drunken Gypo enters the shebeen and approaches a girl who shrinks from him. This girl is a stranger, but, gradually, by double exposure, her form and features change and take focussed shape again as Katie. In a flash we are made acquainted with what would have taken many words to express in a drama.

Another example of the way in which the film, by the possession of this power, deviates from the path pursued by the stage appears in the sound version of *Peter Ibbetson*. In the theatre only a faint and clumsy approach could be made towards realising the peculiar psychological state postulated by the novelist in his hero and heroine. The film accomplished the task easily. From symbolic touches, such as the showing of the railing which separates the two children, the railing which divides the grown man and woman when first they meet again and the prison bars which shut them off physically from one another, to the manipulation of the dream machinery, the film achieves its purpose surely. We are made conscious of the close spiritual connection between the lovers when we watch him being cruelly flogged in jail, switch off for a moment to hear her scream in terrified agony while she stands in her own room miles away and turn back once more to the scene in prison. Readily does the film lend itself to the creation of the dream world into which these lovers, released from the clinging fetters of the flesh, move during their hours of sleep. The vast forests they traverse, the pleasant lawns they tread on, the terrors of the mental storm, the delicate out-lines of the dream palace—all these could be created visu-ally only through the medium of cinematic expression. By no powerful alchemy of machinist or of technical director could there have been hope of producing such an effect in the theatre.

The particular means in the service of the cinema apt to create such impressions are manifold. Direct photography may be employed on occasion; the distortion of the features in the reward notice when the paper is cast on the fire is the real result of the action of the flames and this result has been reproduced directly in the form of a pictorial image. Generally, however, the effects are rendered either by means of camera manipulation or by that of building up special devices. A picture taken a trifle out of focus may suggest several states of mind, each dependent on the context of a film. In *A Midsummer Night's Dream* the out-of-focus images were used to indicate the land of faery, a purely objective approach; but in some emotional film if we are shown a woman in tears a similarly treated picture will at once make us see the world through her eyes. Empathically we become for the moment transported into her mind and her tears have become our own. In another film we are shown, say, a man who, for one reason or another, has had his whole clear vision of the universe destroyed, and here the out-of-focus image becomes less a physical perception than a spiritual mood. Elsewhere the camera may take double shots, so that with some character we lurch drunkenly from a bar-room, seeing things disturbingly and awry. There is indeed hardly any limits set to the manners in which the camera can thus transform reality in accordance with mental states. It can photograph an object in a distorting mirror, and, without realising that we are looking in a mirror, we suddenly see nature in shapes strange and terrifying—changed subjectively so that, instead of remaining observers as we do in the theatre, we become direct participators in the psychological action.

Emotional effects of a kindred sort may be effected by other means. A fade-in may suggest the awakening of some character out of a deep sleep; a fade-out may similarly indicate a lapse into unconsciousness; by double exposure an impression of mental chaos may result, while slow motion or the reverse can easily be given a subjective import. That is to say, those particular devices of the film which in general are used for a purely objective approach have the power of serving a subjective orientation whereby we lose our own individualities as observers and come to view the action through the eyes and through the mind of some particularly selected character.

The importance of all this lies in the fact that such devices are no precious and arcane things. In the very earliest days of the film its resources in this direction were recognised; even Pathé's crude *Faust* of 1905 introduced a "vision" seen in Margaret's mind by making these events appear in a wall-space previously covered by tapestry. Modern films like *Peter Ibbetson* and *Broadway Melody of 1936* are not "art" products: they are the very stuff of Hollywood's industry. Yet in them are being incorporated methods which are seen to be both intimately related to the essential cinematic approach and calculated to introduce a deeper significance into the stories with which they are associated. We are not dealing here with fond theories spun from the brains of idealistic visionaries desirous of making the film a toy for aesthetes and superior intellectuals; we are watching something much more significant— the sure development of an art out of conditions which have made many regard it only as an industry.

PICTORIAL SYMBOLISM

The discussion of these various cinematic devices inevitably leads to the question of pictorial symbolism in the film, and this demands a further consideration of the respective arts of stage and screen. The tragedies of Shakespeare owe their strength and mastery to a combination of many elements—elements of dramatic value and elements of literary power—and of those by no means least in significance are the recurrent images which, as recent critics have demonstrated, run like musical notes through the various plays. In *Macbeth,* for example, we can trace the images of sleep—dream—nightmare—death, of evil feasting and of nature distorted, from the very opening scene of the witches to the final conclusion of the drama. Such images have recently been carefully noted and fully commented upon. Now, at first sight one might be tempted to believe that such a careful tabulation of metaphor and simile in a play were both otiose and false, false because the process of tabulation must of necessity be an intellectual process far removed from the emotional and imaginative appreciation of a theatrical performance. To a certain extent such an objection is justified, but to a certain extent only; for further investigation must convince us that the sixteenth century audience for whom Shakespeare wrote appreciated his plays in a way vastly different from the way in which we appreciate the same plays today. The Elizabethans unquestionably possessed a lively sense of the values in spoken words, were keener in their grasping of verbal significances, had memories more highly trained than those of the present-day audiences. What, therefore, is now to be sought out only with laborious intellectual analysis must have had a direct emotional appeal to Shakespeare's contemporaries. Herein lies one of the principal difficulties for the modern poetic drama; an audience may still be able to appreciate the rhythmic, the musical, worth of words, but that which, in the truly vital poetic drama, must ever accompany that rhythm, the emotional vigour of the poetic symbols, is largely lost. We moderns are, it seems, much more deeply moved by visual symbols than by words; however common is the symbol of the cross, it ever awakens thoughts and emotions when placed in a significant position, a sword is a gleaming sign of force and a flower of charm. In the utilisation of such visual imagery, however, the theatre is manifestly restricted. Symbolic objects may be presented there, it is true, but usually these must remain fixed; there is little opportunity for the introduction of a regular flow of images calculated to excite and stimulate at once the attention and the understanding of the audience. In the cinematic realm, there is nothing which cannot be accomplished in this kind, and accordingly there is the possibility there of awakening to life and of releasing mental processes which in our modern world are apt to remain dormant when words alone are heard.

Already some examples of this cinematic use of the visual symbol have been referred to, but not specifically from this point of view. One such occurred in *Les Miserables* where a character stands in a courtroom with, dimly seen in the background, a large crucifix and, boldly silhouetted in the foreground, a soldier with musket and bayonet. This exemplifies, of course, only the direct and the most simple form of the visage image: beyond that it may proceed with almost unlimited subtlety. Sometimes the image, as here, is subdued; sometimes, as in the well-known stone lions of

The Battleship Potemkin, it is singled out and made prominent, perhaps even setting the tone for the film. In *The Informer,* before the action really starts, we are presented with several misty shots in which are dimly seen a few figures in outline merely, a Black-and-Tan officer, a woman, a man; and here the human persons in silhouette take on the force of symbols. The crumpled paper in the same film which clings like a living thing to Gypo's leg and clutches him the more tenaciously when he tries to shake it off may be taken as another example. Still more effective was the use of double exposure in *Thunder over Mexico,* a kind of imaginative pictorial shorthand; seeing the figures of human beings against the lines of ancient monuments, instantly we were made acquainted with what would have taken many hundreds of words fully to express —and this acquaintance came, not resultant upon intellectual processes, but emotionally. Akin to those was the series of shots, not narrational in aim, which preceded the plot development of *The Age of Innocence.* These, designed to suggest by a series of symbols the pace and conditions of modern life, set out to give tone for the action to follow.

The visual images need, of course, not be confined to one solitary method of presentation. The commonest and the obvious method is, by simple cutting in, to bring two separate shots into close conjunction, one following the other with a break between them or with union provided by a dissolve. Similar effects, however, can readily be secured through the employment of other means. Double exposure, for example, provides a convenient instrument for achieving effects of this kind. While one use of double exposure is to display concurrent events, another, and equally important, is to bring two sharply contrasted ideas or pictures into close association. The precise device used will depend on the particular scene being shown and the effect desired; what we should observe is that each of these devices can be put to varied service and that the cinema has at its command many resources for the securing of similar ends.

The employment of all such images is, naturally, bound up with the Russian theory of montage, and may be carried to an extreme, as it was in Eisenstein's *Romance Sentimentale*. Again, no doubt, we become tired of the device when it is over-emphasised, but nothing is more potent in the hands of skilful directors. The images which colour and inspire the plots of Shakespeare's plays can thus be made to body themselves before the very eyes of spectators, and by the ease with which the cinema turns from shot to shot exquisite and forceful contrast can be effected. To see a room filled with a happy, laughing group of people and to watch that shot fading away into another showing the same room desolate and empty is to experience an emotion which might be conveyed by but few words or none. The sight—with people of today, at least—provides more stimulus to the imagination than the sense of hearing.

At the same time, in dealing with these visual images, one thing ought to be stressed. The visual images themselves should never assume such a pictorial beauty as to make them stand out separately from the rest of the film. A play like Beddoes' *Death's Jest Book* is dramatically weak precisely because the author has created it out of a hundred individual sections, each no doubt exquisitely lyrical and lovely, but by that individual loveliness destroying the dramatic continuity of the whole. Where, then, in a film, any separate shot startles us with wonder and admiration by reason of its beautiful mass and line or by the over-forced nature of its symbolic mood, we may suspect a cinematic blemish, in exactly the same way in which we may suspect a dramatic blemish inherent in a passage of similar qualities appearing in a play. No shot in a film may stand separately any more than an individual scene in a tragedy or a comedy. A "still" provides but a lifeless glimpse of what a whole film really stands for, and little more (even less, because it is more deceptive) can be presented by a single shot or by a single shot-combination.

It is for this reason that those critics who have attacked the ways of the film censorship have ample justification for their wrath. A film is not a mere collection of shots, or at least ought not to be; and in a skilfully directed film the least tampering with the sequence and continuity is likely to destroy or mar its beauty and effectiveness. At this point, however, we approach still a further aspect of cinematic art and before proceeding with an examination of what the method of current censorship implies we must devote a moment or two to an examination of the implications of filmic rhythm.

RHYTHM

The film, as we have seen, is essentially an art of movement. Now this movement, like the movement inherent in a theatrical performance, inevitably involves the introduction of a rhythm peculiar to each work of cinematic art. In accepting such a statement, of course, we are obviously confining our attention to those productions which possess qualities worthy of our esteem. Hundreds of dramatic performances there are in which the rhythmic qualities have been obscured or neglected; and hundreds of films, like-)

wise, exhibit no conscious or innately inspired sense of rhythmic values. We might, perhaps, modify the statement and say that every significant film and drama presents a rhythmic movement, either deliberately conceived or created unconsciously from the artistic sensibilities of its directors.

In the securing of this rhythm various elements may be brought into play. First, naturally, there is the actual tempo of the scenes photographed and projected, which may or may not be identical with that of the original scenes used as the basis for the shots. Thus in *The Informer,* although the subject dealt with the exciting adventures of the Republican Army in Dublin, the rhythm was kept deliberately slow by means of restraining the tempo; there was secured a kind of effect which in the realm of prosody would have been called spondaic. This remains quite distinct from the scope of the action; in this particular film the fictional time occupied a space of only a few hours. Here, of course, the cinematic director employs a means not far different from that which is at the service of the theatrical director; the only essential divergence rests in the fact that, while the latter may slow down or accelerate only the actual persons who appear upon the stage, the former may do that and more, for he has the power of manipulating and controlling the number of frames passed through the projector within a determined period of time and so of fixing the apparent speed of the action.

Much more significantly, however, the cinematic director may introduce rhythm by means of his continuity. The various shots making up the entirety of a film being comparatively short, there will appear in the course of a one-hour showing many independent units, various groups of these units—shot combinations—joining to form larger units, of which there will also be a fair number. If each of these be likened to phrases and paragraphs, it becomes obvious that a definite rhythmic pattern may be woven out of them, if the director and cutter look upon them not merely as portions of a story but as expressive units, each with its own significance. Both length and stress may here be considered, for every shot will possess both a quantitative and a qualitative value. The quantitative depends on the actual number of individual pictures or frames run through the projector in one sequence and consequently upon the number of seconds it will take in the showing; the qualitative, on the other hand, will depend on the emotional stress and strength embodied in the actions depicted. Both of these, and the impression created by them, must be appreciated fully if a film is to be more than a mere conglomeration of separate images. This goes far beyond the simple problem of how much action should be shown or how long a particular action should be held, which concerns wholly the plot-telling or narrational part of a film. It is clearly necessary for a director to assess correctly when precisely the movements of his figures should be cut, for a bare second's additional action may easily destroy what he is desirous of revealing; but, besides that, he must determine the force of his shot in terms of rhythmic, as well as narrational, significance.

This may be made clear by reference to prosody. A poet secures his rhythmic flow and interest by establishing, towards the beginning of his poem, the prevailing metre and then proceeds to work out variations in this norm, the mind of the reader unconsciously superimposing the variation upon the pattern originally set. Thus Shelley starts

> O Wild West Wind, thou breath of autumn's being.

If we employ a / sign to mark a syllable quantitatively long, a x sign to mark one quantitatively weak and a \ sign to mark one of intermediate length, then we may say that that first line establishes a pattern of iambic or rising metre \/|\ /|\ /|x/|x/|x, at the close barely suggesting a variant to come in the form of a trochaic movement. The second line catches up this suggestion,

> Thou from whose unseen presence the leaves dead,

which may be scanned /x|x/|\ /|xx̂|/\ with a strong beat coming first. Lest this variation obscure the basic rhythm, however, the next line catches back the music of the first:

> Are driven like ghosts from an enchanter fleeing,

which once more reveals the rising movement x/|xx/| xx̂|x/|x/|x. The result of all this is that in later stanzas he may easily introduce violent variations, as in

> Shook from the tangled boughs of heaven and ocean,

which scans /xx|/x|/x|/x|/x without our having abanboned the basic iambic pattern x/|x/|x/|x/|x/.

In securing his effect the poet makes use of all the opportunities for variation permitted him. Normally special stress will be laid on a syllable numerically long and a syllable of stress value will be placed in a quantitatively strong position; but often, to obtain variety, this coincidence is abandoned. Thus in the second line of Shelley's poem we are inclined to linger a trifle over the essentially weak word "the" purely because of the place it occupies in the arrangement of the rhythmic pattern; in the third line we correspondingly linger over the essentially weak word "an"; and in the first line words of stress value such as "O", "West" and "thou" appear in quantitatively weak positions.

The fact that Pudovkin has likened the cinematic shots to words gives us assurance for comparing the rhythmic processes of verse with the rhythmic processes of the film, for clearly the various shots may readily be arranged to form a pattern no less appreciable than that secured by the poet. The short shots correspond to the numerically short syllables, the long shots to the syllables numerically long. Variations of a kind precisely similar to those in the poet's music are obtainable in the film. Short shots containing material of powerful emphasis and long shots containing material of less significance may be combined with those in which the quantitative and the qualitative values coincide. Indeed, we might even say that a fixed keeping to such coincidence is likely to result in an effect akin to that produced by a set of verses in which lack of variety induces an impression of monotony and of crude cadence.

That this principle of cinematic art has been but scantily appreciated matters little; important only is the fact that the cinema possesses the means of producing effects perhaps as yet entirely undreamt of. So far we have seen this patterning only in a few sequences, never throughout the entirety of a film; but that does not mean that its complete achievement is unattainable. The visual images presented in the cinema form tools as powerful as ever words were in those of a literary genius and we are as eager to watch and grasp the force of the rhythm created by their means as were men in the past to listen to the poet's music.

Perhaps one further suggestion might here be made. The power that the cinema has of entering into the minds of individual characters may introduce the possibility of securing certain rhythmic overtones beyond those just described. The film, as already has been noted, possesses the extraordinary ability continually to alter and shift its point of view. At one moment, we may seem to be ourselves, observers, looking on at an action, appreciating more or less objectively; the next moment we are seeing things through the eyes of this character or of that, subjectively entering into his mental and physical vision. Nor need these be kept distinct; through some strange magic we find not the slightest difficulty in letting one vision fade imperceptibly into the other. This, in turn, suggests a still further kind of rhythm securable in the cinematic form—the rhythm of eye approach, it might be styled. It seems likely that, for ordinary purposes, no truly significant employment of a pattern obtained by this means were either desirable or possible, but in certain filmic themes the device might be made to yield a thrillingly arresting effect. Closely allied to such rhythmic process is that which arises from camera method. In *Thunder over Mexico* a definite pattern resulted in the mind from the juxtaposition of soft, misty shots and of shots in which were sought depth and a clear-cut quality almost approaching the outlines of a silhouette.

To harmonise these rhythmic processes may seem difficult, indeed might even be thought impossible of achievement; yet the task is no different and no harder than that confronting the poet, who must similarly harmonise in his work a variety of divergent elements. By some strange and as yet unanalysed mental alchemy he succeeds in combining three things—the intellectual content of his words, their sound value and their syllabic significance. The effort is no more easy of accomplishment than that confronting the author of film plays and their director.

From this consideration of the rhythmic qualities which must be, or ought to be, exemplified in all films worthy of esteem, we may return for a moment to that question of film censorship already referred to. Clearly, if someone objected to certain words in Shelley's poem and cut the lines to read

> O West Wind, thou breath of autumn's being,
> Thou from whose presence the leaves
> Are driven, like ghosts from an enchanter,

we should hold up our hands in horror and proclaim against such vandalism. In the theatre, certainly, we have become accustomed to seeing certain sections of a play deleted, but there is one essential difference between a theatrical performance and the presentation of a film. In the former, changes may with some ease be made by the author and director; it is common procedure to alter and improve, either during final rehearsals or during a "try-out," quite apart from any external instructions. A play production is always a malleable thing and so long as the creators of that production are on hand to approve of changes or actually to make the changes no great harm is done. A film, however, once released from the studios is a fixed and completed entity and any alterations made in it must necessarily be, first, in the form of deletions and, secondly, independent of the director's will. Yet boards of censors sit in conclave, chop and change, concerned merely with what they decide is morality, utterly insensitive to any other than ethical values.

Now, two things must be confessed. In a longer work of art—a film or a play—changes may be effected with less injury to the original than in a shorter work of art—a lyric, say. Moreover, most films suffer not a whit from the operation, and some we might well wish cut from an hour's program to one lasting two minutes, yet the danger is there, that, as the cinema develops and improves its artistry, the work of really distinguished and gifted men may be ruined and their further progress thwarted. Sooner or later the work of censoring boards must be carefully considered and their duties defined with specific exactitude. To have all films treated alike, as if they were merely commercial products from which portions might without injury be cut, is fatal to any artistic development within this form.

4

THE SOUND FILM

WHEN sound was first added to the silent forms presented in the cinema, a great outcry arose from those intellectuals who had up to then sponsored and supported the new art, as well as from a number of directors who, aiming more highly than others, felt that they were rapidly mastering the secrets of this medium. Pudovkin at first stoutly opposed the introduction of sound on aesthetic grounds. Writing in 1930 Paul Rotha, likewise condemning reproduction of the human voice, declared that he was

certain that these new forms will never destroy the original and highest form of cinema, the silent, flat film with synchronised or orchestra accompaniment, which is indisputably the most effective medium for the conveyance of the dramatic content of a theme to the mind of an audience.

This judgment he repeated in his next book (1931), where he averred that, although "sound can help the cinema as a means of expression," "speech is proving detrimental to it"; Chaplin he praised because "from the time when the recorded voice was first employed in conjunction with screen images" that actor had "observed the futility of the attempt."

J. G. Fletcher in 1929 categorically dismissed the possibilities which might reside in the combination of visual and audible elements:

THE SOUND FILM

A complete boycott of "talking films" should be the first ᵗ
of anyone who has ever achieved a moment's pleasure fr₁
the contemplation of any film

expressed clearly his point of view. In the same year
Katharine Gerould declared that, if the talkies prevailed,
"then the art of the motion-picture, with its immense possibilities, will be in our own generation as 'lost' as the
Egyptian art of embalming."

These judgments were written only a few years ago;
but Time has many revenges. Time, even the short time
that has elapsed between 1926 and the present, has demonstrated the falsity at least of such prognostications as are
embodied in Rotha's words and seems to have gone further
towards a disproving of the aesthetic standards implied in
Fletcher's appeal. The sound film has fully established itself
in the esteem of the public; by no possible imagining can
we credit the return to favour of the silent film; and recent
years have shown such a marked advance in the former's
artistic excellence that we believe it to contain potentialities far in advance of anything achieved or even imagined
ten years ago.

That popular success in itself does not imply, of course,
the most artistic choice needs no special emphasis. The
public has shown itself at fault in the past, and indeed there
are many still who deplore the loss of good old days, haloed
with the light of fond recollection, when no voice proceeded from the silent expanse of the screen. Of necessity,
we must consider the validity of their position, and, in
order to accomplish this task impartially, we are compelled
to make several admissions.

When Al Jolson came forward with *The Jazz Singer* and *The Singing Fool* a monkey wrench unquestionably was firmly flung into the cinematic machinery. From 1914 to 1926 there had been steady progress, and in the films of 1922-1925 some remarkable things were being accomplished. Charlie Chaplin produced *The Pilgrim* in 1923, *The Gold Rush* in 1925 and *The Circus* in 1927. Robert Wiene's inventive and suggestive *The Cabinet of Dr. Caligari* was a film of 1919, James Cruze's *The Covered Wagon* of 1923; F. W. Murnau's *The Last Laugh* and Eisenstein's *The Battleship Potemkin* both were released in 1925. Out of these was developing a very pretty piece of critical theory, and it certainly looked as though the cinema, which for so long had dealt with impossible melodramatics and stupidly farcical situations, were coming to its own. A vast gulf yawned between the clumsy inanities of *The Fireman* and the subtleties of *The Gold Rush*. Directors and public alike were begining to sense potentialities they had hitherto never even conceived, and positive achievement seemed already to have been realised. Many in 1925 were prophesying great things for the years 1926 to 1930.

In reality, these years showed the cinema almost at its nadir. Sound came, and by one fell swoop most of the fondly established theories came crashing dismally to earth. It had been argued that the cinema was purely an art of visual appeal; that consequently everything should be subordinated to pictorial images; that sub-titles even were fundamentally unnecessary. In the earlier films continuity titles had been constant accompaniments of the displayed action, and by their means direct information and even portions of supposedly spoken speech were freely brought before the attention of the audience. That, argued the theorists, was wrong; the whole story ought to be developed by action and by suggestive symbols; these should stand unaided, and the art that used them seek no assistance, however slight, from the art of literature. The cinema, continued these theorists, is thus the most universal of all the arts. Literature is appreciated only by persons who are familiar with the particular language in which a book is written; painting has its limitations, for the basis of Western art is not that of the oriental; even music depends on a special training, so that the melodies of the Chinese strike strangely on our ears and Bach is incomprehensible in India. The cinema alone possesses the quality of complete universality. Based on fundamental things, it is the literature and the art of humanity. Before it opens out a vast, hitherto unimagined prospect, thrillingly enticing in its unexplored wonders.

Then sound: in a moment sound destroyed and shattered all this conceptioning. The cinema, according to the theorists, was cast back into hybrid mediocrity.

That something of this kind did actually occur, and that most certainly the promise of the years 1922-1925 was destroyed we must agree. We have to admit, too, that sound at first was very terrible. Those who attended performances of those first sound films will recall the alarming bass notes of the heroine and the hesitating uncertainty of the hero's tenor. You were never sure what was to come next and dwelt in constant dreadful expectancy. For some of us the new form had an exciting value of its own and we were prepared, knowing how much science had already accomplished, to credit a future refinement and measure

of perfection. But to those whose dreams had been rudely
broken by raucous voices, the sounds that came from the
screen must have seemed ominous prognostications of
doom and disaster. Even now many persons will not believe that the process of registering sounds on film-strips is
the finest kind of recording hitherto achieved, or, admit-
ting so much, stoutly deny the right of any words at all
to interfere with the progress of the filmic story.

The third admission is this. Having discovered the sound
film, or rather, having sound unwillingly thrust upon them,
the producing companies, in a frantic agony of competi-
tive desperation, immediately bethought them of the treas-
ures of the stage. A play had action and words, they
argued; the new sound film needed action and words;
therefore it seemed reasonable to suppose that herein lay
material ready for cinematic exploitation. Broadway and
Shaftesbury Avenue were ransacked; from Paris and Berlin and Rome cables poured in to the offices announcing
the success of this or that new drama; and scripts, eagerly
sought for, rose in value. Authors and theatrical managers
hastened to make hay in the shining of this cinematic sun;
and the film, which had been developing its own technique, swept back to depend on the stage once more. All
seemed lost.

In critical prose, the theorists put forward their many
objections to the introduction of sound. They demonstrated
to their own satisfaction that, the film being essentially an
art of sight, the bringing in of sound rendered it impure.
They emphasised the power of the cinema to control speed
of movement and declared that with the coming of sound
all this movement necessarily was slowed up. They had
hailed the freedom of the cinema from the restrictions of

the stage, and saw a return to full-face recording, with the movement of lips harmonised to the words that were spoken. They witnessed the rapid disappearance of the visual symbols so inherently cinematic.

Only after the passing of five or six years did the development of the cinema recover itself; indeed, the last two years are those which have brought us back to the conditions of 1925; but in bringing us back, they have also taken us forward and we are able to obtain a clearer view of filmic values than was possible in the earlier years of disruption.

MUSICAL ACCOMPANIMENT

In approaching this subject, it is to be realised that the film never has been without sound accompaniment. From the earliest "nickelodeon" days, music from a tinkling piano or a more formal orchestra has gone along with the display of the pictures on the screen. The reason is not far to seek. Normally, in life we associate sound and movement; on the stage sound hardly ceases unless for some particular purpose. Occasionally maybe the dramatist or director wishes to make comic capital out of a scene in which the characters remain silent; more commonly stage silence arouses a feeling of serious tension. It is the quietness before the breaking of a storm. To witness, without hearing a sound, a pure piece of miming, unless the miming be done in a wholly conventional manner, would become either tedious or over-straining; it is indeed observable that the vaudeville comedian whose skill lies in his actions nearly always demands an instrumental accompaniment from the orchestra. The film, in this, must bow to the same conventions as the stage. A restlessness would

develop were we to witness only the actions, a restlessness
dependent upon the potential alertness of our auditory
nerves. We should expect sound and none would come.
The musical accompaniment to silent films, therefore, simply occupied our attention and prevented the disappoint-
ment resultant upon a thwarted expectancy.

Often enough, this musical accompaniment assumed
mimetic form. First of all, the music was clearly selected
to accord with the situations. Delicate and melodious
strains kept time with the lovers, and deep bass notes harmonised with the appearance of the heavy villain. From
this the accompaniment proceeded to the actual suggestion
at least of the sounds which would in reality have been
heard in the given situations. Not all episodes lent themselves to this, but an organ would play a hymn tune in a
church shot, wind instruments would play a march as the
soldiers passed by, a sea symphony would come with the
waves and rain music in a shot of deluge. Hence was but
a step to the utilisation of special non-musical devices
employed during the performances of some films—knock-
ing at a door, rattling of pistol shots, pounding of horses'
hooves.

So that, even before the introduction of the sound film,
a definite approach had been made towards the introduction of mimetic sounds, in addition to the visual images.
For some reason, these were felt by audiences and directors
to be desirable. The sound-film, however, is fundamentally the talking-film, and with words enters in an intellectual content entirely different in character from either
the musical accompaniment or the mimetic noises referred
to above. It is this the theorists objected to. Before proceeding to examine these objections, it may be well to

point out that the bringing in of incidental noises by means of synchronised recording can hardly itself be condemned. The recording method certainly is far superior to the sometimes erratic manufacturing of the noises by a member of the orchestra, and by its means the director may secure precisely the pitch and approximately the intensity he desires. The noises, it should be observed, need not be merely mimetic in the sense that they provide the sounds which would accompany real actions, nor need they come only when a particular visual image is cast on the screen. They often indeed may serve either for binding shot to shot or for emphasising the particular rhythm of the film. Thus in *The Informer,* after Gypo Nolan has given the particulars which will bring death to his friend, Frankie MacPhillip, we suddenly become aware of the insistent ticking of a clock on the wall. That shot ends, and in the interim between it and the next the ticking of the clock proceeds; proceeds, too, into the shot which shows Frankie at home with his mother and sister, where motivation is again provided by another wall-clock. Furthermore, this insistent ticking is caught up later by the tapping of a blind man's stick as Gypo slinks away from the Black-and-Tan headquarters. The noise possesses at once a subjective and an objective force: amply motivated in all three shots, its drumming persistency yet seems increased by individual awareness, now of time's passing, now of haunting retribution. Still further, a certain rhythmic beat is established thereby which gives some particular tone to the music with which this film is accompanied.

Sounds of this kind, however, as we have seen, may be kept distinct from words and introduced by those who theoretically would prohibit the use of dialogue. Charlie

Chaplin, for example, added to the silent mime a certain amount of sound effect in *City Lights,* but none of the sound had an intellectual significance. The "blah-blah-blah" of the civic orator was literally that and not built out of satirically conceived words. It is dialogue in formally conceived words, which still sticks in the throats of many.

In general, the objections to dialogue are based on a set of false assumptions, upon an unwillingness to consider the possible advantages to be derived from its use and from argumentation founded on observation of the worst in current film fare. Unquestionably, if dialogue were to mean that the fundamental cinematic methods were to be abandoned in favour of straight shooting, nothing could be said for it. To make the film merely a split-up version of a stage play were absurd; therein lies no future.

CONCENTRATION IN SOUND

The assumption that because a film and a stage play both use words therefore there is a likeness between them reveals its falsity just as soon as we stop to consider this question in detail. No doubt, many films of the present unimaginatively employ earlier technique and so fail to secure the greatest possible effectiveness within their command; even such a film as *The Scoundrel* by Hecht and MacArthur strangely erred in this respect, and, in spite of several interesting individual shots, proved unsatisfactory because its method was a combination of outworn cinematic devices and of devices associated with the stage. No use was made in it of symbolic imagery; nearly all the shots were straightforward ones, showing visually the lips of the speakers as they uttered their words; from close-up and medium shot we moved to close-up and medium shot in wearisome monotony; and the dialogue had not been toned down sufficiently for cinematic purposes.

The first thing we observe about cinematic dialogue is that, whereas in general a stage play demands constant talk, a film requires an absolute minimum of words. The essential basis of the cinema lies primarily in the realm of visual images, and such sound accompaniment as is admitted must be reduced to the barest necessaries. The distinction between the two forms becomes at once apparent if we pause to contrast some nineteenth century melodramas and some modern films in which there is excessive dialogue. The melodramas we shall condemn because their authors, in carelessness or haste, often allowed stage-direction, indicating action, to do the work which ought to have been accomplished by the use of words; while, on the other hand, we shall condemn a film which permits words to do what might have been achieved by means of moving forms on the screen. In essential principles drama and cinema stand distinct and separate; they are allied, no doubt, but allied in no wise other than as painting and sculpture, music and poetry, are allied. Lessing in his *Laocoon* demonstrated clearly that we ought to censure a sculptor for trying to do in marble what his fellow-artist so much more easily and effectively might do in words; and precisely the same holds true for cinema and drama.

Drama, certainly, is a concentrated form, and the author must guard against introducing any words or ideas which are not strictly germane to his theme and necessary for the building-up of his impression; but this concentration is increased a thousand-fold in the film. Part of the reason is that selectivity is more readily achieved in the latter, this selectivity being of certain kinds. First of all, we may take

a typical scene in a play. That scene, let us say, introduces
two men quarrelling. Now, so long as these men remain
in the one location and are not interrupted by a third person, the quarrel scene has to be carried through in its entirety. Once start a conversation on the stage and it is difficult to bring it to a conclusion without developing the
theme in some considerable fulness. The film, on the contrary, may arrest words or actions at any given moment,
and this same scene might, in the hands of the cinematic
director, reveal only the first movements and words, cutting all the intervening portions until the conclusion. The
rest would be supplied by the imagination of the audience.
At once we recognise why it is that a bare minimum of
words is called for in the film and, concurrently, we appreciate the fact that in these snatches of conversation (because
of the camera's ability to cut off the scene when required)
greater point and neatness are demanded. An entirely
diverse technique is summoned into play, for whereas the
dramatic author will habitually aim at smoothness and
continuity, with a dialogue moving steadily towards a good
"curtain," the writer of a screen-play will strive towards
the securing of variety, contrast and rapidly made points.

Further than this, however, does the power of concentration go. In ordinary life we normally see and hear only
what we will ourselves to see or hear. Millions of objects
appear before our eyes but of those millions only a small
proportion actually is recorded in our minds, and of the
corresponding millions of sounds few are consciously appreciated. Apart from this general fact we realise that
sounds take on varying intensities in accordance with the
subjective state of our own minds. As an example we may
choose the ticking of a clock upon a wall. Usually the

noise made by this clock will be completely ignored; although the sound, considered objectively, is constant and continually present, it simply ceases to exist so far as we are concerned. Occasionally for a brief moment the noise of its ticking will impinge itself on our senses, but generally, when this happens, we exercise our wills to dismiss it and again it ceases to exist. Imagine, however, an invalid, racked with fever, lying in the room; his mind is peculiarly sensitive so that to him the clock's ticking assumes an exaggerated importance. Try as he will, he cannot succeed in dismissing it from him and the more he strives to escape, the more insistent and terrifying the sounds become. Imagine, too, another person—a condemned prisoner awaiting the hour of his execution. For him the clock becomes a symbol of inexorable Time moving relentlessly on towards his final minute. The clock's ticking takes on for him also an exaggerated importance, only, instead of being irritating, it stands for a power of destiny he cannot control.

This single example may be sufficient to demonstrate that in real life we hear only certain of the myriad sounds around us and either deliberately select those of which we become conscious or else unconsciously dismiss the mass of those we remain unaware of. Sound is an objective thing, measurable by science; but the hearing of sound is subjective. On the stage, obviously there is considerable possibility of selection in this way—selection of dialogue and selection of "off-stage" noises both; but there can be little opportunity, save in a highly expressionistic play, of presenting either from the points of view of individual characters and consequently the possibility itself is limited. A ticking clock remains the same for all the persons introduced on the stage at one time, and, if we do wish to emphasise its importance for one character, we can do so in hardly any other way save by calling attention to the fact in actual speech.

For various reasons, therefore, dependent upon certain means peculiar to the cinema, filmic dialogue must, if it is to be truly characteristic and make full use of the opportunities offered to it, deviate considerably from dialogue characteristic of the stage. The selectivity is perhaps neither more nor less; it is simply different in kind and fully to appreciate this difference is the business of anyone connected, either creatively or critically, with the cinema.

SOUND CONTROL

The second essential difference between the use of sound (including speech) in the theatre and on the screen is that the former, in a variety of ways, bows absolutely to the will of the author and the director. Two kinds of sound there are which can be presented theatrically—the speech of the actors and "off-stage" noises. A little reflection, however, will show that both are extremely restricted in their range. The words spoken by the actors are restricted to the scope of utterance possessed by the performers themselves—for in this we cannot go beyond nature; and if for the "off-stage" noises any mechanical means is employed in the projection of the sounds clearly there is a fettering because of the danger of introducing too violent contrasts between the natural tones and those mechanically manufactured. In the cinema, on the other hand, all the sounds are mechanically reproduced and even although modern recording has achieved a fine sensitivity in rendering we can no more escape the consciousness that the sounds we hear are being presented to us through a medium than we can avoid the realisation that the forms thrown upon the screen are, not reality, but two-dimensional reproductions of reality. This means that the entire range of the sound effects in the film is immeasurably extended. In the process of projection the natural tones of the performers' voices may deliberately be made to acquire an increased flexibility and scope. Through the opportunities thus granted a singer's voice may be rendered into something which we could never hope to hear on the concert platform. Faulty notes can be deleted and a measure of perfection secured by a process of dovetailing all those portions which are flawless combined with that of cutting out those which introduce elements of a less satisfactory quality. Without creating any disturbance or confusion in the minds of the audience the power is granted to the director of developing and controlling a cinematic sound world even as he was granted the means of developing and controlling a cinematic time and a cinematic space.

Because of this extended range, allied to cognate qualities in the sound projection, the actual conversation which the players are to be given for utterance presents a series of problems new and distinct. By means of the purely cinematic tone much may be done acoustically towards the creation of mood and interest which, on the stage, would have to be accomplished through the use of intellectually conceived words. Furthermore, the fact that the words spoken by the actors and what would correspond to "off-stage" noises are harmonised by their both passing through the one medium permits of the introduction of effects securable but rarely and then with extreme difficulty in the theatre. It must, for example, be obvious to all that the suggestion on the stage of crowd noises generally fails in the impression which the dramatist or the director desires to produce. Whether a group of persons is trained to murmur and shout behind the scenes or a loud-speaker is employed, the device usually leaves much to be wished for. Just such effects form excellent cinematic material. Already we have seen how freely and impressively the camera may bring crowds within the range of its vision; masses of people whose presence in the theatre might seem forced and artificial may create powerful impression on the screen. In the same way the field of sound is so extended in the cinema that the acoustic qualities associated with these pictures may effectively be introduced there. Since all the sound heard comes to us through a mechanical medium, there can be no sense of discrepancy or conflict. Nor need this remain solely within the sphere covered by theatrical practice. *The Ghost goes West* introduced several shots which showed visually the Capitol at Washington and the Houses of Parliament in London, with accompanying sounds supposed to be the broadcasting of speeches on both sides of the Atlantic. Clearly this was a device which could reach realisation only in the cinema; for the theatre it would have been impossible.

Still more important is the fact that this mechanical reproduction, besides having the means of increasing the range of natural sound, provides opportunities for alteration and distortion. In the filmic version of *A Midsummer Night's Dream* one of the most effective scenes was that displaying the lovers' quarrel. A few rapid shots showed Hermia and Lysander, Helena and Demetrius in angry recrimination, and throughout the projection of these shots, without a break, we heard their voices in a confused babel of words. On the stage, of course, conversation among a group of characters may be made to overlap, but there could be no chance of proceeding so far as this in the building of an impression of voices excitedly distraught and confusedly intermingled. This example from *A Midsummer Night's Dream*, however, goes but one step beyond nature; no hint is provided there of the greater lengths to which the deliberate alteration of sound may go. One may state that there is no transformation of common tones and noises which is impossible in the cinema; for comic effect or for tragic we may do whatsoever we will with nature. Indeed, when we examine this subject, we realise that precisely the same means of manipulation exist in the realm of sound as exist in the realm of visual images. Slow motion and accelerated motion can be applied to sounds and to the objects of sight as we may desire. We may use the device of double exposure and lay one series of sounds or noises upon another. We may even project words in reverse just as we may show characters on the screen proceeding in backward motion. The fade-in, the fade-out and the dissolve—all of these have their acoustic counterparts; by their means it is easy to have one set of sounds intermingle with another set, to create just such a juxtaposition as we have seen possible in the field of visual images.

How far this control removes the writing of a screenplay from the writing of a stage-drama must be immediately manifest. Acoustic montage has to be applied here in the same way as visual montage is applied to the images fixed on the frames. We are dealing here, not with a selection of sounds from nature, but with a collection of sounds recorded on strips of film, each in its own way distinct from the original which gave it birth, all to be wrought into a harmony by the skill of the author and director.

SOUND SUBJECTIVITY

On the power which the film possesses of abstracting from objective reality particular sounds heard by individual characters and on its power to transform these sounds at will clearly depends the film's ability to suggest, by oral means, psychological processes at which the stage can but hint. With sounds as with visual images, there is the same ease in moving from an objective to a subjective approach. Without the slightest difficulty, a shot, or a series of shots, may be introduced giving the sounds heard by one selected character and not by others introduced in the plot. We might have, for instance, a medium shot showing four persons with no accompaniment save the dialogue given to them, and then a close shot showing one of these persons accompanied by such sounds (external noises in addition to chosen words) as that particular individual is hearing at the moment.

Before going further, it is well to emphasise here that, while dramatic dialogue must always be directly presented, filmic dialogue may be introduced in a variety of ways, of which by far the least interesting is that which shows persons speaking. Absolute synchronisation of lip-movement and of words uttered may be desirable and necessary, but we do not always need, in fact we rarely need, to see the lips at work while the sounds impinge themselves on our ears. In the realm of visual movement, as we have seen, there is the possibility in the cinema of presenting merely part of an object; the pawnbroker's hands therein stand for the whole figure of the man who, in a dramatic treatment of the Dickensian theme, would have had to be brought physically on the stage. Precisely similar opportunities are offered in the realm of sound, for the film may freely provide the words of persons whom we do not see, not because these persons are concealed behind screens or curtains, but because we choose to focus our attention elsewhere. Even in that small passage from *The Barretts of Wimpole Street* there is demonstrated a typical utilisation of this device. Flush is let into the hall; from an inner room comes a voice, the voice of Barrett, and, hearing it, the dog drops his tail and slinks upstairs. While we are looking at Flush, we hear Barrett. No doubt this particular effect, save for the acting of the dog, might be reproduced on the stage; but from this we proceed further. By means of groupings and of positions, a theatrical director may suggest what particularly he wants his audience to observe, but never may we be positively assured that the indications will be appreciated or carried out in realisation. Within the cinematic sphere, the director is sole judge of what the audience shall see and hear; because of the means at his command he can rest assured that every single thing he chooses will be brought fully to the attention of the spectators and that there will be no chance of having certain dearly cherished and carefully planned effects lost or disregarded through the straying of attention elsewhere. From his point of view, therefore, dialogue assumes functions and must be made to serve purposes entirely different from those associated with theatrical conversation.

Here another aspect of the subject calls for consideration. On the stage (unless in some bizarre and highly experimental productions) the dialogue heard by the audience is associated directly with the characters set at the moment within the proscenium frame. This, as has been demonstrated, need not hold for the cinema where sound heard and objects seen may be, if desired, wholly separated. The result is that the filmic author and director are granted certain opportunities denied to the dramatist and the theatrical director. Sound and visual images may agree in synchronisation, indeed, it is possible to agree that commonly this combination will form the staple basis of any ordinary film. On the other hand, infinite variety is achievable in different directions. An impression of strong contrast may be evoked by showing, say, a picture of a man in despair while a jazz melody insistently throbs in our ears. Another impression may be summoned forth by making the two (the visual and the acoustic) agree without synchronisation in mood and spirit. The scene of grief might, for example, be given increased tension and poignancy by having the picture accompanied, not by words, but by the whimpering or moaning as of some animal in pain. Or else, perhaps, the words are left and the visual images changed, as in a scene where we hear the voices of two lovers murmuring their endearments while on the screen we watch the slow ripple of waves upon the sand or the gentle tossing of boughs in a forest. Further opportunities may be exemplified by a series of shots in *Strike Me Pink* where during the singing of a song suggestive of violent emotion the visual images were presented in a series of exceedingly short, sharply delineated and abruptly divided pictures. The possibilities of securing variety by such means are indeed unmeasured. All we need to do in order to appreciate this is to think of some simple situation —let us say, a miser bent over his treasured gold—and imagine the diverse ways in which the film might treat it.

We might have the miser soliloquising, with lip movements synchronised, or silent himself with a whispering voice suggesting his inner thoughts, or silent again with the groaning of some hungry wretch coming to us from outside his window, or silent still with the accompaniment of immaterialised and fantastic sounds expressive in some way of his greed; or else we might completely change the approach, allowing the jingling clink of the coins as he counts them to become accompaniments to pictures which do not introduce the figure of the miser at all—pictures calculated, by their imagic agreement or by their contrast, to bring forth more strongly the impression desired.

In order to make this absolutely clear it is possibly best to retrace our steps a moment and take a perfectly simple example of filmic non-agreement in acoustic and visual terms. Such an example is provided in that scene of *The Barretts of Wimpole Street* when Barrett enters Elizabeth's room in the midst of Henrietta's hilarious polka:

BEDROOM FULL SHOT—
Henrietta has stopped dead in the centre of the room. The others stand rooted to their places. The silence is deadly.

CUT TO:
CLOSE SHOT FLUSH
He descends quietly from the foot of Elizabeth's couch and pads discreetly—CAMERA PANNING WITH HIM—over to his basket. He clambers in, and lies down, his back to the camera.

CUT TO:
ELIZABETH'S ROOM—CLOSE SHOT BARRETT
He stands motionless just beyond the threshold looking before him with a perfectly expressionless face.

Voice of Elizabeth

Good evening, Papa.

The camera then proceeds to pick up Barrett again and we see him speaking: but a moment later the same device is repeated:

CLOSE SHOT HENRIETTA & OCTAVIUS

Henrietta

I—I beg your pardon, Papa.

Voice of Barrett

And may I ask what you were doing as I came into the room?

Henrietta

I was showing Ba how to polk.

CUT TO:

CLOSE UP BARRETT

He looks incredulous disgust.

Barrett

To . . . polk?

Voice of Henrietta

How to dance the polka.

Barrett

I see.

An analysis of this sequence indicates the rapid shifting of attention. First, it is concentrated upon Henrietta, arrested suddenly in her dance (visual only); then it moves to Flush, symbolic of the spirit of the human actors, cowed by Barrett's presence (visual, for symbolic effect); is fixed upon Barrett, with Elizabeth's voice coming through (visual and indirect sound); turns back to Henrietta, with the voice of Barrett heard (visual and both direct and indirect sound); and finally concentrates on Barrett with Henrietta's faltering accents indicating her fear (visual and both direct and indirect sound). Variety is provided here and an emphasis, possibly not greater than might have been secured on the stage, but assuredly divergent in essential principle from that.

The use of the unseen voice has many applications in the filmic telling of a story. Only occasionally on the stage, by the use of non-directional recording apparatus or by that of the aside, can an approach be made towards the creation of words apart from those spoken in conversation by the actors seen by the audience. God's voice may thus descend from the clouds to a devout Noah, O'Neill may employ the aside in *Strange Interlude* to suggest inner thought, unexpressed externally in life, and Shakespeare may have his heroes unburden their hearts in words through the medium of soliloquy. Such methods, however, seem only too often forced and strained, while of means to project the unarticulated voices of madness and hallucination there are none. All this may readily be accomplished in the cinema. In the same way that *The Informer* showed momentarily a subjective mental image in Gypo Nolan's mind while his eyes rested on the model of the liner, so momentarily are presented the voices which well up within his own consciousness and to him appear audible as those actually spoken by his companions. When his conscience recreates the image of the murdered Frankie, Frankie's voice takes shape and warns him that he is lost, that without the aid of his friend's brains he can do naught. Similarly, too, in *The Scoundrel* words, which may be those of fate or merely the hallucinations of a dying man, sound while we look upon the floating body in the whirling waste of waves. The mother in *So Red The Rose* hears her son calling, and, as we ride with her when she sets out to find his body, the mental voice comes whisperingly through to us. Immense possibilities are here, both in the creation of themes specifically designed for the film and in the re-treatment of themes already known to the stage. A film of *Hamlet* thus might articulate much more of the hero's imaginings than the stage soliloquies allowed, and Joan of Arc's supposedly heaven-sent admonitions could take actual filmic form before an audience. By the employment of a whispered intensity, these words could never be mistaken for the words of living persons consciously uttering their thoughts; spectators, however untutored, would find no difficulty in appreciating their force and significance.

LINKAGE BY SOUND

Already something has been said concerning the linking of shots in the cinema, but this subject, introducing a fresh use of sound, deserves a trifle more attention. In a theatrical performance, as we have seen, the divisions in the action are relatively few and not many opportunities are offered to the director for the binding together of part and part. Occasionally an attempt is made in this way; recent examples were provided by Georg Bruckner's *Elizabeth and Essex* and the same author's *Races,* when words spoken in one scene were caught up in the scene immediately following or running concurrently. The device, however, is not essentially dramatic and even when skilfully handled, generally lacks conviction. At the most it may be employed in one single section of a play. We found the movement of the savage tribal chant into the hymn-singing of Munro's *Progress* exceedingly effective, but the employment of a similar concatenation in other scenes would have been deemed monotonous or ridiculous.

In a film, on the other hand, the shots are so numerous and the intermission periods so brief that linking of one set of images to another becomes generally desirable and certainly easy of attainment. That linkage usually is secured by visual means, but sound presents the opportunity of diversifying the method of binding the shots and of producing slightly different emotional results. A simple example of such sound linkage appears in the Micawber scenes of *David Copperfield*, where the wailing of the child joins shot and shot together; that child is shown in one picture, as we wait for the next shot its wailing cry is still heard, and while we watch the second shot, although the child itself is not in the picture, the cry persists. The ticking of the clock in *The Informer* illustrates a further use of this device, three distinct scenes being connected by its means. Difficult indeed would it be exactly to analyse our aesthetic and emotional reactions during the hearing of this sound. In one respect, the realistic motivation is complete—that is to say, in the latter example there is no reason why we should not hear the ticking of the second clock. On the other hand, we realise two things: first, that the ticking is exaggeratedly loud and, second, that it has harmonised with or forms a continuation of the sound given forth by the other. With the latter we shared empathically in Gypo's nervous expectation, and with the former, although Gypo is not present, indeed has remained far off in the Black and Tan headquarters, we watch the action at least partly through his imagination. The movements of the characters are objective, certainly, but at the same time we know that these movements are precisely those which Gypo was conjuring up in his brain while he dwelt on the effect of the information he had given. The linkage here is thus not entirely objective; we are carried forward from shot to shot emotionally.

Further possibilities in treatment of cinematic dialogue and in linkage effects were revealed in a short sequence of an otherwise not too imaginative film, *The Man Who Broke the Bank at Monte Carlo.*

In that sequence we are taken to Interlaken where the hero, Ronald Colman, has made the acquaintance of the heroine, Joan Bennett. The business of the director is to show the progress of their friendship. On the stage all that could have been accomplished would have been the presentation of a single scene in which Colman testified to his adoration. Normally in cinematic treatment there would have been a series of scenes each with a short passage of conversation between the pair; but in this particular story it was obviously expedient to keep the girl as silent as possible while, on the other hand, the particular terms Colman found to testify to his love did not really matter. All we were concerned with was the fact that he had fallen madly in love with her and told her so. The entire story, therefore, was narrated in three closely associated shots. In the first the two were riding, in the second they were boating and in the third they stood after dinner upon the terrace of the hotel. These unrelated pictorial shots were bound by words; during the first we heard Colman utter six words, the beginning of a sentence, during the second he was carrying on that sentence, and during the third the sentence was completed. Nothing could have been better devised to suggest the constant reiteration of his passion, while the association of the pictures with the words clearly indicated the various occasions he took to reveal his state of mind. Visually, orally and by combined linkage effect the impression was effectively and arrestingly given.

Closely connected with this question goes the question of sub-titles. Sub-titles, we might have imagined, would have naturally vanished with the disappearance of the silent film, but we can still see them in at least a few of the current products. In general, they are to be condemned, although very occasionally they may serve a special purpose of their own. The test, probably, ought to be whether they can be dispensed with or their information supplied by more normal cinematic methods. Judged according to this standard, their use in three or four recent films was faulty. *The Informer* started with a perfectly needless reference to Judas casting down the thirty pieces of silver. The quotation printed on the screen did nothing to add either to the story or to the appreciation of Gypo's character; rather did it serve to distract because it raised an assumption that something was to be developed in the theme which was never carried out and never even projected. *Les Miserables,* similarly, started with a few words of information which aided not a whit towards the understanding of the plot. Perhaps preliminary notes of this kind are not wholly to be deplored, but, if introduced, they had better come as frank directional information along with the name of the actors, reproducing thus what might have gone in a theatre program note. It seems a mistake to put them in Gothic or other "harmonising" letters and to throw them on the screen as the first shot of the film itself.

Much more dangerous are the titles within a film. One of

this kind suddenly intruded itself in the course of *David Copperfield,* where a caption drew our attention to the fact that, having pursued the fortunes of the young David, we were now to follow his career in manhood. Even more disturbing were those in *Peter Ibbetson.* Among them was a sentence telling us that Peter was confined in a prison, set amid bleak northern moors. To have displayed these moors before us, to have suggested the dank and the dreary wastes, would have been a simple cinematic task; the sub-title was manifestly a wrong procedure. Another similar employment of the printed words appeared in *The Little Minister.* There one shot shows Babby scribbling her note in the minister's Bible; the next action shot reveals the minister himself finding this note on opening the Bible while he stands in the pulpit. Between the one and the other a number of days is supposed to elapse, and, to indicate this, a notice "On the following Sunday . . ." was inserted. Once more we cannot escape feeling that the lapse of time could have been indicated by means, either visual or oral, more in accord with the cinematic style. Final examples may be taken from *A Tale of Two Cities.* Here there was a foreword title, giving a fairly long quotation stating that this "was the best of times" and "the worst of times . . . in short, it was a period very like the present." Into this foreword title faded a scene on Shooter's Hill, the Dover Road, with, superimposed upon it, a caption reading "England—The Dover Road, A Certain Evening Late in the 18th Century." Later on we were shown an obviously French roadway with characteristic rows of poplars and once more came the superimposed caption, "France." Hardly any better examples could be found than these. Maybe a "program note" might have been admitted, but the initial quotation was of doubtful value, while the information about the Dover road and the French roadway was either otiose or a confession of weakness. For the whole series of titles there was no excuse. Nor was there excuse for the title which accompanied an aristocratic banquet scene:—"This was the Warning," with its long-winded terms. When the revolution starts and messengers are sent galloping over the land, the visual pictures were amply sufficient to emphasise the action, and consequently another superimposed title was worse than valueless:—"Over the Countryside the Message of Hate went forth: Death to the Aristos! Death to the Innocent as well as the Guilty! Death to all Aristos! Death to their Friends! Death to their Servants! Smite them all, the Root and the Branch! Death!" Equally false was the commentary, "And from the Slum of St. Antoine came the Answer: 'Down with the Bastille'," while this plethora of printed signs reached its most absurd expression in a series of questions:— "Why?" "WHY?" "WHY?" we read in increasing size of letters and in increasing wonderment. Even a well prepared scenario like *Anna Karenina* superimposed a useless "Moscow" over a picture which, because it concentrated on "the characteristic domes of the Kremlin," clearly told its own story.

That the creator of a screen-play and a director are here presented with a serious difficulty is, of course, not to be denied, but we may at the same time assert that the solving of the problem ought to be attempted cinematically and not in the way of literary narrative. Filmically both the passage of time and the establishing of setting had better be indicated either by means of visual symbols or, if absolutely necessary, by means of spoken words. The former method is generally the more satisfactory; but in the sound film words, too, may be used for this purpose as they are used in a stage play, although, with the much greater concentration demanded by the cinema, rarely is there the opportunity granted for leisurely time exposition. Each word has to do so much more in a film than in a play that but sparing use can be made of oral indications of this kind.

Normally, we may agree that, in spite of the difficulties, mere falling back on informative captions is an unimaginative escape; ample justification is there for saying that, by symbolic images—visual or verbal—a way should be found for bringing the lapse of time or the locality directly before the public. Occasionally a device of the kind employed in *So Red the Rose* may be employed—the providing of information by some titles disguised as filmic material, in this instance through what purported to be Civil War bulletins chalked on a board; but such a device, although wrought into the general plan, clearly is not to be used with any frequency. However transformed, it remains a printed caption, and to that almost anything is preferable. Even the use of an unseen announcer's voice, the Voice of Time, would have been better than the introduction of the printed words in *David Copperfield*. Strangely enough, this device, although known on the stage from an early period, seems not to have been much exploited in the film. There would appear to be no valid reason why it should not meet a need, although, as with all things in cinematic art, experience from actual trial alone could provide a definite answer.

DRAMA AND SCREEN PLAY

Having thus surveyed some of the basic principles involved in the sound film, we may turn to a brief consideration of the film scenario or screen-play in its entirety. Already have been demonstrated the essential facts that cinematic dialogue must be much more economic in its effects than dialogue in a play, that we expect in it not the complete development of a conversation from beginning to end but a series of suggestions concerning that conversation's course, that the subjective frequently must be called into service alongside the objective, and that the words introduced often must play a double part, directly presenting a scene and indirectly linking that scene to the one immediately following. Dependent on these principles is another, that, in order to secure economy, visual images are preferable to words if these visual images are sufficient to convey the impression desired. Fundamental to the cinema is that which is presented to the eye; this must ever take chief place. Words spoken occupy a secondary position; and printed words may only occasionally be called into service. *A Tale of Two Cities* presented one sequence which illustrates this clearly. Mme. Defarge has just told La Vengeance that the man who had kept Dr. Manette in prison for eighteen years was the Marquis St. Evremonde and has added that, for other reasons as well, this nobleman occupies "a place of honour" on her "register." This information could hardly have been presented visually; therefore the dialogue is right and just. Right and just, too, are the following wholly visual shots:—

CAMERA PANS DOWN the shawl that she is knitting, until we come to almost the top of the shawl. The knitting is covered with simplified designs of the crests of armorial bearings of the aristocratic families. The first is the same as the crest of the carriage door of the Marquis St. Evremonde. From the crest on her register,

DISSOLVE TO:

THE SAME CREST

On a carriage door of a coach, which is moving quickly. PULL CAMERA BACK and reveal the Marquis, sitting nonchalantly and casually—speaking to an attendant, Moreau.

After a series of shots introducing words and actions (the coach brought to a stop when it runs over the little child of Gaspard and setting off again) there is a further dissolve into a picture of

CHATEAU EVREMONDE

The Marquis' carriage comes over moat, and comes to stop at porte-cochere. He alights amid lackeys—turns, goes off stage.

This, again, is followed by:—

THE CHATEAU EVREMONDE. CLOSE SHOT THE COAT OF ARMS OVER THE MAIN DOOR.

There can be no doubt but that by such visual means the implications of the story and the relationship of the characters are fully and effectively portrayed. On the other hand we may reasonably criticise adversely the latter part of *The Informer,* a film otherwise well planned, because of its failure to permit the visual precedence over the oral. The story of this film was largely told in visual pictures up to the last court-martial scene, and that scene somehow proved less satisfying than the earlier shots. The reason well may lie in the fact that words there were substituted for movements. Movement there was, of course, but not

sufficient attention had been paid to the necessity of securing an absolute economy in the speeches and of allowing
the eyes to serve as instruments for the imagination. How
fully possible this is was shown in *Chapayev*, where the
character and achievements of the hero were delineated
visually in such a manner that a spectator who knew no
Russian could, even without the aid of sub-titles, follow at
least the main outlines of the plot and appreciate Chapayev's virtues and vices as conceived by the director.

It is but natural that, since the film started with silent
images cast on a screen, greater proficiency should in general be displayed in the controlling and determining of
visual sequences than in welding words into suitable cinematic form. Of this, too, a good example is provided in *A
Tale of Two Cities*. Whereas the shots showing the capture
of the Bastille were brilliantly managed (in the screen-play
conception, if not in actual direction), with judicious
variety both in the incidents delineated and in the camera
angles, the conversational portions of the film were weak.
Soliloquy was permitted to intrude when Carton meditated
on the distinction between himself and Darnay; and soliloquy must be judged a thing essentially belonging to the
stage, a convention determined by the theatre's restrictions
in the possibility of displaying inner thought. In many
parts, too, the words came in long monotonous sequences,
lacking diversity. In the screen-play, throughout two entire
pages Carton and Darnay converse without any attempts
being made to co-ordinate movement in the pictures presented and movement in the words. The storming of the
Bastille, on the other hand, exhibited careful planning and
genuine appreciation of cinematic values. Bare feet clatter-
ing over cobblestones, independent shots showing selected

citizens leaving their shops to join the crowd, the mob marching, that mob joined by others, the mob seen from the castle walls, the drawbridge rising and bearing with it a young man who is eventually forced to fall, rapid short shots of individual members of the mob and of the troops, the firing of the cannon, the arrival of the French soldiers, and the final fall of the fortress. The way in which this was handled, particularly the skill used in quickening the tempo and reducing the length of the shots in accordance with the increase in tension and excitement, left little to be desired. The contrast between the methods employed here and those employed in the treatment of dialogue is thoroughly characteristic.

While emphasising the importance of the visual images, we must at the same time note that sound is not a mere appendage in the film. The introduction of words has brought into being a new form, these words and their power frequently determining the shape which a film play will take. Perhaps, in order to emphasise this a few concrete examples may be taken, and first it will be convenient to start with one where it is possible to compare closely stage and cinematic versions of the same theme. Of all modern plays perhaps *The Barretts of Wimpole Street* is among the best-known, and consequently it will not be unfitting to select that and the accompanying screen-play for examination. In the play's second act, as will be recalled, several themes were developed—principally those of Henrietta's love of Surtees Cook and of Elizabeth's first meeting with Robert Browning. The whole of the action during this series of scenes—indeed during the entire length of the stage-play—was set in Elizabeth's room.

A comparison of this with the corresponding episodes in the film becomes highly instructive. First of all, there is, of course, no act division. Following the play, the film makes Elizabeth ask Wilson to draw the curtains and extinguish the lamp, but the movement that follows introduces several essentially cinematic features. The camera proceeds from a general shot of the room to a close-up of Elizabeth, and thence "pans" over to a close-shot of the window. During the second of these we see "one of the faded flowers in the vase" shed "its petals on the table."

Deliberately this shot is made to dissolve in order to provide continuity of impression: the scene just shown drifts into another of the same window framing a winter view. The camera now draws nearer, tilts downwards and presents us with a glimpse of the street below where we see Henrietta emerging with a surreptitious air from the doorway. Here comes the first major departure from the stage action. Besier obviously was forced to employ a trick in order to get Surtees Cook within Elizabeth's room, and, equally obviously he was denied the opportunity of showing anything of the clandestine meetings between Cook and Henrietta. The ubiquitous camera, however, can tilt itself downwards and, having caught Henrietta outside, may follow her until she meets her lover at the nearby pillar-box. The few phrases of the stage Henrietta's reported conversation are legitimately expanded here into a section of dialogue which serves to indicate the relations between this pair and the force which separates them.

The next shot in the film shows Elizabeth on her couch, reading a book before an open fire. Wilson moves in to clear away the dishes, and there ensues the substance of the play's dialogue concerning the unfinished lunch and the in-

comprehensibilities of *Sordello*. This is presented by means
of the general shot referred to, a close shot of Wilson as
she stops in surprise, a medium shot of Elizabeth and Wilson while the former reads the passage from Browning's
poem. Immediately upon the close of this action (without
any break) Arabel and Bella enter, Bella then announcing
her engagement. At this there is a cut to a close shot of
the door, through which Henrietta comes dazedly.
Through several shots the conversation proceeds until
Bella leaves, confident of her power to win Barrett's con-
sent for the appearance of Henrietta at her marriage. Left
alone with Elizabeth, Henrietta tells that Surtees Cook has
asked her to marry him and that "of course she accepted
him—and said that she couldn't." This is interrupted by
the arrival of a note from Browning, announcing that he
is downstairs and waiting to see Elizabeth. Here the screen
version, by presenting a reading of the note and some
accompanying comments, adds a trifle to the dialogue of
the play. After some hesitation Browning is admitted. First
we see Elizabeth nervously waiting; Henrietta's voice is
heard; Browning enters and greets her. With some considerable movement of the camera, this scene continues up
to the beginning of the discussion concerning his poetry.
Then we get a close-up of Flush, "sitting up in his basket,
gazing interestedly at the visitor." This shot is caught up by
Browning's turning to the dog and addressing some of his
remarks to it. Through a series of varied shots the scene
proceeds, while Elizabeth confronts him with the obscuri-
ties of *Sordello*. That finished, a long—probably too long—
shot follows in which Browning testifies to his adoration.
Then the talk ceases: Elizabeth rises shakily and manages
to reach the window, her movement being momentarily

broken by a short glimpse of Flush as "he watches his mistress with grave eyes." From above we see the street as Elizabeth sees it and watch the figure of Browning marching bravely down it.

Thus ends the second main section of the film, corresponding to the play's second act. Clearly the action follows that of the drama fairly closely, but precisely because of this close approximation we may discern more easily the differences between the dramatic and the cinematic methods. Flush plays no part in this act on the stage; unless with a specially trained dog his performance therein would have been entirely impossible. In the film, on the other hand, he can be made to play an important rôle and symbolically to arouse the audience's imagination. A mere comic element in the drama, he becomes almost a protagonist in the film, for it is he who both begins and closes the entire action. The exploitation of his rôle is perfectly justifiable. Justifiable, too, is the symbolic treatment of the falling petals. The effect would have been insecurable on the stage both because of physical difficulties presented in producing such a trick and because the distance of the spectators would rob the device of any real significance. It is just such a device as the cinema legitimately may use. Still more important is the use made of a combined objective and subjective approach towards certain things—concentration on what she sees and concentration on the picture of Elizabeth herself.

All of these, however, lie within the sphere of visual images, and at the moment we are concerned mainly with sound. Much of the play's conversation in this section of the film has been curtailed, and rightly so in view of the different conditions in presentation; but one episode has been added, the direct displayal of Henrietta's love affair. Without a doubt, we feel that the insertion of this episode was right, and, believing so, at once we recognise that, just as the theatre has certain *scènes à faire* without seeing which an audience is dissatisfied, in the cinematic narrative other *scènes à faire* are demanded, including material which in a play we should be content to have described for us. Following along this line of thought, we may well ask ourselves the question whether indeed more deviation still was not demanded in this cinematic treatment of *The Barretts of Wimpole Street*. In particular one might argue that in the cinema more preparation is demanded for Browning's entrance than is provided by the sudden sending-in of the letter; one might express the belief that several shots showing Browning in his own surroundings would have been desirable, thus by presenting contemporaneous events in his apartment and in Elizabeth's sitting-room bringing that tension which is peculiarly securable by these cinematic means. Indeed, there is a need for just such a scene here as is given later in the screen-play when, after watching Elizabeth write her letter to Browning, we find the scene fading into the poet's study, and there listen to Wilson's words, first to the housekeeper and later to Browning himself. The presence in this study of books by and articles on Elizabeth is used to emphasise the passionate devotion he accords her. In the play we know it is impossible to see Browning at the moment he receives her note; realising that no difficulty is presented in the cinematic treatment, this is a scene we positively demand. There can be no doubt but that this is not only thoroughly in harmony with the cinematic technique but also a very effec-tive way of telling Browning's story; and we recognise that something of this kind was required also before the poet's appearance in Elizabeth's room.

Already examples have been given of the way in which concurrent events of this kind may be effectively introduced by means of visual images alone; an indication of the manner in which they may be used to build up a filmic narrative by combined employment of sound and image is provided by the beginning of *Private Lives*. This film, after a general shot of a marriage ceremony, opens with a composition shot of a church interior taken over the back of the minister:

Bride and bridegroom stand side by side at the chancel rail. Sybil looks up at Elyot with a demurely happy smile to which he responds with some restraint. The hymn ends. The parson, book in hand, takes a step towards the bridal pair.

The Parson

Dearly beloved brethren, we are gathered together here, in the sight of God and . . .
As he speaks, DISSOLVE INTO INT(ERIOR) FRENCH *MAIRIE*—COMP(OSITION) SHOT—DAY (Shooting from back of *Maire*). The voice of the English Parson dissolves into that of the little *Maire,* bearded, beribboned and important, who is gabbling the concluding half of the Civil marriage service in fluent French. Victor, the bridegroom, seems a little dubious as to the propriety of this French ceremony; Amanda is quite at ease, not to say amused.

There follows here a comic interlude, during which the *Maire* continues reciting his service. At the end of this

He returns—ignoring the laughter of the villagers—to the bridal pair CAMERA PANNING WITH HIM and continues

his rapid gabbling of the service as we DISSOLVE INTO
EXT(ERIOR) SKY—LONG SHOT—DAY
From the heart of a great white cloud comes the sound of a
plane in flight and in a moment the plane itself emerges
from the clouds and flies toward camera.
DISSOLVE INTO
INT(ERIOR) PLANE — CLOSE SHOT — SYBIL AND
ELYOT.

This shot, concentrating on the young couple as they sit
in the plane, introduces some dialogue which indicates
that Sybil is Elyot's second bride. It in turn dissolves into

EXT(ERIOR) FERRY—MEDIUM SHOT
Victor's roadster is being towed across a river on an old
fashioned ferry worked by a sturdy peasant from the bank.
The monotonous squeak proceeds from the winch the man is
turning.
CAMERA MOVES TO A CLOSE SHOT of Victor and
Amanda. Victor holds on his lap a neat and shining little
lunch basket. Amanda leans against Victor's shoulder interestedly examining the contents. Victor looks down at her
tenderly.

Some dialogue again follows and during it we learn that
Amanda has been previously married to Elyot. At once
the significance and relationship of the two sets of shots
become apparent; and when we turn from these to first the
exterior and then the interior of a Riviera hotel the purpose of both comes with tense expectancy to us. Anxiously
we watch Elyot and Sybil alight from their taxi and get
supplied with a terrace suite, followed by Victor and
Amanda who likewise are accommodated with a terrace
suite on the same floor.

The gradual drawing together of two apparently unrelated episodes, with only occasional and vague clues, provided partly by visual images, partly by words, seems one of the specific functions of cinematic narrative. This method may, of course, be used both for comic and for serious effect: it may be employed to arouse laughter, or romantic expectancy, or the terror of an almost tragic emotion. On the rhythm of the shots and the temper introduced into them will depend the effect they have on us. From this consideration must spring a realisation of what an opportunity was lost in *The Barretts of Wimpole Street*. Cinematically, the story offered a good chance for such double action in the Elizabeth Barrett-Robert Browning relationship; nay further, for the adequate unfolding of the story more was required than the sudden receipt by the former of the latter's note. Maybe there was a justification here for keeping as closely as possible to the theme development of the play in that this play was so well known that serious deviations might have met with a considerable amount of adverse comment. So far the method employed may be defended; but considering this film as a film, and therefore as something entirely distinct from any stage production, we might well demand freer handling and greater use of that which the cinema may give which the stage cannot.

An examination of other films leads to similar judgments. Let us take a simple example, *Bonnie Scotland*, in which the irrepressible Laurel and Hardy were featured. In that we started with a street in a small Scots town; the pair go to an hotel, stating that they have come to claim a legacy; they proceed to the solicitor's office where, to show their identity, they display jail cards and explain they have crossed the Atlantic in a cattle-boat. No doubt, by these sequences a few elements of surprise are secured, but one may well ask the question whether, in view of the fact that we have here a series of scenes taking place in what is fundamentally one locality (the Scots town), the method employed is not closer to the dramatic than to the cinematic. The journey on the cattle-boat and the jail experiences are indicated mainly by a kind of retrospective narrative; and retrospective narrative is alien to the general methods of the film. One may suggest that much more comic effect might have been attained by opening the film in a Mid-Western prison, with following scenes of escape, pursuit, safe stowage in a cattle-boat and arrival in the Scots town. By this means the story would have been told in more effectively cinematic terms.

Another example, taken from a serious film, *A Tale of Two Cities,* corroborates this judgment. Undoubtedly the freedom of the film brings it nearer in structure to the novel than the drama, where a conventional limitation and restriction is demonstrably essential; but simply to follow the plan of a novel in the preparing of a screen-play is a procedure as erroneous as the faithful reproduction on the screen of dramatic form. This, unfortunately, is the scheme of *A Tale of Two Cities.* Starting with a quotation, we take up the contents of Dickens's first chapter, see the Dover Mail lumbering up Shooter's Hill and hear the mysterious message, "Recalled to Life." Next we come to the Royal George Hotel, Dover, where Lorry tells Lucie Manette of her father's imprisonment and rescue. Straightaway, we move over to Paris and have presented before us the tabloided contents of Dickens' chapter in which he describes so magnificently the broken barrel and the trickling blood-red wine spreading along the narrow street. Next we are introduced to Defarge's wine-shop whither Lucie comes to reclaim her father. No doubt the sequence of incidents does not lack interest, but the arrangement seems much better adapted for the purposes of prose narrative than for those of the cinema. The information regarding Dr. Manette's imprisonment must perforce be presented retrospectively as must several other matters relating to the principal *dramatis personæ*. A much more effective arrangement might easily have been found than this simple one of following the novel's structure, and no doubt increased interest might have arisen from a carrying of the action back beyond the point from which it is made to start. Long passages of informative dialogue such as that between Lucie Manette and Lorry appear generally unfitted for treatment in the film.

Quite apart from narrative values, too, the presence of sound must in the future play a determining part in the creation of the screen-play. One example, and that a simple one, may serve. On the stage an effect may be produced of stillness moving into swift action or of quietness giving way to loud sound. Such effects, however, will be conditioned by the physical limitations of the stage and by the sets necessarily employed. By filmic methods something more and of a different kind may be secured. At the beginning of *Top Hat,* for example, the first shot shows a wall-plate informing us that the building we are about to enter is The Thackeray Club, London; a second shot displays a notice saying that silence must be observed by members in the club rooms, the way being thus prepared for a shot of a lounge in which a dozen men are seated, each solemnly buried behind a copy of *The Times.* Among them, clearly anxious impishly to create a disturbance, sits Fred Astaire. The silence and decorum are intensified further by the angry glances and expressions of offended dignity when a waiter inadvertently clinks one wine-glass against another and when Astaire himself makes his newspaper rustle in the process of unfolding it. The path is cleared for a strong contrast. The immediately obvious contrast comes when Astaire, leaving the lounge, stands at the doorway and startles the members by executing a few staccato dance steps; but a much more important contrast follows when at length, in his own apartment, his nimble feet start to beat out their amazing rhythms. The ease with which a film can move from set to set offers innumerable opportunities for sound contrasts of this larger kind and manifestly these opportunities must condition to a certain extent the composition of the preliminary screen-play.

That, within the past two or three years, vast advances have been made in technical knowledge and in artistic sensibility to cinematic requirements needs no demonstration; but obviously complete mastery has not yet been attained. For the securing of that mastery is required not only a great amount of experimentation but also an exhaustive examination of cinematic devices and of cinematic principles, such as the stage has had in its possession for centuries. Critical rules cannot hope to make creative dramatists, but the dramatists of all ages have benefited much from the painstaking analysis which has been devoted to the work of their predecessors.

Weakness in the preparation of cinematic scripts may be due to a variety of causes, not least of which perhaps is the fact that many authors write for the screen with their left hand. They are interested in the money rather than sincerely moved to tell a story or express an idea.

But this cannot be taken alone. Perhaps Will Hays comes nearer to the truth when he says that

Recognition of the motion pictures as an art by the great universities (will mark) the beginning of a new day in motion picture work. It (will pave) the way for the motion picture's Shakespeares.

This is no strained and fantastic statement. It means simply that through the aid of the detailed analysis and critical evaluation similar to that which the drama has been accorded, the ground will be prepared for surer mastery of effect; from the principles thus established the cinematic form of expression will be provided with that sense of purpose already attained by other arts of more extended ancestry. Shakespeare could not have been without the preparation made for him by the humanistic work of the academies; the "University wits," trained in the study of literature, were his immediate predecessors and masters.

For this the cinema is waiting.

5

FILM REALITY: THE CINEMA AND
THE THEATRE

ONE question of fundamental importance remains for
consideration. When we witness a film, do we anticipate
something we should not expect from a stage performance,
and, if so, what effect has this upon our appreciation of
film acting? At first, we might be tempted to dismiss such
a query or to answer it easily and glibly. There is no essential difference, we might say, save in so far as we expect
greater variety and movement on the screen than we do
on the stage; and for acting, that, we might reply, is
obviously the same as stage acting although perhaps more
stabilised in type form. Do we not see Charles Laughton,
Cedric Hardwicke, Ernest Thesiger, Elizabeth Bergner
now in the theatre, now in the cinema? To consider
further, we might say, were simply to indulge in useless
and uncalled for speculation.

Nevertheless, the question does demand just a trifle more
of investigation. Some few years ago a British producing
company made a film of Bernard Shaw's *Arms and the
Man*. This film, after a few exciting shots depicting the
dark streets of a Balkan town, the frenzied flight of the
miserable fugitives and the clambering of Bluntschli onto
Raina's window terrace, settled down to provide what was
fundamentally a screen-picture of the written drama. The
dialogue was shortened, no doubt, but the shots proceeded
more or less along the dramatic lines established by Shaw

and nothing was introduced which he had not originally conceived in preparing his material for the stage. The result was that no more dismal film has ever been shown to the public. On the stage *Arms and the Man* is witty, provocative, incisively stimulating; its characters have a breath of genuine theatrical life; it moves, it breathes, it has vital energy. In the screen version all that life has fled, and, strangest thing of all, those characters—Bluntschli, Raina, Sergius—who are so exciting on the boards, looked to the audience like a set of wooden dummies, hopelessly patterned. Performed by a third-rate amateur cast their lifeblood does not so ebb from them, yet here, interpreted by a group of distinguished professionals, they wilted and died—died, too, in such forms that we could never have credited them with ever having had a spark of reality. Was there any basic reason for this failure?

THE CAMERA'S TRUTH

The basic reason seems to be simply this—that practically all effectively drawn stage characters are types and that in the cinema we demand individualisation, or else that we recognise stage figures as types and impute greater power of independent life to the figures we see on the screen. This judgment, running so absolutely counter to what would have been our first answer to the original question posited, may seem grossly distorted, but perhaps some further consideration will demonstrate its plausibility. When we go to the theatre, we expect theatre and nothing else. We know that the building we enter is a playhouse; that behind the lowered curtain actors are making ready, dressing themselves in strange garments and transforming their natural features; that the figures we later see on the boards are never living persons of king and bishop and clown, but merely men pretending for a brief space of time to be like these figures. Dramatic illusion is never (or so rarely as to be negligible) the illusion of reality: it is always imaginative illusion, the illusion of a period of make-believe. All the time we watch Hamlet's throes of agony we know that the character Hamlet is being impersonated by a man who presently will walk out of the stage-door in ordinary clothes and an autograph-signing smile on his face. True, volumes have been written on famous dramatic characters—Greek, Elizabethan English and modern Norwegian—and these volumes might well seem to give the lie to such assumptions. Have not Shakespeare's characters seemed so real to a few observers that we have on our shelves books specifically concerned with the girlhood of his heroines—a girlhood the dramas themselves denied us?

These studies, however, should not distract us from the essential truth that the greatest playwrights have always aimed at presenting human personality in bold theatric terms. Hamlet seizes on us, not because he is an individual, not because in him Shakespeare has delineated a particular prince of Denmark, but because in Hamlet there are bits of all men; he is a composite character whose lineaments are determined by dramatic necessity, and through that he lives. Fundamentally, the truly vital theatre deals in stock figures. Like a child's box of bricks, the stage's material is limited; it is the possibilities in arrangement that are well-nigh inexhaustible. Audiences thrill to see new situations born of fresh sociological conditions, but the figures set before them in significant plays are conventionally fixed and familiar. Of Romeos there are many, and of Othellos legion. Character on the stage is restricted and stereotyped and the persons who play upon the boards are governed, not by the strangely perplexing processes of life but by the established terms of stage practice. Bluntschli represents half a hundred similar rationalists; the idealism of thousands is incorporated in Sergius; and Raina is an eternal stage type of the perplexing feminine. The theatre is populated, not by real individuals whose boyhood or girlhood may legitimately be traced, but by heroes and villains sprung full-bodied from Jove's brain, by clowns and pantaloons whose youth is unknown and whose future matters not after the curtain's fall.

In the cinema we demand something different. Probably we carry into the picture-house prejudices deeply ingrained in our beings. The statement that "the camera cannot lie" has been disproved by millions of flattering portraits and by dozens of spiritualistic pictures which purport to depict fairies but which mostly turn out to be faintly disguised pictures of ballet-dancers or replicas of figures in advertisements of night-lights. Yet in our heart of hearts we credit the truth of that statement. A picture, a piece of sculpture, a stage-play—these we know were created by man; we have watched the scenery being carried in back stage and we know we shall see the actors, turned into themselves again, bowing at the conclusion of the performance. In every way the "falsity" of a theatrical production is borne in upon us, so that we are prepared to demand nothing save a theatrical truth. For the films, however, our orientation is vastly different. Several periodicals, it is true, have endeavored to let us into the secrets of the moving-picture industry and a few favored spectators have been permitted to make the rounds of the studios; but from ninety per cent of the audience the actual methods employed in the preparation of a film remain far off and dimly realised. "New York," we are told,

struts when it constructs a Rockefeller Center. A small town chirps when it finishes a block of fine cottages. The government gets into the newspapers for projects like Boulder Dam. It takes Hollywood approximately three days to build Rome and a morning to effect its fall, but there is very little hurrah about it. The details are guarded like Victorian virtue.

There is sound reticence on the part of a community that is usually articulate about its successes. Hollywood is in the business of building illusion, not sets. . . . The public likes to feel that the stork brought *The Birth of a Nation*. It likes to feel that a cameraman hung in the clouds—mid-Pacific—the day that Barrymore fought the whale.

That audience, accordingly, carries its prejudices with it intact. "The camera cannot lie"—and therefore, even when we are looking at Marlene Dietrich or Robert Montgomery, we unconsciously lose sight of fictional surroundings and interpret their impersonations as "real" things. Rudolph Valentino became a man who had had innumerable Sheikish adventures, and into each part she took the personality of Greta Garbo was incorporated. The most impossible actions may be shown us in a film, yet Laurel and Hardy are, at their best, seen as individuals experiencing many strange adventures, not as virtuoso comedians in a vaudeville act.

How true this is was demonstrated by a film, *Once in a Blue Moon,* which has been shown only in a few theatres. The general tone of *Once in a Blue Moon* was burlesque. In it was a "take-off" of certain Russian films, incidental jibes at a few popular American examples, and occasional skits directed at prominent players; Jimmy Savo took the rôle of Gabbo the Great while one of the actresses made up to look like Katherine Hepburn. The result was dismal. In Charlie Chaplin's free fantasy there is life and interest; throughout the course of *Once in a Blue Moon* vitality was entirely lacking. Nor was the reason far to seek. We cannot appreciate burlesque in the cinema because of the fact that in serious films actor and rôle are indistinguishable; on the stage we appreciate it since there, in serious plays, we can never escape from separating the fictional character and its creator. Stage burlesque is directed at an artistic method, generally the method employed by an individual player in the treatment of his parts. To caricature Irving was easy; hardly would a cinematic travesty of Arliss succeed. The presentation of this single film proved clearly the difference in approach on the part of cinema and theatre public respectively. These, so generally considered identical, are seen to be controlled by quite distinct psychological elements.

Charlie Chaplin's free fantasy has been referred to above. This, associated with, say, the methods of Rene Clair, might well serve to demonstrate the true resources of the film; comparison with the erring tendencies of *Once in a Blue Moon* brings out clearly the genuine frontiers of the cinematic sphere. In *The Ghost Goes West* there was much of satire, but this satire was directed at life and not at art and, moreover, was kept well within "realistic" terms. Everything introduced there was possible in the sense that, although we might rationally decide that these events could not actually have taken place, we recognized that, granted the conditions which might make them achievable, they would have assumed just such forms as were cast on the screen. The ghost was thus a "realistic" one, shown now in the guise of a figure solid and opaque and now in that of a transparent wraith, capable of defying the laws of physics. In a precisely similar way is the fantasy of a Chaplin film bound up with reality. We know that the things which Charlie does and the situations in which he appears are impossible but again, given the conditions which would make them possible, these are the shapes, we know, they would assume. Neither René Clair nor Charlie Chaplin steps into the field occupied by the artistic burleque; neither are "theatrical." The former works in an independent world conceived out of the terms of the actual, and the latter, like George Arliss in a different sphere, stands forth as an individual experiencing a myriad of strange and fantastic adventures.

The individualising process in film appreciation manifestly demands that other standards than those of the stage be applied to the screen-play. In the theatre we are commonly presented with characters relatively simple in their psychological make-up. A sympathetically conceived hero or heroine is devoted in his or her love affairs to one object; at the most some Romeo will abandon a visionary Rosaline for a flesh-and-blood Juliet. For the cinema, on the other hand, greater complexity may be permitted without loss of sympathy. The heroine in So Red the Rose is first shown coquetting with her cousin, suggestion is provided that she has not been averse to the attentions of a young family friend, she sets her cap at a visiting Texan and grieves bitterly on receiving news of his death, and finally she discovers or rediscovers the true love she bears to the cousin. All this is done without any hint that she is a mere flirt; her affections are such as might have been those of an ordinary girl in real life and we easily accept the filmic presentation in this light. On the stage the character could not have been viewed in a similar way; there we should have demanded a much simpler and less emotionally complicated pattern if our sympathies were firmly to be held.

The strange paradox, then, results:—that, although the cinema introduces improbabilities and things beyond nature at which any theatrical director would blench and murmur soft nothings to the air, the filmic material is treated by the audience with far greater respect (in its relation to life) than the material of the stage. Our conceptions of life in Chicago gangsterdom and in distant China are all colored by films we have seen. What we have witnessed on the screen becomes the "real" for us. In moments of sanity, maybe, we confess that of course we do not believe this or that, but, under the spell again, we credit the truth of these pictures even as, for all our professed superiority, we credit the truth of newspaper paragraphs.

TYPE CASTING

This judgment gives argument for Pudovkin's views concerning the human material to be used in a film—but that argument essentially differs from the method of support which he utilised. His views may be briefly summarised thus:—types are more desirable in film work because of the comparative restrictions there upon make-up; the director alone knows the complete script and therefore there is little opportunity for an individual actor to build up a part intelligently and by slow gradations; an immediate, vital and powerful impression, too, is demanded on the actor's first entrance; since the essential basis of cinematic art is montage of individual shots and not the histrionic abilities of the players, logic demands the use of untrained human material, images of which are wrought into a harmony by the director. Several of the apparent fallacies in Pudovkin's reasoning have been discussed above. There is, thus, no valid objection to the employment of trained and gifted actors, provided that these actors are not permitted to overrule other elements in the cinematic art and provided the director fully understands their essential position. That casting by type is desirable in the film seems, however, certain. Misled by theatrical ways, we may complain that George Arliss is the same in every screen-play he appears in; but that is exactly what the cinema demands. On the stage we rejoice, or should rejoice, in a performer's versatility; in the cinema unconsciously we want to feel that we are witnessing a true reproduction of real events, and consequently we are not so much interested in discerning a player's skill in diversity of character building. Arliss and Rothschild and Disraeli and Wellington are one. That the desire on the part of a producing company to make use of a particular "star" may easily lead to the deliberate manufacturing of a character to fit that star is true; but, after all, such a process is by no means unknown to the theatre, now or in the past. Shakespeare and Molière both wrote to suit their actors, and Sheridan gave short sentimental scenes to Charles and Maria in *The School for Scandal* because, according to his own statement, "Smith can't make love—and nobody would want to make love to Priscilla Hopkins."

To exemplify the truth of these observations no more is demanded than a comparison of the stage and screen versions of *The Petrified Forest*. As a theatrical production this play was effective, moving and essentially harmonised with the conventions applying to its method of expression; lifeless and uninteresting seemed the filming of fundamentally the same material. The reasons for this were many. First was the fact that the film attempted to defy the basic law which governs the two forms; the theatre rejoices in artistic limitation in space while the film demands movement and change in location. We admire Sherwood's skill in confining the whole of his action to the Black Mesa but we condemn the same confining process when we turn to see the same events enacted on the screen. Secondly, since a film can rarely bear to admit anything in the way of theatricality in its settings, those obviously painted sets of desert and mountain confused and detracted from our appreciation of the narrative. A third reason may be sought for in the dialogue given to the characters. This dialogue, following the lines provided for the stage play, showed itself as far too rich and cumbersome for cinematic purposes; not only was there too much of it, but that which sounded exactly right when delivered on the boards of the theatre (because essentially in tune with theatrical conventions) seemed ridiculous, false and absurd when associated with the screen pictures. Intimately bound up with this, there has to be taken into account both the nature and the number of the *dramatis personæ*. Sherwood's stage characters were frankly drawn as types—an old pioneer, a killer, an unsuccessful littérateur, an ambitious girl, a veteran, a business-man, a business-man's wife—each one representative of a class or of an ideal. Not for a moment did we believe that these persons were real, living human beings; they were typical figures outlining forces in present-day society. This being so, we had no difficulty in keeping them all boldly in our minds even when the whole group of them filled the stage. When transferred to the screen, however, an immediate feeling of dissatisfaction assailed us; these persons who had possessed theatrical reality could have no reality in the film; their vitality was fled; they seemed false, absurd, untrue. Still further, their number became confusing. The group of representative types which dominated the stage proved merely a jumbled mass on the screen, for the screen, although it may make use of massed effects of a kind which would be impossible in the theatre, generally finds its purposes best served by concentration on a very limited number of major figures. The impression of dissatisfaction thus received was increased by the interpretation of these persons. Partly because of the words given to them, all the characters save Duke Mantee seemed to be actors and nothing else. There was exhibited a histrionic skill which might win our admiration but which at the same time was alien to the medium through which it came to us. A Leslie Howard whose stage performance was right and just became an artificial figure when, before the camera, he had to deliver the same lines he had so effectively spoken on the stage. From the lack of individualisation in the characters resulted a feeling of confusion and falsity; because of the employment of conventions suited to one art and not to another vitality, strength and emotional power were lost.

PSYCHOLOGICAL PENETRATION

The full implications of such individualisation of film types must be appreciated, together with the distinct approach made by a cinema audience to the persons seen by them on the screen. Because of these things, allied to its possession of several technical devices, the cinema is given the opportunity of coming into closer accord with recent tendencies in other arts than the stage. Unquestionably, that which separates the literature of today from yesterday's literature is the former's power of penetrating, psychoanalytically, into human thought and feeling. The discovery of the sub-conscious has opened up an entirely fresh field of investigation into human behaviour, so that whereas a Walter Scott spread the action of a novel over many years and painted merely the outsides of his characters, their easily appreciated mental reactions and their most obvious passions, James Joyce has devoted an extraordinarily lengthy novel to twenty-four hours in the life of one individual. By this means the art of narrative fiction has been revolutionised and portraiture of individuals completely altered in its approach.

Already it has been shown that normally the film does not find restrictions in the scope of its material advantageous; so that the typical film approaches outwardly the extended breadth of a Scott novel. In dealing with that material, however, it is given the opportunity of delving more deeply into the human consciousness. By its subjective method it can display life from the point of view of its protagonists. Madness on the stage, in spite of Ophelia's pathetic efforts, has always appeared rather absurd, and Sheridan was perfectly within his rights when he caricatured the convention in his Tilburina and her address to all the finches of the grove. On the screen, however, madness may be made arresting, terrifying, awful. The mania of the lunatic in the German film, M, held the attention precisely because we were enabled to look within his distracted brain. Seeing for moments the world distorted in

eccentric imaginings, we are moved as no objective presentation of a stage Ophelia can move us.

Regarded in this way, the cinema, a form of expression
born of our own age, is seen to bear a distinct relationship
to recent developments within the sphere of general artistic
endeavour. While making no profession to examine this
subject, one of the most recent writers on *This Modern
Poetry,* Babette Deutsch, has expressed, *obiter dicta,* judgments which illustrate clearly the arguments presented
above. "The symbolists," she says, "had telescoped images
to convey the rapid passage of sensations and emotions.
The metaphysicals had played in a like fashion with ideas.
Both delighted in paradox. The cinema, and ultimately the
radio, made such telescopy congenial to the modern poet,
as the grotesqueness of his environment made paradox inevitable for him." And again:

The cinema studio creates a looking-glass universe where,
without bottles labeled "Drink me" or cakes labeled "Eat me"
or keys to impossible gardens, creatures are elongated or telescoped, movements accelerated or slowed up, in a fashion suggesting that the world is made of india-rubber or collapsible
tin. The ghost of the future glimmers through the immediate
scene, the present dissolves into the past.

Akin to these marvels is the poetry of such a man as
Horace Gregory. In his *No Retreat: New York, Cassandra,*
"the fluent images, the sudden close-ups, the shifting angle
of vision, suggest the technique of the cinema." The
method of the film is apparent in such lines as these:

Give Cerberus a non-employment wage, the dog is hungry.
This head served in the war, Cassandra, it lost an eye;

That head spits fire, for it lost its tongue licking the paws
of lions caged in Wall Street and their claws
were merciless.

Follow, O follow him, loam-limbed Apollo, crumbling before
Tiffany's window: he must buy
himself earrings for he meets his love tonight,
(Blossoming Juliet
emptied her love into her true love's lap)
dies in his arms.

If the cinema has thus influenced the poets, we realise
that inherently it becomes a form of art through which
may be expressed many of the most characteristic tendencies in present-day creative endeavour. That most of
the films so far produced have not made use of the
peculiar methods inherent in the cinematic approach
need not blind us to the fact that here is an instrument
capable of expressing through combined visual and vocal
means something of that analytical searching of the spirit
which has formed the pursuit of modern poets and novel-
ists. Not, of course, that in this analytic and realistic
method are to be enclosed the entire boundaries of the
cinema. The film has the power of giving an impression
of actuality and it can thrill us by its penetrating truth to
life: but it may, if we desire, call into existence the strangest of visionary worlds and make these too seem real. The
enchanted forest of *A Midsummer Night's Dream* will
always on the stage prove a thing of lath and canvas and
paint; an enchanted forest in the film might truly seem
haunted by a thousand fears and supernatural imaginings.
This imaginary world, indeed, is one that our public has
cried for and demanded, and our only regret may be that
the producers, lacking vision, have compromised and in

compromising have descended to banalities. Taking their
sets of characters, they thrust these, willy-nilly, into scenes
of ornate splendour, exercising their inventiveness, not to
create the truly fanciful but to fashion the exaggeratedly
and hyperbolically absurd. Hotels more sumptuous than
the Waldorf-Astoria or the Ritz; liners outvying the pre-
tentions of the Normandie; speed that sets Malcolm Camp-
bell to shame; melodies inappropriately rich—these have
crowded in on us again and yet again. Many spectators are
becoming irritated and bored with scenes of this sort, for
mere exaggeration of life's luxuries is not creative artistically.

That the cinema has ample opportunities in this direction
has been proved by Max Reinhardt's *A Midsummer Night's
Dream,* which, if unsatisfactory as a whole and if in many
scenes tentative in its approach, demonstrated what may be
done with imaginative forms on the screen. Apart from the
opportunity offered by Shakespeare's theme for the presentation of the supernatural fairy world, two things were
specially to be noted in this film. The first was that certain
passages which, spoken in our vast modern theatres
with their sharp separation of audience and actors, become mere pieces of rhetoric devoid of true meaning and
significance were invested in the film with an intimacy and
directness they lacked on the stage. The power of the
cinema to draw us near to an action or to a speaker served
here an important function, and we could at will watch a
group of players from afar or approach to overhear the
secrets of a soliloquy. The second feature of interest lay in
the ease with which the cinema can present visual symbols
to accompany language. At first, we might be prepared to
condemn the film on this ground, declaring that the imagi-

native appeal of Shakespeare's language would thereby be lost. Again, however, second thoughts convince us that much is to be said in its defence; reference once more must be made to a subject already briefly discussed. Shakespeare's dialogue was written for an audience, not only sympathetic to his particular way of thought and feeling, but gifted with certain faculties which today we have lost. Owing to the universal development of reading, certain faculties possessed by men of earlier ages have vanished from us. In the sixteenth century, men's minds were more acutely perceptive of values in words heard, partly because their language was a growing thing with constantly occurring new forms and strange applications of familiar words, but largely because they had to maintain a constant alertness to spoken speech. Newspapers did not exist then; all men's knowledge of the larger world beyond their immediate ken had to come from hearing words uttered by their companions. As a result, the significance of words was more keenly appreciated and certainly was more concrete than it is today. When Macbeth, in four lines, likened life to a brief candle, to a walking shadow and to a poor player, one may believe that the ordinary spectator in the Globe theatre saw in his mind's eye these three objects referred to. The candle, the shadow and the player became for him mental realities.

The same speech uttered on the stage today can hardly hope for such interpretation. Many in the audience will be lulled mentally insensible to its values by the unaccustomed movement of the lines, and others will grasp its import, not by emotional imaginative understanding, but by a painful, rational process of thought. A modern audience, therefore, listening to earlier verse drama, will normally require a direct stimulus to its visual imagination—a thing entirely unnecessary in former times. Thus, for example, on the bare Elizabethan platform stage the words concerning dawn or sunlight or leafy woods were amply sufficient to conjure up an image of these things; latter-day experiments in the production of these dramas in reconstructed "Shakespearian" theatres, interesting as these may be and refreshing in their novelty, must largely fail to achieve the end, so easily and with such little effort reached among sixteenth century audiences. We need, now, all the appurtenances of a decorated stage to approach, even faintly, the dramatist's purpose. This is the justification for the presentation of Shakespeare's tragedies and comedies not in a reconstructed Globe theatre, but according to the current standards of Broadway or of Shaftesbury Avenue.

The theatre, however, can only do so much. It may visually create the setting, but it cannot create the stimulus necessary for a keener appreciation of the imagic value of Shakespeare's lines. No method of stage representation could achieve that end. On the screen, on the other hand, something at least in this direction may be accomplished. In *A Midsummer Night's Dream* Oberon's appearance behind dark bespangled gauze, even although too much dwelt on and emphasised, gave force to lines commonly read or heard uncomprehendingly—"King of Shadows," he is called; but the phrase means little or nothing to us unless our minds are given such a stimulus as was here provided. Critics have complained that in the film nothing is left to the imagination, but we must remember that in the Shakespearean verse is a quality which, because of changed conditions, we may find difficulty in appreciating. Its strangeness to us demands that an attempt be made to render it more intelligible and directly appealing. Such an attempt, through the means of expression granted to the cinema, may merely be supplying something which will bring us nearer to the conditions of the original spectators for whom Shakespeare wrote.

Normally, however, verse forms will be alien to the film. Verse in itself presupposes a certain remoteness from the terms of ordinary life and the cinema, as we have seen, usually finds its most characteristic expression in the world that immediately surrounds us. The close connection, noted by Babette Deutsch, between cinematic expression and tendencies in present-day poetry will declare itself, not in a utilisation of rhythmic speech but in a psychological penetration rendered manifest through a realistic method.

THE WAY OF THE THEATRE

If these arguments have any validity, then clearly a determined revision is necessary of our attitude towards the stage of today. That the theatre ought not servilely to follow cinematic methods seems unnecessary of proof, even although we may admit that certain devices of the film may profitably be called into service by playwright and director. *She Loves Me Not* with ample justification utilised for the purpose of stage comedy a technique which manifestly was inspired by the technique strictly proper to the cinema, and various experiments in the adapting of the filmic flash-back to theatrical requirements have not been without significance and value. But this way real success does not lie; the stage cannot hope to maintain its position simply by seizing on novelties exploited first in the cinema, and in general we must agree that the cinema can, because of its peculiar opportunities, wield this technique so much more effectively that its application to the stage seems thin, forced and artificial.

This, however, is not the most serious thing. Far more important is the fundamental approach which the theatre during recent years has been making towards its material. When the history of the stage since the beginning of the nineteenth century comes to be written with that impartiality which only the viewpoint of distant time can provide, it will most certainly be deemed that the characteristic development of these hundred odd years is the growth of realism and the attempted substitution of naturalistic illusion in place of a conventional and imaginative illusion. In the course of this development stands forth Ibsen as the outstanding pioneer and master. At the same time, this impartial survey may also decide that within the realistic method lie the seeds of disruption. It may be recognised that, while Ibsen was a genius of profound significance, for the drama Ibsenism proved a curse upon the stage. The whole realistic movement which strove to impose the conditions of real life upon the theatre may have served a salutary purpose for a time, but its vitality was but shortlived and, after the first excitement which attended the witnessing on the stage of things no one had hitherto dreamt of putting there had waned, its force and inspiring power was dissipated. Even if we leave the cinema out of account, we must observe that the realistic theatre in our own days has lost its strength. No doubt, through familiarity and tradition, plays in this style still prove popular and, popular success being the first requirement demanded of dramatic art, we must be careful to avoid wholesale condemnation; *Tobacco Road* and *Dead End* are things worthy of our esteem, definite contributions to the theatre of our day. But the continued appearance and success of naturalistic plays should not confuse the main issue, which is the question whether such naturalistic plays are likely in the immediate future to maintain the stage in that position we should all wish it to occupy. Facing this question fairly, we observe immediately that plays written in these terms are less likely to hold the attention of audiences over a period of years than are others written in a different style; because bound to particular conditions in time and place, they seem inevitably destined to be forgotten, or, if not forgotten, to lose their only valuable connotations. Even the dramas of Ibsen, instinct with a greater imaginative power than many works by his contemporaries and successors, do not possess, after the brief passing of forty years, the same vital significance they held for audiences of the eighties and nineties. If we seek for and desire a theatre which shall possess qualities likely to live over generations, unquestionably we must decide that the naturalistic play, made popular towards the close of the nineteenth century and still remaining in our midst, is not calculated to fulfil our highest wishes.

Of much greater importance, even, is the question of the position this naturalistic play occupies in its relations to the cinema. At the moment it still retains its popularity, but, we may ask, because of cinematic competition, is it not likely to fail gradually in its immediate appeal? The film has such a hold over the world of reality, can achieve expression so vitally in terms of ordinary life, that the realistic play must surely come to seem trivial, false and inconsequential. The truth is, of course, that naturalism on the stage must always be limited and insincere. Thousands have gone to *The Children's Hour* and come away fondly believing that what they have seen is life; they have not realised that here too the familiar stock figures, the type characterisations, of the theatre have been presented before them in modified forms. From this the drama cannot escape; little possibility is there of its delving deeply into the recesses of the individual spirit. That is a realm reserved for cinematic exploitation, and, as the film more and more explores this territory, does it not seem probable that theatre audiences will become weary of watching shows which, although professing to be "lifelike," actually are inexorably bound by the restrictions of the stage? Pursuing this path, the theatre truly seems doomed to inevitable destruction. Whether in its attempt to reproduce reality and give the illusion of actual events or whether in its pretence towards depth and subtlety in character-drawing, the stage is aiming at things alien to its spirit, things which so much more easily may be accomplished in the film that their exploitation on the stage gives only an impression of vain effort.

Is, then, the theatre, as some have opined, truly dying? Must it succumb to the rivalry of the cinema? The answer to that question depends on what the theatre does within the next ten or twenty years. If it pursues naturalism further, unquestionably little hope will remain; but if it recognises to the full the conditions of its own being and utilises those qualities which it, and it alone, possesses, the very thought of rivalry may disappear. Quite clearly, the true hope of the theatre lies in a rediscovery of convention, in a deliberate throwing-over of all thoughts concerning naturalistic illusion and in an embracing of that universalising power which so closely belongs to the dramatic form when rightly exercised. By doing these things, the theatre has achieved greatness and distinction in the past. We admire the playhouses of Periclean Athens and Elizabethan England; in both a basis was found in frank acceptance of the stage spectacle as a thing of pretence, with no attempt made to reproduce the outer forms of everyday life. Conventionalism ruled in both, and consequently out of both could spring a vital expression, with manifestations capable of appealing not merely to the age in which they originated but to future generations also. Precisely because Æschylus and Shakespeare did not try to copy life, because they presented their themes in highly conventional forms, their works have the quality of being independent of time and place. Their characters were more than photographic copies of known originals; their plots took no account of the terms of actuality; and their language soared on poetic wings. To this again must we come if our theatre is to be a vitally arresting force. So long as the stage is bound by the fetters of realism, so long as we judge theatrical characters by reference to individuals with whom we are acquainted, there is no possibility of preparing dialogue which shall rise above the terms of common existence.

From our playwrights, therefore, we must seek for a new foundation. No doubt many journeymen will continue to pen for the day and the hour alone, but of these there have always been legion; what we may desire is that the dramatists of higher effort and broader ideal do not follow the journeyman's way. Boldly must they turn from efforts to delineate in subtle and intimate manner the psychological states of individual men and women, recognising that in the wider sphere the drama has its genuine home. The cheap and ugly simian chatter of familiar conversation must give way to the ringing tones of a poetic utterance, not removed far off from our comprehension, but bearing a manifest relationship to our current speech. To attract men's ears once more to imaginative speech we may take the method of T. S. Eliot, whose violent contrasts in *Murder in the Cathedral* are intended to awaken appreciation and interest, or else the method of Maxwell Anderson, whose *Winterset* aims at building a dramatic poetry out of common expression. What procedure is selected matters little; indeed, if an imaginative theatre does take shape in our years, its strength will largely depend upon its variety of approach. That there is hope that such a theatre truly may come into being is testified by the recent experiments of many poets, by the critical thought which has been devoted to its consummation and by the increasing popular acclaim which has greeted individual efforts. The poetic play may still lag behind the naturalistic or seemingly naturalistic drama in general esteem, but the attention paid in New York to Sean O'Casey's *Within the Gates* and Maxwell Anderson's *Winterset* augurs the beginning of a new appreciation, while in London T. S. Eliot's *Murder in the Cathedral* has awakened an interest of a similar kind. Nor should we forget plays not in verse but aiming at a kindred approach; Robert Sherwood's *The Petrified Forest* and S. N. Behrman's *Rain from Heaven,* familiar and apparently realistic in form, deliberately and frankly aim at doing something more than present figures of individuals; in them the universalising power of the theatre is being utilised no less than in other plays which, by the employment of verse dialogue, deliberately remove the action from the commonplaces of daily existence.

Established on these terms native to its very existence and consequently far removed from the ways of the film, the theatre need have no fear that its hold over men's minds will diminish and fail. It will maintain a position essentially its own to which other arts may not aspire.

THE WAY OF THE FILM

For the film are reserved things essentially distinct. Possibility of confusion between the two has entered in only because the playhouse has not been true to itself. To the cinema is given a sphere, where the subjective and objective approaches are combined, where individualisation takes the place of type characterisation, where reality may faithfully be imitated and where the utterly fantastic equally is granted a home, where Walt Disney's animated flowers and flames exist alongside the figures of men and women who may seem more real than the figures of the stage, where a visual imagery in moving forms may thrill and awaken an age whose ears, while still alert to listen to poetic speech based on or in tune with the common language of the day, has forgotten to be moved by the tones of an earlier dramatic verse. Within this field lies the possibility of an artistic expression equally powerful as that of the stage, though essentially distinct from that. The distinction is determined by the audience reactions to the one and to the other. In the theatre the spectators are confronted by characters which, if successfully delineated, always possess a quality which renders them greater than separate individuals. When Clifford Odets declares that by the time he came to write his first play, *Awake and Sing!* he understood clearly that his

interest was not in the presentation of an individual's problems, but in those of a whole class. In other words, the task

was to find a theatrical form with which to express the mass
as hero—

he is doing no more than indicate that he has the mind
and approach of a dramatist. All the well-known figures
created in tragedy and comedy since the days of Aristoph-
anes and Æschylus have presented in this way the lineaments of universal humanity. If the theatre stands thus for
mankind, the cinema, because of the willingness on the
part of spectators to accept as the image of truth the moving forms cast on the screen, stands for the individual. It
is related to the modern novel in the same respect that the
older novel was related to the stage. Impressionistic and
expressionistic settings may serve for the theatre—even
may we occasionally fall back on plain curtains without
completely losing the interest of our audiences; the cinema
can take no such road, for, unless in frankly artificially
created films (such as the Walt Disney cartoon), we cling
to our preconceived beliefs and clamour for the three-dimensional, the exact and the authentic. In a stage play such as
Yellow Jack we are prepared to accept a frankly formal
background, because we know that the actors are actors
merely; but for the treatment of similar material in *The
Prisoner of Shark's Island* and *The Story of Pasteur* cinematic authenticity is demanded. At first glance, we might
aver that, because of this, the film had fewer opportunities for artistic expression than the stage; but further consideration will demonstrate that the restrictions are amply
compensated for by an added scope. Our illusion in the
picture-house is certainly less "imaginative" than the illusion which attends us in the theatre, but it has the advan-
tage of giving increased appreciation of things which are

outside nature. Through this the purely visionary becomes almost tangible and the impossible assumes shapes easy of comprehension and belief. The sense of reality lies as the foundation of the film, yet real time and real space are banished; the world we move in may be far removed from the world ordinarily about us; and symbols may find a place alongside common objects of little or no importance. If we apply the theory of "psychological distance" to theatre and film we realise the force of each. For any kind of aesthetic appreciation this distance is always demanded; before we can hope to feel the artistic qualities of any form we must be able to set ourselves away from it, to experience the stimulus its contemplation creates and at the same time have no call to put the reactions to that stimulus into play. This distance obviously may be of varying degrees; sometimes it is reduced, sometimes it provides a vast gulf between the observer and the art object. Furthermore the variation may be of two kinds—variation between one art and another, and variation between forms within the sphere of a single art. Music is further removed from reality than sculpture, but in music there may be an approach towards commonly heard sounds and in sculpture abstract shapes may take the place of familiar forms realistically delineated. Determination of the proper and legitimate approach will come from a consideration of the sense of distance between the observer and the object; the masterpieces in any art will necessarily be based on an adaptation to the particular requirements of their own peculiar medium of expression.

Applying this principle to theatre and cinema, we will recognise that whereas there is a strong sense of reality in audience reactions to the film, yet always there is the fact that the pictures on the screen are two-dimensional images and hence removed a stage from actual contact with the spectators. What may happen if successful three-dimensional projection is introduced we cannot tell; at present we are concerned with a flat screen picture. This gulf between the audience and the events presented to them will permit a much greater use of realism than the stage may legitimately employ. The presence of flesh-and-blood actors in the theatre means that it is comparatively easy to break the illusion proper to the theatre and in doing so to shatter the mood at which any performance ought to aim. This statement may appear to run counter to others made above, but there is no essential contradiction involved. The fact remains that, when living person is set before living person—actor before spectator—a certain deliberate conventionalising is demanded of the former if the aesthetic impression is not to be lost, whereas in the film, in which immediately a measure of distance is imposed between image and spectator, greater approaches to real forms may be permitted, even although these have to exist alongside impossibilities and fantastic symbols far removed from the world around us. This is the paradox of cinematic art.

Herein lies the true filmic realm and to these things the cinema, if it also is to be true to itself, must tend, just as towards the universalising and towards conventionalism must tend the theatre if it is to find a secure place among us. Fortunately the signs of the age are propitious; experiments in poetic drama and production of films utilising at least a few of the significant methods basically associated with cinematic art give us authority for believing that within the next decade each will discover firmer and surer foothold and therefore more arresting control over their material. Both stage and cinema have their particular and peculiar functions; their houses may stand side by side, not in rivalling enmity, but in that friendly rivalry which is one of the compelling forces in the wider realm of artistic achievement.

BIBLIOGRAPHY

BIBLIOGRAPHY

While the following list of books does not profess to be exhaustive, an effort has been made to present a fairly comprehensive survey of writings on the subject of the film. Purely technical and scientific aspects have, of course, been largely neglected and only such articles as seemed to have a bearing on aesthetic problems have been deliberately admitted; even so, articles of this kind appearing in cinematic periodicals listed in the second portion of the present bibliography have not been included. The whole field of amateur cinematography finds no place here and but few references have been given to material on film actors, minor social problems, the legal status of the cinema and the like. It should be noted also that, with several exceptions, pamphlets and reports by various cultural and official organisations have not been separately indexed; among the most important of such organisations are *The International Institute of Educational Cinematography* (League of Nations, publications in London and Rome), *The Bureau of Commercial Economics, Department of Public Instruction* (Washington), *The National Board of Censorship of Motion Pictures* (New York), *The National Congress of Parents and Teachers: Committee on Motion Pictures* (Washington) and *The Commission on Educational and Cultural Films* (London). The *Library of Congress,* Washington, has since 1912 periodically issued mimeographed *Lists of Recent References on the Moving Picture Industry.* Many cities in England and America have appointed committees concerned with the films in their immediate neighborhood, and some of these have issued pamphlet reports.

Abbott, M. A.: Motion Picture Preferences of Adults and Children (*School Review,* xli, 1933, 278-83)

Abel, Paul: *Kinematographie und Urheberrecht* (Vienna, 1914)

Ackerknecht, Erwin: Verzeichnis deutscher Fachschriften über Lichtspielwesen (*Bildwart-Flugschriften,* ii, 1914, 1-54)

———: *Das Lichtspiel im Dienste der Bildungspflege* (Berlin, 1918).

———: *Lichtspielfragen* (Berlin, 1928)

Agnew, Frances: *Motion Picture Acting* (N. Y., 1913)

Ahern, M. L.: The World gets an Earful (*Commonweal,* xi, 1930, 333-35)

———: Hollywood Horizons (*Commonweal,* xii, 1930, 71-73)

Albán, Eugen: *Charlie Chaplin, film konstens mästare* (Stockholm, 1928)

Alexander, Hans: *Das Film- und Kinobuch* (Leipzig, 1920)

Allendy, A.: *La valeur psychologique de l'image* (in *L'art cinématographique,* I, Paris)

Allighan, Garry: *The Romance of the Talkies* (London, 1929)

Altenloh, Emilie: Zur Soziologie des Kino (*Schriften zur Soziologie der Kultur,* Jena, iii, 1913)

Altman, Georg: *Ça, c'est du cinéma* (Paris, 1931)

———: *Le cinéma russe* (in *L'art cinématographique,* viii, Paris, 1931)

Alvaro, C.: I quarant' anni del cinema (*Nuova Antologia,* ccclxxviii, 1935, 601-04)

Ames, V. M.: *Introduction to Beauty* (N. Y., 1931)

Amiguet, M. F. P.: Remarks on the Cinema" (*Review of Reviews,* lxvii, 1923, 435-36)

Amiguet, P. H.: *Cinéma! Cinéma!* (Lausanne, 1923)

Andersen, C.: *Die deutsche Filmindustrie* (Munich, 1930)

Anderson, A.: Cinema and its Detractors (*English Review,* xxxviii, 1924, 593-98)

Anderson, Milton: *The Modern Goliath: A Study of Talking Pictures* (Los Angeles, 1935)

Anderson, R.: What is to become of the Theater? (*Illustrated World,* xxiv, 1916, 660-65)

Angel, Ernst: *Das Drehbuch* (Potsdam, 1922)

Anoshchenko, Nikolai D.: Кино в Германии (Moscow, 1927)

——: Кино (Moscow, 1929)

——: Рождение кино-фильмы. Экскурсия на кино-фабрику (Moscow, 1930)

——: Звучащая фильма в СССР и за границей (Moscow, 1930)

Ardov. Victor E.: Население кино-республики. Кино-рассказы (Moscow, 1929)

Arnau, F., ed.: *Universal-Filmlexikon* (Berlin, 1933, 2nd edn.)

Arnaud and Boisyvon: *Le cinéma pour tous* (Paris, 1922)

Arnheim, Rudolf: *Film als Kunst* (Berlin, 1932; trs. as *Film,* by L. M. Sieveking and Ian F. D. Morrow, London, 1933)

Arnoldi, E.: Авантюрный жанр и кино (Moscow, 1929)

Arnspiger, Varney C.: *Measuring the Effectiveness of Sound Pictures as Teaching Aids* (N. Y., 1933)

Aronson, J.: The Film and Visual Education (*School and Society,* xxxviii, 1933, 53-55)

Arroy, Jean and Reynaud, J. C.: *Attention! On tourne!* (Paris, 1929)

Ashley, Walter: *The Cinema and the Public* (London, 1934)

Atkinson, E. J. R.: *Key to the Adaptation of the Best of Shakespeare's Plays to the Stage-Cinema Interaction Process for the Production of Drama* (London, 1920)

Bagier, Guido: *Der kommende Film, eine Abrechnung und eine Hoffnung* (Stuttgart, 1928)

Bakshy, Alexander: Cinematograph as Art (*Drama,* No. 22, 1916, 267-84)

——: *The Path of the Modern Russian Stage* (London, 1917)

Bakshy, Alexander: *The Theatre Unbound* (London, 1923)
——: The New Art of the Moving Picture (*Theatre Arts Monthly*, xi, 1927, 277-82)
——:The Road to Art in the Motion Picture (*Theatre Arts Monthly*, xi, 1927, 455-62)
——: The Future of the Movies (*Nation*, cxxvii, 1928, 360-64)
——: The Language of Images (*Nation*, cxxviii, 1928, 720-21)
——: Character and Drama (*Nation*, cxxvi, 1928, 463-64)
——: Freelances; Little Cinema Houses (*Nation*, cxxviii, 1929, 324-26)
——: The Talkies (*Nation*, cxxviii, 1929, 236-38)
——: There are Silent Pictures (*Nation*, cxxix, 1929, 203-04)
——: The Movie Scene; Notes on Sound and Silence (*Theatre Arts Monthly*, xiii, 1929, 97-107)
——: Screen Musical Comedy (*Nation*, cxxx, 1930, 158)
——: As You Were (*Nation*, cxxx, 1930, 106)
——: Enter Japan (*Nation*, cxxxi, 1930, 104)
——: The Shrinking of Personality (*Nation*, cxxxii, 1931, 590)
——: The German Invasion (*Nation*, cxxxii, 1931, 538)
——: Concerning Dialogue (*Nation*, cxxxv, 1932, 151-52)
——: With Benefit of Music (*Nation*, cxxxii, 1931, 359-60)
——: S O S (*Nation*, cxxxiii, 1931, 142)
Balázs, Béla: *Der sichtbare Mensch; oder, Die Kultur des Films* (Vienna, 1924; 2nd edn. 1931)
——: *Der Geist des Films* (Halle, 1930)
——: Movies for the Middle Class (*Living Age*, cccxxxix, 1930, 294-97)
——: The Future of the Films (*Living Age*, cccxxxix, 1930, 294-300)
Balbi, C. M. R.: *Talking Pictures and Acoustics* (London, 1932)

Balcerzak, Wladyslaw: (Przemyst filmowy w Polsce (*Wyzsza szkola handlowa*, Warsaw, v, 1928, 1-56)

Baldwin, O.: The Fatuity of British Films (*Bookman*, London, lxxxiv, 1933, 192)

Balfour, B.: The Art of the Cinema (*English Review*, xxxviii, 1923, 388-91)

Ball, Eustace H.: *The Art of the Photoplay* (N. Y., 1913)

———: *Photoplay Scenarios, How to write and sell them* (N. Y., 1915)

Bamberger, Theron: Will the Films buy it? (*N. Y. Times*, March 3, 1932)

Bamburg, Lilian: *Film Acting as a Career* (London, 1929)

Barker, Ellen F.: *Successful Photoplay Writing* (N. Y., 1914)

———: *The Art of Photoplay Writing* (St. Louis, 1917)

Barlow, S. L. M.: The Movies: an Arraignment (*Forum*, lxvii, 1922, 37-41; reply by M. MacAlarney, *The Movies: in their Defense*, ib. 42-45)

Barron, Samuel: The Dying Theater (*Harper's Magazine*, clxxii, 1935, 108-17)

Barry, Iris: *Let's go to the Pictures* (London, 1926)

Barshak, O.: Кино в деревне (Moscow, 1929)

Batenburg, A. van: *De revolutiefilm* (Rotterdam, 1929)

Bauer, L. V.: The Movies tackle Literature (*American Mercury*, xiv, 1928, 288-94)

Baughan, E. A.: The Art of Moving Pictures (*Fortnightly Review*, cxii, 1919, 448-56)

Bayes, W.: In Defence of the Kinema (*Saturday Review*, cxlv, 1928, 428-29)

Beach, R.: The Author and the Film (*Mentor*, ix, 1921, 31)

Beaton, Welford: In Darkest Hollywood (*New Republic*, lxiii, 1930, 287-89)

———: *Know your Movies* (Hollywood, 1932)

Bell, M.: The Director, his Problems and Qualifications (*Theatre Arts Monthly*, xiii, 1929, 645-49)

Beman, Lamar T.: *Selected Articles on Censorship of the Theatre and Moving Pictures* (N. Y., 1931)

Bennett, Colin N.: *The Guide to Kinematography* (London, 1917)

Berchtold, W. E.: Grand Opera goes to Hollywood (*North American Review,* ccxxxix, 1935, 138-46)

Berg, Gustaf: *Filmen i kulturens tyänst* (Stockholm, 1926)

———: *Två gånger två är fyra* (Stockholm, 1927)

———: *Filmen och statsmakterna* (Stockholm, 1929)

Berge, André: *Cinéma et littérature* (in *L'art cinématographique,* III, Paris)

Berglund, A.: *Hur man blir filmstjärna* (Söderköping, 1930)

Bernard, R.: Le cinéma (*Annales politiques et littéraires,* xciii, 1929, 455-56)

Bernhardt, Felix K.: *Wie schriebt und verwertet man ein Film?* (Berlin, 1926)

Bertram, Alfred: *Der Kinematograph in seinen Beziehungen zum Urheberrecht* (Munich, 1914)

Bertsch, Marguerite: *How to write for the Moving Pictures* (N. Y., 1917)

Betts, Ernest: *Heraclitus, or, The Future of the Films* (London, 1928)

———: Ordeal by Talkie (*Saturday Review,* cxlviii, 1929, 7-8)

———: The Film as Literature (*Saturday Review,* cxliv, 1927, 905-06)

Beucler, A.: *Le comique et l'humour* (in *L'art cinématographique,* I, Paris)

Beuss, W. and Wollenberg, H.: *Der Film im öffentlichen Recht* (Berlin, 1932)

Beyfuss, E. C. A. and Kossowsky, A.: *Das Kulturfilmbuch* (Berlin, 1924)

Bilinsky, B.: *Le costume* (in *L'art cinématographique,* VI, Paris)

Binder, F. A.: *Unsere Filmsterne* (Berlin, 1921)

Blakeston, Oswell: *Through a Yellow Glass* (London, 1928)

Blanchard, Phyllis: The Motion Picture as an Educational Asset (*Pedagogical Seminary,* xxvi, 1919, 284-87)

Blasetti, Alessandro: *Come nasce un film* (Rome, 1932)

Blitz, A.: *Los cien artistas más populares de la cinematografía mundial* (Barcelona, 1919)

Block, R.: Literature of the Screen? (*Bookman*, N. Y., lx, 1924, 472-73)

———: The Ghost of Art in the Movies (*New Republic*, xxxviii, 1924, 310-12)

———: Not Theatre, not Literature, not Painting (*Dial*, lxxxii, 1927, 20-24)

Bloem, W. S.: *Seele des Lichtspiels* (Leipzig, 1922; trs. as *The Soul of the Moving Picture*, N. Y., 1924)

Blumer, Herbert: *Movies and Conduct* (N. Y., 1933)

———: *Movies, Delinquency and Crime* (N. Y., 1933)

Boehmer, Henning von and Reitz, Helm: *Der Film in Wirtschaft und Recht* (Berlin, 1933)

Bogan, L.: True to the Medium (*New Republic*, lii, 1927, 263-64)

Boisyvon: *Le cinéma français* (in *L'art cinematographique*, VII, Paris)

Boitler, Michael S.: Культурный кино-театр (Moscow, 1930)

Bollman, Gladys: *Motion Pictures for Community Needs* (N. Y., 1922)

Boltianskii, Grigorii: Кино-справочник (Moscow, 1929)

Bond, Kirk: Film as Literature (*Bookman*, London, lxxxiv, 1933, 188-89)

Bontempelli, M.: Cinematografo (*Nuova Antologia*, ccclv, 1931, 403-07)

Boone, A. R.: Talkie Troubles (*Scientific American*, cxlvii, 1932, 326-29)

———: History in the Talkies (*Scientific American*, cxlviii, 1933, 70-74)

Borchardt, M.: *Kinofilm-Aufnahmeapparat* (Berlin, 1933)

Boughey, Davidson: *The Film Industry* (London, 1921)

Braak, Menno ter: *Cinema militans* (Utrecht, 1928)

———: *De absolute film* (Rotterdam, 1931)

Bradley, Willard K.: *Inside Secrets of Photoplay Writing* (N. Y., 1926)

Bragaglia, A. G.: *Il film sonoro; nuovi orizzonti della cinematografia* (Milan, 1929)

Bragdon, C.: Mickey Mouse and What He Means (*Scribner's Magazine*, xcvi, 1934, 40-43)

Brande, D.: A Letter on the Movies (*American Review*, iii, 1934, 148-60)

Brandenburg, H.: Was ist eigentlich das Kino? (*Deutsche Rundschau*, ccviii, 1926, 54-57)

Brewster, Eugene V.: *The Ten Essentials for Successful Pictures* (Los Angeles, 1933)

Brie, A.: *Filmzauber* (Berlin, 1919)

Britton, L.: Kino-eye. Vertoff and the Newest Film Spirit of Russia (*Realist*, ii, 1929, 126-38)

Bronnikov, M.: Этюды о творчестве Мари Пикфорд (Leningrad, 1927)

Brown, Bernard: *Talking Pictures* (London, 1931; 2nd edn., 1932)

Brown, Ivor: Art in Search of its Youth (*Saturday Review*, cxxxvii, 1924, 56-57)

Brunel, Adrian: *Filmcraft* (London, 1933)

Brunner, Karl: *Der Kinematograph von heute eine Volksgefahr* (Berlin, 1913?)

——: *Das neue Lichtspielgesetz im Dienste der Volks- und Jugendwohlfahrt* (Berlin, 1920)

Bryher: *Film Problems of Soviet Russia* (Territet, Switzerland, 1929)

Buchanan, Andrew: *Films: The Way of the Cinema* (London, 1932)

Buchanan, D. W.: The Art of the European Film (*Queen's Quarterly*, xl, 1933, 568-76)

Buchner, Hans: *Im Banne des Films* (Munich, 1927)

Buckle, Gerard F.: *The Mind and the Film* (London, 1926)

Bugaiev, B. N.: На переводѣ. Синематографъ (in Вѣсы., No. 7, Moscow, 1907)

Bull, Lucien: *La cinématographie* (Paris, 1928)

Buñuel, Luis and Dali, Salvador: An Andalusian Dog (*This Quarter*, v, 1932, 149-57)

Burg, O.: *Manuskripte für Film und Bühne* (Vienna, 1929)

Burnett, R. G. and Martell, E. D.: *The Devil's Camera: Menace of a Film-ridden World* (London, 1932)

Busse, K.: Film als Kunst? (*Preussische Jahrbücher,* ccxxviii, 1932, 138-43)

Calzini, R.: Sequenze e dissolvenze del festival cinematografico veneziano (*Nuova Antologia,* ccclxxxi, 1935, 282-93)

Cameron, J. R.: *Talking Movies* (N. Y., 1927)

———: *Motion Pictures with Sound* (N. Y., 1929)

———: *Motion Picture Projection and Sound Pictures* (Woodmont, Conn. 5th edn., 1933)

Cameron, J. R. and Dubray, J. A.: *Cinematography and Talkies* (N. Y., 1932)

Canuda: *L'usine aux images* (Paris, 1927)

Carlston, Wallace A.: The Animated Cartoon (*Movie Pictorial,* ii, 1915, 625-27)

Carman, M. E.: Ricochets and Retrospects (*Canadian Forum,* xii, 1932, 476-77)

———: Attractions and Detractions (*Canadian Forum,* xii, 1932, 438-39)

Carr, Catherine and others: *The Art of Photoplay Writing* (N. Y., 1914)

Carter, Huntly: *The New Theatre and Cinema of Soviet Russia* (N. Y., 1925)

———: *The New Spirit in the Russian Theatre* (N. Y., 1929)

———: Cinema and Theatre: the Diabolical Difference (*English Review,* lv, 1932, 313-20)

———: *The New Spirit in the Cinema* (London and N. Y., 1930)

Cauda, Ernesto: *Cinematografia sonora* (Milan, 1930)

Charensol, George: *Panorama du cinéma* (Paris, 1930)

———: *40 ans de cinéma* (Paris, 1935)

Charques, R. D.: The Technique of the Films (*Fortnightly Review,* cxxx, 1928, 504-11)

Charques, R. D.: The Future of Talking Films (*Fortnightly Review*, cxxxii, 1929, 88-98)

———: The Essentials of a Film (*English Review*, xlviii, 1929, 91-95)

Charters, W. W.: Developing the Attitudes of Children (*Education*, liii, 1933, 353-57)

———: Motion Pictures and Youth (N. Y., 1933)

Chéronnet, L.: The German Cinema (*Living Age*, cccxliii, 1933, 441-44)

Chesmore, Stuart: Behind the Cinema Screen (London, 1934)

Chesterton, G. K.: Generally Speaking (London, 1928)

Churchill, W.: Everybody's Language; Can Silent Movies come back? (*Collier's*, xcvi, 1935, 24)

Clairmont, Leonard: Konsten att filma (Stockholm, 1930)

Clayton, B.: The Cinema (*Quarterly Review*, ccxxxiv, 1920, 177-89)

———: The Cinema and its Censor (*Fortnightly Review*, cxv, 1921, 222-28)

———: The Talking Pictures (*Nineteenth Century*, cv, 1929, 820-27)

———: Shakespeare and the Talkies (*English Review*, xlix, 1929, 739-52)

Clement, Ina: Teaching Citizenship via the Movies (N. Y., 1918)

———: Visualizing Citizenship (N. Y., 1920)

Clements, T.: Censoring the Talkies (*New Republic*, lix, 1929, 64-66)

Cohen, J. S.: This Year of Sound (*Theatre Arts Monthly*, xiii, 1929, 650-55)

Coissac, G. M.: Les ombres chinoises et les projections (Paris, 1911)

———: Histoire du cinématographe de ses origines à nos jours (Paris, 1925)

———: Les coulisses du cinéma (Paris, 1929)

Colby, E.: Literature and the Movies (*American Review*, ii, 1924, 368-71)

Collard, Charles: *Le cinématographe et la criminalité infantile* (Brussels, 1919)

Collins, F. L.: The Talk of the Town (*Delineator*, civ, 1929, 13)

Colombini, Umberto: *Hollywood, visione che incanta* (Turin, 1929)

Condon, F.: Before Sound (*Saturday Evening Post*, ccvi, 1934, 34)

———: All because of the Sunshine (*Saturday Evening Post*, ccvii, 1934, 30)

Conradt, Walther: *Kirche und Kinematograph* (Berlin, 1910)

Consiglio, Alberto: *Introduzione a un' estetica del cinema e altri scritti* (Naples, 1932)

Consitt, Frances: *The Value of Films in History Teaching* (London, 1931)

Coonleigh, J. C.: Succeeding with Scenarios (*Drama*, xiii, 1923, 362; xiv, 30)

Corrigan, B.: Harlequin in America (*Canadian Forum*, xiv, 1933, 62-65)

Costa, Enrico: *Il proiezionista di film sonori* (Milan, 1933)

Cotta, Johannes: *Der Kientopp* (Dresden, 1918)

Cousins, E. G.: *Filmland in Ferment* (London, 1932)

Coustet, Ernest: *Le cinéma* (Paris, 1921)

———: *Traité pratique de cinématographie* (Paris, n. d.)

Cowan, Lester: *Recording Sound for Motion Pictures* (London, 1931)

Craig, Gordon: Cinema and its Drama (*English Review*, xxxiv, 1922, 119-22)

Crandall, Ernest L.: Possibilities of the Cinema in Education (*Annals of the American Academy of Political and Social Science*, cxxviii, 1926, 109-15)

Craven, T.: The Great American Art (*Dial*, lxxxi, 1926, 483-92)

Croy, Homer: The Infant Prodigy of our Industries (*Harper's Magazine*, cxxxv, 1917, 349-58)

———: *How Motion Pictures are made* (N. Y., 1918)

Croy, Homer: The Future of the Educational Film (*Educational Film Magazine*, 1919, 6-7)

Czapek: *Die Kinematographie* (Dresden, 1908)

Dahlgreen, Reinhold: *Tonfilmwidergabe* (Stuttgart, 1932)

————: *Handbuch für Lichtspielvorführer* (Berlin, 1928)

Dale, Edgar: Helping Youth to Choose Better Movies *Parents' Magazine*, ix, 1934, 26)

————: *How to Appreciate Motion Pictures* (N. Y., 1934)

————: *The Content of Motion Pictures* (N. Y., 1935)

Dali, Salvador: *Babaouo, scénario inédit, précédé d'un abrégé d'une histoire critique du cinéma* (Paris, 1932)

Dalrymple, I.: Film Censorship (*Spectator*, clv, 1935, 895-96)

Danton, F. M.: *Per diventare artisti cinematografici* (Messina, 1932)

Dark, Sidney: The Art of the Film (*Saturday Review*, cliv, 1932, 640)

Davy, C.: Is there a Future for Talkies? (*Bookman*, London, lxxxvi, 1934, 248)

Dean, Basil: The Talking Pictures (*Nineteenth Century*, cvi, 1929, 823-27)

Dearborn, G. V.: Children at the Movies (*School and Society*, xl, 1934, 127-28)

Debries, Erwin: *Hollywood wie es wirklich ist* (Zurich, 1930)

Delluc, Louis: *Cinéma et Cie* (Paris, 1919)

————: *Charlot* (Paris, 1920)

————: *Drames de cinéma* (Paris, 1923)

Delmont, Joseph: *Wilde Tiere im Film* (Stuttgart, 1925)

Delpeuch, André: *Le cinéma* (Paris, 1927)

Demeter, K.: Die soziologischen Grundlagen des Kinowesens (*Deutsche Rundschau*, ccviii, 1926, 57-62)

Dench, Ernest A.: *Motion Picture Education* (Cincinnati, 1917)

————: *Playwriting for the Cinema* (London, 1914)

————: *Making the Movies* (N. Y., 1915)

Deval, J.: Le film parlant? (*Annales politiques et littéraires,* xciii, 1929, 51-52)

Devereux, Frederick L.: *The Educational Talking Picture* (Chicago, 1933)

Diamant-Berger, H.: *Le cinéma* (Paris, 1920)

Dickinson, T. H.: The Theory and Practice of the Censorship (*Drama,* No. 18, 1915, 248-61)

Diebold, B.: Film und Drama (*Neue Rundschau,* xliii, 1932, 402-10)

Dieckmann, Friederike: *Das Kino, sein Wesen und die Möglichkeiten seiner Gestaltung* (Wolfenbüttel, 1921)

Diehl, Oskar: *Mimik im Film* (Munich, 1922)

Diele, H.: *Kino und Jugend* (Warendorf, 1913)

Dienstag, P.: *Der Arbeitsvertrag des Filmschauspielers und Filmregisseurs* (Berlin, 1929)

Dimick, Howard T.: *Photoplay Making* (Ridgewood, N. J., 1915)

Disher, M. W.: Classics into Films (*Fortnightly Review,* cxxx, 1928, 784-92)

Donnelly, F. P.: The Craft of the Screen (*Commonweal,* ix, 1929, 369-71)

Dost, W.: *Geschichte des Films* (Halle, 1925)

Drinkwater, John: *The Life and Adventures of Carl Laemmle* (N. Y., 1931)

Dubray, J. A. and Cameron, J. R.: *Cinematography and Talkies* (N. Y., 1932)

Ducom, J.: *Le cinématographe scientifique et industriel* (Paris, 1911; 2nd edn., 1931)

Duhamel, G.: Misère et grandeur du cinéma (*Annales politiques et littéraires,* xcix, 1932, 449-52)

Dukes, Ashley: English Scene: chiefly about Screenwriting (*Theatre Arts Monthly,* xviii, 1934, 822-29)

Dulac, G.: *Les esthétiques, les entraves, la cinégrafie intégral* (in *L'art cinématographique,* II, Paris)

Dullin, C.: *L'émotion humaine* (in *L'art cinématographique,* I, Paris)

Dupernex, E.: *The Soul in Screenland* (London, 1927)

Dupont, A. and Podehl, F.: Wie ein Film geschrieben wird und wie man ihn verwertet (Berlin, 1926)

Dusmesnil, R.: Musique et cinéma (*Mercure de France*, ccxlvii, 1933, 454-58)

Duyn, G. van: *Psychologische beschouwingen over film en bioskoopbezoeker* (Baarn, 1926)

Dysinger, Wendell S. and Rucknick, Christian A.: *The Emotional Responses of Children to the Motion Picture Situation* (N. Y., 1933)

Eastman, F.: What's wrong with the Movies? (*Homiletic Review*, cvi, 1933, 175-79)

Eaton, Walter P.: Class-consciousness and the "Movies" (*Atlantic Monthly*, cxv, 1915, 48-56)

Ecclestone, J.: The Cinema (*Nineteenth Century*, xciv, 1923, 634-39)

Eckstein, Ernst: *Deutsches Film- und Kinorecht* (Mannheim, 1924)

Eddy, R.: The Movies as a Factor in Public Education (*Education*, liv, 1934, 306-07)

Edelson, Z. A. and Filippov, B. M., ed: Профсоюзы и искусство (Leningrad, 1927)

Eger, Lydia: *Kinoreform und Gemeinden* (Dresden, 1920)

———: *Der Kampf um das neue Kino* (Munich, 1922)

Elliott, Eric: *The Anatomy of Motion Picture Art* (Territet, Switzerland, 1928)

Ellis, Carlyle: Art and the Motion Picture (*Annals of the American Academy of Political and Social Science*, cxxviii, 1926, 54-57)

Ellis, Don Carlos: *Motion Pictures in Education* (N. Y., 1923)

Elston, L.: What is new in Movieland (*Canadian Magazine*, lxxvii, 1932, 19)

———: The What and the Why of Movie Censorship (*Canadian Magazine*, lxxix, 1933, 6)

Emerson, John: *Breaking into the Movies* (N. Y., 1921)

Engelbrecht, K.: *Kinokultur. Kritische Gänge durch die Gegenwart* (Leipzig, 1923)

Engl, J.: *Der tönende Film* (Brunswick, 1927)

Epstein, Jean: *Cinéma* (Paris, 1921)
————: *La poésie d'aujourd'hui* (Paris, 1921)
Erenburg, Ilja: *Die Traumfabrik* (Berlin, 1931)
Ernst, Morris L. and Lorentz, Pierre: *Censored; the Private Life of the Movie* (N. Y., 1930)
Ervine, St. John: Talkie-talkies (*Spectator,* cxlii, 1928, 681-82)
————: The Cinema and the Child (*Fortnightly Review,* cxxxvii, 1932, 426-43)
Esenwein, Joseph B. and Leeds, A.: *Writing the Photoplay* (Springfield, Mass., 1913)
Eulderink, Fr.: *Wij filmen* (Bloemendaal, 1932)
Evans, M.: The Movies and the Highbrows (*Bookman,* N. Y., lxvii, 1928, 533-37)
Fain, Gaël: *Une industrie-clé intellectuelle* (Paris, 1928)
Farquharson, J.: *Picture Plays and how to Write them* (London, 1916)
Faure, Élie: *The Art of Cineplastics* (trs. by W. Pach: Boston, 1923)
Faure, J.: Du film muet au film parlant (*L'Illustration,* clxxiv, 1929, 447-48)
Fawcett, L'Estrange: *Films; Facts and Forecasts* (London, 1927)
————: *Writing for the Films* (London, 1932)
————: Problems of the Film Story (*Saturday Review,* clv, 1933, 480-81)
Feo, Luciano de: *L'activité de l'Institut international du cinématographe éducatif en 1930* (Rome, 1930)
Ferdinand, F. and Ferdinand-Bielietz, E.: *Wie werde ich Kino-Darsteller?* (Vienna, 1916)
Ferguson, O.: Artists among the Flickers (*New Republic,* lxxxi, 1934, 103-04)
Fernández Cuenca, Carlos: *Fotogenia y arte* (Madrid, 1927)
————: *Historia anecdótica del cinema* (Madrid, 1930)
Fescourt, Henri: *Le cinéma, des origines à nos jours* (Paris, 1932)
Filippov, Boris: Кино в рабочем клубе (Moscow, 1926)

Finger, Willy: *Deutschkunde und Kinodrama* (Berlin, 1921)

Fischer, Walther: *Das belebte Bild* (Vienna, 1931)

Flaherty, M. R.: Sentimentality and the Screen (*Commonweal*, xx, 1934, 522-23)

Fletcher, John G.: *The Crisis of the Film* (Seattle, 1929)

Floherty, John J.: *Moviemakers* (N. Y., 1935)

Florey, Robert: *Filmland* (Paris, 1923)

————: *Deux ans dans les studios américains* (Paris, 1925)

Flügge, Karl A.: *Entartungserscheinungen im Kino* (Kassel, 1924)

Fonss, Olaf: *Films-Erindringer gennem 20 Aar* (Copenhagen, 1930)

Forch, Carl: *Der Kinematograph und das sich bewegende Bild* (Vienna, 1913)

Forman, Henry J.: *Our Movie Made Children* (N. Y., 1933)

Foster, W. T.: *Vaudeville and Motion Picture Shows, a Study of Theaters in Portland, Oregon* (Portland, Ore., 1914)

Foulon, O.: *Die Kunst des Lichtspiels* (Aachen, 1924)

Fox, Charles D.: *Mirrors of Hollywood* (N. Y., 1925)

Fraccaroli, A.: *Hollywood, paese d'avventura* (Milan, 1929)

Frank, Leonhard: *Die Entgleisten* (Berlin, 1929)

Franken, M. T. H. and Ivens, Joris: *De techniek van de kunstfilm* (Rotterdam, 1932)

Franklin, Harold B.: *Sound Motion Pictures, from the Laboratory to their Presentation* (N. Y., 1929)

Freeburg, Victor O.: *The Art of Photoplay Making* (N. Y., 1918)

————: *Pictorial Beauty on the Screen* (N. Y., 1923)

Freeman, Frank N. ed: *Visual Education* (Chicago, 1924)

Freeman, J.: *Voices of October* (N. Y., 1929)

Friedland, Nadejda: Сегодняшний быт германского кино (Moscow, 1930)

Fuchsig, Heinrich: *Rund um den Film* (Vienna, 1929)

Fülop-Miller, René: *Die Phantasiemaschine* (Berlin, 1931)

Funk, Alois: *Film und Jugend* (Munich, 1934)

Furduev, Vadim V.: Кино завтра (Moscow, 1929)

Furnas, J. C.: Moral War in Hollywood (*Fortnightly Review*, cxliii, 1935, 73-84)

Gad, U.: *Der Film. Seine Mittel, seine Ziele* (Berlin, 1920)

Gance, Abel: *La beauté à travers le cinéma* (Paris, 1926)

———: *Le temps de l'image est venu* (in *L'art cinématographique*, II, Paris)

Gance, Abel, Epstein, Jean and Clair, René: *Cinéma; scénario, études et chroniques* (Paris, 1928)

Garbo, Greta: What the Public wants (*Saturday Review*, clvi, 1931, 857)

Gaupp, R. and Lange, Konrad: *Die Kinematographie als Volksunterhaltungsmittel* (Munich, 1913; 2nd. edn., 1922)

Gavriushin, Constantin L.: Советские киношколы (Moscow, 1929)

Gemmert, F. J.: *Kinematograph* (Berlin, 1920, 3rd. edn.)

George, W. H.: *The Cinema in School* (London, 1935)

Gerould, Katharine F.: The Movies (*Atlantic Monthly*, cxxviii, 1921, 22-30)

———: The Nemesis of the Screen (*Saturday Evening Post*, cxciv, 1922, 12)

———: The Lost Art of Motion Pictures (*Century Magazine*, cxviii, 1929, 496-506)

Gershanek, Sinai: *A Motion Picture Bibliography* (Chicago, 1916)

Gerstein, E.: Four Films of New Types (*Theatre Arts Monthly*, xi, 1927, 295-98)

Ghione, E.: *Le cinéma italien* (in *L'art cinématographique*, VII, Paris)

Giese, Eberhard: *Der Kinoschund und die Jugend* (Bielefeld, 1919)

Gillette, D. C.: The Amusement Octopus (*American Mercury*, xi, 1927, 91-99)

Gilman, C. C.: Better Movies, but how? (*Woman's Journal*, xv, 1930, 7-9)

Giovanetti, E.: *Il cinema e le arti meccaniche* (Palermo, 1930)

Giovanetti, E.: Il crodo di Hollywood (*Nuova Antologia,* ccclxvi, 1932, 126-33)

Giusti, Arnaldo: *Lezioni di cinematica* (Turin, 1933)

Godwin, M.: Sociology, Fate, Form and Films (*New Republic,* lxvii, 1931, 72-73)

Goldobin, A.: Кино на территории СССР по материалам провинциональной прессы (Moscow, 1924)

Goldovskii, E. M.: Освещение кино-ателье (Moscow, 1927)

Goldwyn, Samuel: *Behind the Screen* (London, 1924)

Golias, Eduard, ed.: *Film and Schute. Beiträge zur Frage der pädagogisch-didaktischen Verwertbarkeit des Films* (Vienna, 1925)

Goll, I.: *Die Chapliniade. Eine Kinodichtung* (Dresden, 1920)

González Alonso, Luis: *Manual de cinematografía* (Madrid, 1929)

Gordon, Jan and Cora: *Star-dust in Hollywood* (London, 1931)

Gordon, William L.: *How to Write Moving Picture Plays* (Cincinnati, 1913; 2nd edn., 1915)

Görres, K.: *Das Lichtspielgesetz im Lichte des Verwaltungsrechts* (Baden, 1921)

Gotwalt, V.: Кинематографъ (Moscow, 1909)

Graadt van Roggen, C. J.: *Het linnen venster* (Rotterdam, 1931)

Grafly, D.: America's Youngest Art (*American Magazine of Art,* xxvi, 1933, 336-42)

Grau, Hermann: *Technik und Film* (Berlin, 1932)

Grau, R.: *The Theatre of Science* (N. Y., 1914)

Green, Fitzhugh: *The Screen finds its Tongue* (N. Y., 1930)

Gregor, Joseph: *Der Zeitalter des Films* (Vienna, 1932)

Gregor, Joseph and Fülop-Miller, René: *Das amerikanische Theater und Kino* (Vienna, 1931)

Gregory, C. L.: *Motion Picture Photography* (N. Y., 1927)

Grière, J. C.: L'avenir du cinéma (*Mercure de France,* cclxiii, 1935, 501-04)

Grierson, J.: The Future of British Films (*Spectator,* cxlviii, 1932, 691-92)

Griffith, D. W.: The Motion Pictures (*Mentor,* ix, 1921, 2-12)

——: Are Motion Pictures Destructive of Good Taste? (*Arts and Decoration,* xix, 1923, 12-13)

——: The Movies 100 Years from now (*Collier's,* lxxiii, 1924, 7)

Griffith, Mrs. D. W.: *When the Movies were Young* (N. Y., 1925)

Griffith, H.: The Films and the British Public (*Nineteenth Century,* cxii, 1932, 190-200)

Groth, F. von: *Der Filmschriftsteller* (Vienna, 1919)

Grundy, C. R.: Cinema and Culture (*Connoisseur,* lxxxvi, 1930, 277-78)

Guilmardet, J.: Le septième art et la parole (*Mercure de France,* ccxxxiii, 1932, 85-101)

Gurlitt, L.: Кинематографъ, какъ популизаторъ искусства въ жизни и въ школѣ (St. Petersburg, 1914)

Gürster, E.: Film und Theater (*Deutsche Rundschau,* ccxvii, 1928, 91-94)

Guttmann, R.: *Die Kinomenscheit* (Vienna, 1916)

Gvialev, Evgenii D.: Советские фильмы за границей (Moscow, 1929)

Haas, Arthur: *Physik des Tonfilms* (Berlin, 1934)

Hacker, Leonard: *Cinematic Design* (Boston, 1931)

Häfker, H.: *Die Aufgaben der Kinematographie in diesem Kriege* (Munich, 1915)

——: *Der Kino und die Gebildeten* (Munich, 1915)

Halter, Hermann: *Die Kino-Frage* (Meiringen, 1921)

Hamilton, C.: The Art of the Moving-Picture Play (*Bookman,* N. Y., xxxii, 1911, 512-16)

——: The Esperanto of the Eye (*Literary Review,* iii, 1923, 889-90)

Hampton, Benjamin B.: *A History of the Movies* (N. Y., 1931)

Hannon, William M.: *The Photodrama; its Place among the Fine Arts* (New Orleans, 1915)

214 FILM AND THEATRE

Hapgood, N.: Will Hays and what the Pictures do to us (*Atlantic Monthly*, cli, 1933, 75-84)

Harms, R.: *Philosophie des Films* (Leipzig, 1926)

——: *Kulturbedeutung und Kulturgefahren des Films* (Karlsruhe, 1927)

Harrison, L. R.: *Screencraft* (N. Y., 1916)

Hatschek, Paul: *Wass muss jeder vom Film und Tonfilm wissen?* (Berlin, 1933)

Hays, Will H.: The Motion Pictures and their Censors (*Review of Reviews*, lxxv, 1927, 393-98)

——: *See and Hear* (N. Y., 1929)

Hazlitt, H.: Revolution with Sound Effects (*Century Magazine*, cix, 1929, 3-5)

——: Pictures from Plays (*Nation*, cxxxiii, 1931, 343)

Hellwig, Albert: *Die Filmzensur* (Berlin, 1914)

——: *Die Reform des Lichtspielrechts* (Leipzig, 1920)

——: *Die Grundsätze der Filmzensur* (Munich, 1923)

——: *Schundfilme. Ihr Wesen, ihre Gefahren und ihre Bekämpfung* (Halle, 1911)

Hémardinquer, Pierre: *Le cinématographe sonore* (Paris, 1932)

Henry, R. L.: The Cultural Influences of the Talkies (*School and Society*, xxix, 1929, 149-50)

Hepworth, C. M.: *Animated Photography* (London, 1897)

Herkt, Günther: *Der Tonfilmtheater* (Berlin, 1931)

Hermans, Fons: *Jeugd en bioskoop* (Antwerp, 1932)

Herring, Robert: The Movies (*London Mercury*, xiv, 1926, 303-05)

Herrmann, H.: Vom Wesen des Films (*Deutsche Rundschau*, ccxliii, 1935, 219-23)

Herzberg, Max J. ed.: *Photoplay Studies* (Newark, N. J., 1935)

Heymann, Robert: *Der Film und die Karikatur* (Berlin, 1929)

Hitchcock, A. M.: The Relation of the Picture Play to Literature (*English Journal*, iv, 1915, 292-98)

Hoagland, H. C.: *How to Write a Photoplay* (N. Y., 1912)

Hoffmann-Harnisch, W.: Der Tonfilm, der jüngste Wunder unsrer Zeit (*Westermanns Monatshefte*, cxlv, 1928, 421-26)

Hofmannsthal, Hugo von: Substitutes for Dreams (*London Mercury*, ix, 1923, 177-80)

Holaday, Perry W.: *Getting Ideas from the Movies* (N. Y., 1933)

Hollis, Andrew P.: *Motion Pictures for Instruction* (N. Y., 1926)

Holm, E.: *Das Objektiv im Dienste der Photographie* (Berlin, 1902; 2nd. edn., 1906)

Honeg, K.: *Die Wahrheit über das Kino* (Friedrichshagen, 1921)

Hooker, B.: Shakespeare and the Movies (*Century Magazine*, xciii, 1916, 298-304)

———: The Movies: A Critical Prophecy (*Century Magazine*, xciii, 1917, 857-68)

Hopwood, H. V.: *Living Pictures; their History, Photoproduction and Practical Working* (London, 1899; new edn., 1915)

Horne, M. C.: *The Cinema in Education and as an Amusement and Entertainment* (London, 1919)

Horstmann, Henry C. and Tousley, Victor H.: *Motion Picture Operation* (London, 1920)

Howard, S.: Hollywood on the Slide (*New Republic*, lxxii, 1932, 350-53; reply by A. B. Kuttner, *They're not so bad as they're painted*, ib. lxxiii, 1932, 129-30)

Hoyer, T. B. F.: *Russische filmkunst* (Rotterdam, 1932)

Hubert, A.: *Hollywood* (Leipzig, 1929)

Hughes, Elinor: *Famous Stars of Filmdom* (Boston, 1931)

Hughes, Glenn: Making the Film pay for the Theatre (*Theatre Arts Monthly*, xvi, 1932, 561-65)

Hughes, R.: The Art of Moving Picture Composition (*Arts and Decoration*, xix, 1923, 9-10)

———: Aspects of the Cinema (*Outlook*, lvii, 1926, 8)

———: Calamity, with Sound Effects (*New Outlook*, clxii, 1933, 21-26)

Hughes, R.: A Brief for Hollywood (*Saturday Evening Post*, ccvi, 1934, 23)

———: Early Days in the Movies (*Saturday Evening Post*, ccvii, 1935, 18)

Hulfish, D. S.: *The Motion Picture; its Making and its Theatre* (Chicago, 1909)

———: *Cyclopaedia of Motion-Picture Work* (Chicago, 1911)

———: *Motion-Picture Work* (Chicago, 1913)

Hullinger, E. W.: Free Speech for the Talkies? (*North American Review*, ccxxvii, 1929, 737-43)

Hunter, William: *Scrutiny of the Cinema* (London, 1932)

Hutchens, J.: L'enfant terrible: The Little Cinema Movement (*Theatre Arts Monthly*, xiii, 1929, 694-97)

Huxley, A. L.: *Essays New and Old* (London, 1926)

Iezuitov, Nikolai M.: Пути художественного фильма (Moscow, 1934)

Irwin, W.: *The House that Shadows built* (N. Y., 1928)

Isaacs, Edith J. R.: Let's go to the Movies! (*Theatre Arts Monthly*, xix, 1935, 399-410)

Jackson, Arrar: *Writing for the Screen* (London, 1929)

Jacobs, Lewis: *Film Writing Forms* (N. Y., 1934)

Jacobsohn, Kurt: *Das Arbeiten mit farbenempfindlichen Platten und Filmen* (Berlin, 1929)

Jaensch, Wolfgang: *Wie man filmt* (Berlin, 1929)

———: *Filmt gij nog niet?* (Rotterdam, 1929)

Jalabert, R. P. L.: *Le film corrupteur* (Paris, 1921).

Jamme, L.: Realism (*Saturday Evening Post*, ccvi, 1934, 72)

Jannings, Emil: Why I left the Films (*Living Age*, cccxxxviii, 1930, 554-57)

Jason, Alexander: *Der Film in Ziffern und Zahlen* (Berlin, 1924)

———: *Handbuch der Filmwirtschaft* (Berlin, 1933)

Jasper, Gerhard: *Vom Film* (Berlin, 1934)

Jeanne, R.: La crise cinématographique (*Revue des Deux Mondes*, VIII, xvii, 1933, 118-39)

Jeanne, R.: Quarante ans de cinéma (*Revue des Deux Mondes*, VIII, xxx, 1935, 907-22)

Jellinek, Guido: *Due nuovi sistemi di cinematografia in rilievo* (Milan, 1932)

Joachim, H.: *Die neueren Fortschritte der Kinematographie* (Leipzig, 1921)

———: *Die kinematographische Projektion* (Halle, 1928)

Johnston, William A.: The Structure of the Motion Picture Industry (*Annals of the American Academy of Political and Social Science*, cxxviii, 1926, 20-29)

Jones, B. E. ed: *The Cinematograph Book* (N. Y., 1915)

———: *How to make and operate Moving Pictures* (N. Y., 1916)

Jones, G. F.: *Sound Film Reproduction* (London, 1931)

Jones, Harold E. and Conrad, H. S.: *Psychological Studies of Motion Pictures* (Berkeley, Calif., 1928-1929)

Jones, Henry Arthur: The Dramatist and the Photoplay (*Mentor*, ix, 1921, 29)

Jordaan, L. J.: *Dertig jaar film* (Rotterdam, 1932)

Kahan, Hans: *Dramaturgie des Tonfilms* (Berlin, 1930)

Kahn, Otto H.: *Of Many Things* (N. Y., 1926)

Kalbus, Oskar: *Der deutsche Lehrfilm in der Wissenschaft und im Unterricht* (Berlin, 1922)

Kasteel, Jan van: *Film als kunst* (Amsterdam, 1928)

Katsigras, Alexander I.: Что такое кино (Moscow, 1929)

———: Как работать с кино-передвижкой в деревне (Moscow, 1929)

Kaufman, Naum O.: Упонское кино (Moscow, 1929)

Kaufmann, Nicholas: *Filmtechnik und Kultur* (Stuttgart, 1931)

Kellogg, A.: Minds made by the Movies (*Survey Graphic*, xxii, 1933, 244-50)

Kendall, G. P.: *Film Titling* (London, 1935)

Kennedy, Joseph P.: *The Story of the Films* (Chicago, 1927)

Kent, G.: A New Crisis in the Motion Picture Industry (*Current History*, xxxiii, 1931, 887-91)

Kent, Sidney R.: The Motion Picture of To-morrow
     (*Annals of the American Academy of Political and
     Social Science,* cxxviii, 1926, 30-33)
Kerr, Alfred (introd. by): *Russische Filmkunst* (Berlin,
     1927)
Kidd, R.: The Censorship of Films (*New Statesman,* ix,
     1935, 170-71)
Kinross, M.: The Screen from this side (*Fortnightly Re-
     view,* cxxxvi, 1931, 499-512)
Klabund: *Wie ich den Sommernachtstraum im Film sehe*
     (Berlin, 1925)
Kloppers, P.: *In het toonverrijk der film* (Amsterdam,
     1931)
Klumph, Inez and H.: *Screen Acting* (N. Y., 1922)
Knepper, Max: *Sodom and Gomorrah: The Story of Holly-
     wood* (Los Angeles, 1935)
Knospe, P.: *Der Kinematograph im Dienste der Schule*
     (Halle, 1913)
Knowles, Dorothy: *The Censor, the Drama and the Film,
     1900-1934* (London, 1934)
Knowlton, Daniel C. and Tilton, J. W.: *Motion Pictures in
     History Teaching* (New Haven, Conn., 1929)
Knox, E. V.: Cinema English (*Living Age,* cccxxxviii,
     1930, 187-89)
Koebner, F. W.: *Hinter die Filmkulissen* (Berlin, 1929)
Koller, Arnold: *Schlüssel zum Film-Szenen-Schema
     "Solum"* (Lucerne, 1923)
————: *Der Film aus dem Volk* (Leipzig, 1924)
Konwiczka, Hans: *Kinematograph* (Leipzig, 1913)
Koon, Cline M.: *Motion Pictures in Education in the
     United States* (Chicago, 1934)
Köper, J. C. and Brepohl, F. W.: *Vorschlage zu einem
     Reformkino* (Nurnberg, 1919, 3rd. edn.)
Koster, Simon: *Duitsche filmkunst* (Rotterdam, 1932)
Kracauer, S.: *Zur Lage des Tonfilms* (*Neue Rundschau,*
     xlii, 1931, 287-88)
Kreiselmeier, L.: *Der Film in Schule* (Berlin, 1925)

Kress, E.: *Historique du cinématographe* (Paris, 1912)

Krieger, Ernst and Sterzenbach, Ralph: *Das Schul- und Volksbildungskino* (Leipzig, 1922)

Krows, A. E.: Literature and the Motion Picture (*Annals of the American Academy of Political and Social Science,* cxxviii, 1926, 70-73)

———: *The Talkies* (N. Y., 1930)

Krutchenich, A.: Фонетика театра (Moscow, 1923)

Krylov, S. M.: Кино вместо водки (Moscow, 1928)

Kühlein, T.: *Projektionskunst* (Leipzig, 1928)

Kuenzig, B.: *Der Verlagsvertrag des Filmrechts* (Eilenberg, 1928)

Kuleshov, L.: Практика кинорежиссуры (Moscow, 1935)

———: Репетиционный метод в кино (Moscow, 1935)

Kunte, J.: *Das Kino. Ein Mahn- und Warnruf an Eltern und Jugend* (Vienna, 1917)

Künzel, Max: *Wie werde ich Filmschauspieler, Filmschauspielerin?* (Nurnberg, 1921)

Kurtz, R.: *Expressionismus und Film* (Berlin, 1926)

Labadié, J.: L'évolution technique du cinématographe (*L'Illustration,* cxcii, 1935, 304-06)

Ladd-Franklin, C.: *Colour and Colour Theories* (N. Y., 1929)

Laemmle, Carl: From the Inside (*Saturday Evening Post,* cc, 1927, 10, 18 and 28)

Laing, A. B.: Designing Motion Picture Sets (*Architectural Record,* lxxiv, 1933, 59-64)

Lalois, Maurice: *Cinq mois à Hollywood avec Douglas Fairbanks* (Paris, 1929)

Lambert, C.: Music in the Kinema (*Saturday Review,* cxlvii, 1929, 498-99)

Lambert, Richard S. ed: *For Filmgoers Only* (London, 1934; lectures by the editor, A. Buchanan, C. A. Lejeune, P. Rotha)

Lampe, F. D.: *Der Film in Schule und Leben* (Berlin, 1924)

Landry, L.: *Formation de la sensibilité* (in *L'art cinémato-graphique*, II, Paris)

Lane, Tamar: *What's Wrong with the Talkies?* (London, 1923)

Lang, A.: *Théâtre et cinéma* (in *L'art cinématographique*, III, Paris)

Lange Konrad: *Das Kino in Gegenwart und Zukunft* (Stuttgart, 1920)

Lange, Konrad and Gaupp, R.: *Die Kinematographie als Volksunterhaltungsmittel* (Munich, 1913; 2nd edn., 1922)

Langer, Resi: *Kinotypen vor und hinter die Filmkulissen* (Halle, 1919)

Lasky, J. L.: Hearing Things in the Dark (*Collier's*, lxxxiii, 1929, 8-9)

Lassally, Arthur: *Bild und Film im Dienste der Technik* (Halle, 1919)

Lauwerys, J. A., ed.: *The Film in the School* (London, 1935)

Lawson, W. P.: *The Movies* (N. Y., 1915)

Lazarev, Petr P. and others: Культурфильма (Moscow, 1929)

Lee, Herman van: *De wonderen der filmwereld* (Utrecht, 1926)

Leeds, A. and Esenwein, Joseph B.: *Writing the Photoplay* (Springfield, Mass., 1913)

Lefol, Gaston: *Cinémas* (Paris, 1921)

Lega, Giuseppe: *Il fonofilm: l'arte e la tecnica della cinematografia parlata e sonora* (Florence, 1933)

Lehmann, H.: *Die Kinematographie, ihre Grundlagen und ihre Anwendungen* (Leipzig, 1911; 2nd edn., 1919)

Lejeune, C. A.: *Cinema: A Review of Thirty Years' Achievement* (London, 1931)

———: British Films and Others (*Fortnightly Review*, cxliii, 1935, 285-94)

Lembke, Fr.: *Das Kino im Dorfe* (Berlin, 1920)

Lemke, H.: *Die Kinematographie der Gegenwart* (Leipzig, 1912)

Lenoble, G.: Памятка начинающему сценаристу (Moscow, 1929)

Lescarboura, Austin: *Behind the Motion Picture Screen* (N. Y., 1919)

——: *The Cinema Hand-book* (N. Y., 1921; London, 1922)

Levenson, J.: The Censorship of the Movies (*Forum*, lxix, 1923, 1404-14)

Levinson, A.: The Nature of the Cinema (*Theatre Arts Monthly*, xiii, 1929, 684-93)

——: *Pour une poétique du film* (in *L'art cinématographique*, IV, Paris)

Levman, Boris S.: Рабочий зритель в кино (Moscow, 1930)

Lewin, William: Standards of Photoplay Production (*English Journal*, xxi, 1932, 799-810)

——: *Photoplay Appreciation in American High Schools* (N. Y., 1934)

Lherbier, Marcel: *Le cinématographe et l'espace* (in *L'art cinématographique*, IV, Paris)

Lichatchev, B. S.: Кино в России (Leningrad, 1927)

Lichtveld, L.: *De geluidsfilm* (Rotterdam, 1933)

Liddy, Lewis W.: *Photoplay Instructions* (San Francisco, 1913)

Lilly, J.: Hope for Hollywood (*Outlook*, clviii, 1931, 206)

Lindsay, Vachel: *The Art of the Moving Picture* (N. Y., 1915; London, 1922)

Lipp, Hermann and Felix, Franz: *Führer durch das Wesen der Kinematographie* (Berlin, 1918; 2nd edn., 1921)

Lolling J.: *Kino und Schule* (Berlin, 1914)

Lomas, H. M.: *Picture Play Photography* (London, 1914)

Lorant, Stefan: *Wir vom Film* (Berlin, 1929)

Lore, Colden: *The Modern Photoplay and its Construction* (London, 1923)

Lorentz, P.: Stillborn Art (*Forum*, lxxx, 1928, 364-72)

Lorentz, Pierre and Ernst, Morris L.: *Censored; the Private Life of the Movie* (N. Y., 1930)

Louttit, C. M.: Motion Pictures and Youth (*Journal of Applied Psychology*, xviii, 1934, 307-16)

Loving, Pierre: Is the Play vanishing? (*Drama*, xii, 1922, 311-12)

Lozowick, L.: The Soviet Cinema (*Theatre Arts Monthly*, xiii, 1929, 664-75)

Lubschez, Ben Jehuda: *The Story of the Motion Picture*, 65 B. C. to 1920 A. D. (N. Y., 1920)

Lucas, E. V.: Moving-Picture Prospects and Retrospects (*Living Age*, cccxviii, 1923, 564-70)

Luciani, S. A.: *L'antiteatro. Il cinema come arte* (Rome, 1928)

Lullack, Frederich: *Titeltechnik* (Halle, 1933)

Lunatcharski, Anatolii V.: Кино на западе и у нас (Moscow, 1928)

————: *Der russische Revolutionsfilm* (Berlin, 1929)

Lutz, Edwin G.: *Animated Cartoons* (N. Y., 1926)

————: *The Motion Picture Cameraman* (N. Y. and London, 1927)

Lytton, Grace: *Scenario Writing Today* (Boston and N. Y., 1921)

MacAlarney, R. E.: The Movies: in their Defense (*Forum*, lxvii, 1922, 42-45)

Macbean, L. C.: *Kinematograph Studio Technique* (N. Y., 1922)

McClusky, Frederick D.: *Visual Instruction* (N. Y., 1932)

McCrory, John R.: *How to Draw for the Movies* (Kansas City, 1918)

McDonald, I. T.: What's Back of the Screen? (*Commonweal*, ix, 1929, 624-26; reply by F. P. Donnelly, *ib.* ix, 1929, 720)

Macgowan, K.: The Artistic Future of the Movies (*North American Review*, ccxiii, 1921, 260-65)

Mack, M.: *Wie komme ich zu Film?* (Berlin, 1919)

————: *Die zappelnde Leinwand* (Berlin, 1920)

McKay, H. C.: The Romance of the Movies (*American Photography*, xxvii, 1933, 751-56)

Mac-Orlan, *Le fantastique* (in *L'art cinématographique, I, Paris*)

Magnaghi, Ubaldo: *Le ombre e lo schermo* (Milan, 1933)

Magnus, Erwin: *Lichtspeil und Leben* (Berlin, 1924)

Maillet, G.: L'avenir du film silencieux (*Mercure de France*, ccxv, 1929, 209-13)

Mallet-Stevens, R.: *Le décor* (in *L'art cinématographique, VI, Paris*)

———: *Le décor moderne au cinéma* (Paris, 1928)

Maraun, F.: Wann wird der Tonfilm wieder Film? (*Westermanns Monatshefte*, clviii, 1935, 206-08)

Marble, A. L.: The Movies and the Appreciation of Drama (*Photo-Era*, lxiv, 1930, 163-64)

———: Teaching with the Talkies (*Photo-Era*, lxiv, 1930, 218)

Marchand, René and Weinstein, Pierre: *Le cinéma russe* (Paris, 1927)

Marchant, Sir James: *The Cinema in Education* (London, 1925)

Marcks, G. and Günther, W.: *Lehr- und Kulturfilm* (Berlin, 1933)

Margadonna, Ettore M.: *Cinema, ieri e oggi* (Milan, 1932)

Markgraf, Bruno: *Kampf des Kino! Warum?* (Leipzig, 1913)

Marshall, N.: Music in the Talkies (*Bookman*, London, lxxxiv, 1933, 191)

Martyn, H.: The New Art Film (*Canadian Forum*, xi, 1931, 479)

Masetti, Umberto: *I grandi films* (Rome, 1932)

Martini, W.: *Tonfilm-Technik in Frage und Antwort* (Berlin, 1933)

Matthews, Brander: Are the Movies a Menace to the Drama? (*North American Review*, ccv, 1917, 447-54)

Maurois, André: *La poésie du cinéma* (in *L'art cinématographique*, III, Paris)

Maxwell, G.: The Fascination of the Films (*Fortnightly Review*, cxx, 1923, 453-59)

May, Bruno: *Das Recht des Kinematographen* (Berlin, 1912)

Meighen, E. L. M.: *Le code du cinéma* (Paris, 1921)

Meinel, Walter: *Hilfsbuch für die Prüfung des Kinovorführers in Frage und Antwort* (Berlin, 1925, 2nd edn.)

Mencken, H. L.: *Prejudices* (6th series, N. Y., 1927)

Mendel, G. V.: *Ins Zauberreich des Films* (Berlin, 1930)

Menzies, W. H. C.: Cinema Design (*Theatre Arts Monthly*, xiii, 1929, 676-83)

Messel, R.: *This Film Business* (London, 1928)

Meunier-Surcouf, C.: *Hollywood au ralenti* (in *L'art cinématographique*, V, Paris)

Meyer, Franz E.: *Die Besteuerung des Lichtspielgewerbes durch die deutschen Grosstädte* (Greifswald, 1922)

Miehling, Rudolph: *Sound Projection* (N. Y., 1929; 2nd edn., 1930)

Mierendorff, C.: *Hätte ich das Kino!* (Berlin, 1920)

Mihály, Denes von: *Der sprechende Film* (Berlin, 1928)

Miklashevski, Constantin: Звуковое кино (Berlin, 1929)

Milne, Peter: *Motion Picture Directing* (London, 1922)

Minney, R. J.: *Hollywood by Starlight* (London, 1935)

Mirsky, D. S.: The Background of the Russian Films (*London Mercury*, xxiv, 1931, 53-64)

——: Soviet Films (*Virginia Quarterly Review*, vii, 1931, 522-32)

——: *Literature and Films in Socialist Russia* (N. Y., 1932)

Mitchell, Alice M: *Children and Movies* (Chicago, 1929)

Mitchell, R.: *Creative Theatre* (N. Y., 1929)

Moholy-Nagy, L.: *Malerei, Photographie, Film* (Munich, 1925; 2nd edn., 1928)

Monosson, L. T.: The Soviet Cinematography (*Journal of the Society of Motion Picture Engineers*, xv, 1930, 509-27)

Montagu, Ivor: *The Political Censorship of Films* (London, 1929)

Moorad, G. L.: Chinese Talkies (*Asia*, xxxv, 1935, 614-19)

Moore, D.: Music and the Movies (*Harper's Magazine,* clxxi, 1935, 181-88)

Moreck, Curt: *Sittengeschichte des Kinos* (Dresden, 1926)

Moris, Roger: *Le cinéma* (Montpellier, 1930)

Morlion, Felix: *Filmleiding* (Tilburg, 1933)

Moussinac, Léon: *La naissance du cinéma* (Paris, 1925)

———: *Le cinéma soviétique* (Paris, 1928)

———: *Panoramique du cinéma* (Paris, 1929)

———: *Cinéma: Expression sociale* (in *L'art cinématographique,* IV, Paris)

Muensterberg, Hugo: *The Photoplay: a Psychological Study* (N. Y., 1916)

Mühsam, Kurt and Jacobsohn, E.: *Lexikon des Films* (Berlin, 1926)

Mullen, S. M.: Walt Disney, Master of Cartoons (*Scholastic,* xxvi, 1935, 10-11)

———: Following the Films; all Motion Pictures have a Basic Theme (*Scholastic,* xxvi, 1935, 28)

Mullett, M. B.: David W. Griffith, Greatest Moving Picture Producer in the World (*American Magazine,* xci, 1921, 32-35)

Mumin, Reinhard: *Die Lichtbühne* (Berlin, 1920)

Mur, Leo: Бумажные броненосцы (Фельетоны о сценариях) (Moscow, 1929)

Muratov, P. P.: Кинематографъ (Современныя записки), Paris, 1925-26, 287-312)

Murawski, F.: *Die Kinematographie und ihre Beziehungen zu Schule und Unterricht* (Dresden, 1914)

Nadell, Aaron: *Projecting Sound Pictures* (London, 1931)

Nanni, A.: *Tecnica e arte del film* (Milan, 1931)

Napolitano, G. C.: Prima e dopo il parlato (*Nuova Antologia,* ccclxii, 1932, 140-44)

Nathan, G. J.: The Pictorial Phonograph (*American Mercury,* xvii, 1929, 374-75)

———: A Living Corpse (*American Mercury,* xvi, 1929, 504-05)

———: The Play is still the Thing (*Forum,* lxxxvi, 1931, 36-39)

Neblette, C. B.: The Place of the Motion Picture in Modern Life (*Photo-Era*, lvii, 1926, 175-80)

Neergaard, Ebbe: *Hvorfor er Filmen sådan?* (Copenhagen, 1931)

Nelson, J. A.: *The Photoplay* (Los Angeles, 1913)

Nestriepke, S.: *Wege zu neuer Filmkultur* (Berlin, 1929)

Nichols, R.: Cinema-to-be (*Spectator*, cxlvi, 1931, 103-04)

Niessen, Karl: *Der "Film" eine selbständige deutsche Erfindung* (Emsdetten, 1934)

Noack, Victor: *Das Kino* (Leipzig, 1913)

Nordmann, C.: L'illusion cinématographique (*Revue des Deux Mondes*, VIII, vii, 1932, 1933-40)

Nussy, Marcel: *Le cinématographe et la censure* (Montpellier, 1929)

Oberholtzer, E. P.: *The Morals of the Movie* (Philadelphia, 1922)

———: The Moving Picture: Obiter Dicta of a Censor (*Yale Review*, ix, 1920, 620-32)

O'Dell, Scott: *Representative Photoplays Analysed* (Hollywood, 1924)

Ogden, R.: The Art of René Clair (*Bookman*, London, lxxxii, 1932, 64-66)

Ortman, Marguerite: *Fiction and the Screen* (Boston, 1935)

Orton, William: But is it Art? (*Atlantic Monthly*, cxlix, 1932, 586-97)

Ott, Richard: *Die Organisation im Film- und Theaterbetrieb* (Berlin, 1920)

———: *Wie führe ich mein Kino?* (Berlin, 1922)

———: *Das Film-Manuskript, sein Wesen, sein Aufbau und seine Erfordernisse* (Berlin, 1926)

Otten, J. F.: *Amerikaansche filmkunst* (Rotterdam, 1931)

Ottley, D. C.: *The Cinema in Education* (London, 1935)

Overmans, J.: *Theater und Kino in neuen Deutschland* (Frankfurt, 1920)

Page, Arthur W. and others: *Modern Communication* (Boston and N. Y., 1932)

Palmer, Frederick: *Photoplay Plot Encyclopaedia* (Hollywood, 1922)

Palmer, Frederick: *The Author's Photoplay Manual* (Hollywood, 1924)
———: *Technique of the Photoplay* (Hollywood, 1924)
Parker, G.: The Author and the Motion Pictures (*Mentor,* ix, 1921, 14-19)
Parker, Sir Gilbert: What about Motion Pictures? (*Bookman,* N. Y., liv, 1921, 313-17)
Parker, R. A.: The Art of the Camera (*Arts and Decoration,* xv, 1921, 369)
Parsons, I. M.: The Future of the Talkies (*Saturday Review,* cxlix, 1930, 382-83)
Parsons, L. O.: *How to Write for the Movies* (Chicago, 1915)
Patterson, Frances T.: *Cinema Craftsmanship* (N. Y., 1920; 2nd edn., 1921)
———: The Sedulous Ape (*New Republic,* li, 1927, 177-79)
———: *Scenario and Screen* (N. Y., 1928)
———: *Motion Picture Continuities* (N. Y., 1930)
———: Descent into Hollywood (*New Republic,* lxv, 1931, 239-40)
Paul, Peter: *Das Filmbuch* (Berlin, 1914)
Paulau, Josep: *El cinema soviètic* (Barcelona, 1932)
Paushkin, Michael M.: Кино через пять лет (Moscow, 1930)
Peacocke, Leslie T.: *Hints on Photoplay Writing* (Chicago, 1916)
Peden, Charles: *Newsreel Man* (N. Y., 1932)
Peet, C.: Jumbled Talkies (*Outlook,* cliii, 1929, 292-94)
———: A Letter to Hollywood (*Outlook,* clvi, 1930, 612; reply by J. R. Metcalf, *ib.* clvii, 1931, 80)
———: French Film Studios (*Outlook,* clix, 1931, 403)
———: German Studios (*Outlook,* clix, 1931, 249)
Perry, Clarence A.: *The Attitude of High School Students towards Motion Pictures* (N. Y., 1923)
Perucca, Eligio: Problemi fisici del film parlato (*Annuario della r. Scuola di Ingegnieria di Torino,* Turin, 1932)

Peters, Charles C.: *Motion Pictures and Standards of Morality* (N. Y., 1933)

Petersen, Ruth C. and Thurstone, L. L.: *Motion Pictures and the Social Attitudes of Children* (N. Y., 1933)

Petrie, C.: The Historical Film (*Nineteenth Century,* cxvii, 1935, 613-23)

Petrov, Evgenii: Актер перед кино-аппаратом (Moscow, 1929)

Petsche, M.: The French Cinema (*Living Age,* cccxlix, 1935, 243-47)

Petzet, Wolfgang: *Verbotene Filme* (Frankfurt, 1931)

Pfleiderer, Wolfgang: *Lichtbild und Film* (Frankfurt, 1927)

Phillips, H. A.: *The Photodrama* (Larchmont, N. Y., 1914)

Piccini, Giulio: *Le novelle del cinematografo* (Florence, 1910)

Pierre-Quint, L.: *Signification du cinéma* (in *L'art cinématographique,* II, Paris)

Pisani, Ferri: *Au pays du film* (Paris, 1923)

———: *Le cinéma américain* (in *L'art cinématographique,* VII, Paris)

Pitchford, R. and Coombs, F.: *The Projectionist's Handbook* (London, 1933)

Pitkin, Walter B. and Marston, William M.: *The Art of Sound Pictures* (N. Y., 1930)

Playfair, Sir Nigel: Theatre and the Films (*English Review,* lii, 1931, 336-41)

Podehl, F. and Dupont, A.: *Wie ein Film geschrieben wird und wie man ihn verwertet* (Berlin, 1926)

Popov, Iakov S.: Кино-сьемочные аппараты (Moscow, 1929)

Pordes, Victor E.: *Das Lichtspiel: Wesen, Dramaturgie, Regie* (Vienna, 1919)

Potamkin, H. A.: Music and the Movies (*Musical Quarterly,* xv, 1929, 281-96)

Pouaille, H.: *Charles Chaplin* (Paris, 1927)

Poulain, É.: *Contre le cinéma . . . Pour le cinéma* (Besançon, 1917)

Pravdoliubov, V. A.: Кино и наша молодежь на основе данных педологии (Moscow, 1929)

Prels, Max: *Kino* (Berlin, 1919; 2nd edn., 1926)

Privé, J. C.: Avenir du cinéma (*Mercure de France,* ccxxii, 1930, 257-99)

Pudovkin, V. I.: *Film Technique* (trs. by Ivor Montagu, London, 1929) (German trs. as *Filmregie und Filmmanuskript,* Berlin, 1928; Italian trs. Rome, 1932)

——: Актер в фильме (Leningrad, 1931) (Trs. as *Film Acting,* London, 1935)

Radlov, Sergei: Угроза кинематографу (Аполлонъ, St. Petersburg, 1917, No. 8-10, 46-48)

Radnor, Leona: *The Photoplay Writer* (N. Y., 1913)

Rafalovitch, Daniel L.: Кино-Америка сегодня (Leningrad, 1929)

Rageot, G.: Le théâtre cinématographique et le cinéma artistique (*Revue politique et littéraire,* lix, 1921, 28-30)

——: Comédiens de théâtre et comédiens de cinéma (*Revue politique et littéraire,* lxi, 1923, 602-04)

——: Le cinématisme (*L'Illustration,* clxvii, 1926, 484-85)

——: Et le cinéma? (*L'Illustration,* clxxxiii, 1932, 311-12)

Ramsaye, Terry: *A Million and One Nights* (N. Y., 1926, 2 vols.)

——: The Motion Picture (*Annals of the American Academy of Political and Social Science,* cxxviii, 1926, 1-19).

Randall, G.: Cinema and the Censor (*Outlook,* lxi, 1928, 254)

Randone, B. and Solito, G.: *Guida film* (Rome, 1932)

Rapée, E.: The Future of Music in Moviedom (*Etude,* xlvii, 1929, 649-50)

Rascoe, Burton: The Motion Pictures; an Industry, not an Art (*Bookman,* N. Y., liv, 1921, 193-99)

Rath, W.: *Kino und Bühne* (Munich, 1912)

Rathbun, J. B.: *Motion Picture Making and Exhibiting* (Chicago, 1914)

Raucourt, Jules: *L'amour du cinéma* (Ostend, 1926)

Ravitch, N.: Кино на Востоке (Moscow, 1929)

Reitz, Helm and Boehmer, Henning von: *Der Film in Wirtschaft und Recht* (Berlin, 1933)

Renshaw, S.: *Children's Sleep: A Series of Studies on the Influence of Motion Pictures* (N. Y., 1933)

Rensselaer, A. van: Photoplay Writing and the Photoplay Market (*Bookman*, N. Y., lvi, 1922, 229-304)

Reuss, Prince Henry of: The Talkies and the Stage (*Living Age*, cccxxxix, 1930, 298-300)

Reuter, Leon: *Filmstjärnor* (Stockholm, 1927)

Reyes, Alfonso: *Simpatías y diferencias* (Madrid, 1922)

Reynolds, Frederick W. and Anderson, Carl: *Motion Pictures and Motion Picture Equipment* (Washington, 1920)

Reynolds, Q.: Shooting Stars (*Collier's*, xcv, 1935, 12)

Rhodes, Harrison: Majestic Movies (*Harper's Magazine*, cxxxviii, 1919, 183-94)

Richard, A. P.: *La technique* (in *L'art cinématographique*, VI, Paris)

Richards, O. W.: The Terminology proposed for Motion Picture Films (*Science*, lxxxii, 1935, 102-03)

Richardson, F. H.: *Motion Picture Handbook* (N. Y., 1912; frequently reprinted)

Richter, Hans: *Der Spielfilm. Aufsätze zu einer Dramaturgie des Films* (Berlin, 1920)

———: *Filmgegner von Heute: Filmfreunde von Morgen* (Berlin, 1929)

Riesenfeld, H.: Music and Motion Pictures (*Annals of the American Academy of Political and Social Science*, cxxviii, 1926, 58-62)

Rinehart, M. R.: Sounds in Silence (*Ladies Home Journal*, xlix, 1932, 10)

Ring, R. L.: *Kallprat om film* (Stockholm, 1928)

Rippo, Giosuè: *L'operatore di cinematografo* (Turin, 1933)

Rogers, Gustavus A.: *The Law of the Motion Picture Industry* (N. Y., 1916)

Roos, Elizabeth de: *Fransche filmkunst* (Rotterdam, 1931)

Rorty, J.: The Dream Factory (*Forum*, xciv, 1935, 162-65)

Rose, D.: Silence is Requested (*North American Review,* ccxxx, 1930, 127-28)

Rosenthal, Solomon P.: *Change of Socio-economic Attitudes under Radical Motion Picture Propaganda* (N. Y., 1934)

Ross, E. N.: *Scenario Writing* (Philadelphia, 1912)

Rossi, Canevari R.: *Trattato teorico pratico internazionale di diritto cinematografico* (Milan, 1933)

Rotha, Paul: *The Film till Now* (London, 1930)

————: *Celluloid: The Film To-day* (London, 1931)

————: A Museum for the Cinema (*Connoisseur,* lxxxvi, 1930, 34-37)

Rott, Leo: *Die Kunst des Kinos* (Vienna, 1921)

Rouff, M.: Méditations à la porte d'un studio (*Mercure de France,* ccxxix, 1931, 5-21)

Rous, Friederich: *Der Weg zum Tonfilm* (Troppau, 1933)

Rowland, Stanley: The Future of the Cinema (*Quarterly Review,* cclviii, 1932, 63-78)

Rucknick, Christian A. and Dysinger, Wendell S.: *The Emotional Responses of Children to the Motion Picture Situation* (N. Y., 1933)

Rulon, Philip J.: *The Sound Motion-Picture in Science Teaching* (Cambridge, Mass., 1933)

Sabott, Edmund: *Das Wunderkind. Eine Geschichte vom Film* (Berlin, 1925)

Salmon, Heinz: *Die Kunst im Film* (Dresden, 1921)

Sambra, Fausto: *Come si diventa "artisti" cinematografici e drammatici* (Venice, 1932)

Samuleit, Paul and Borm, Emil: *Der Kinematograph als Volks- und Jugendbildungsmittel* (Berlin, 1912)

Sargent, Epes W.: *The Technique of the Photoplay* (N. Y., 1912; 2nd edn., 1916)

Saugnet, H.: La musique et l'art muet (*L'Europe nouvelle,* xiv, 1931, 1340-41)

Scheuing, F. M.: *Motion Picture Acting* (N. Y., 1913)

Schieber, Anna: *Zwei Kino-Konferenzen* (Stuttgart, 1919)

Schmidl, Poldi: *O, diese Kinos!* (Mühlhausen, 1922)

Scholte, Henrik: *Nederlansche filmkunst* (Rotterdam, 1933)

Schopen, E.: *Das Kulturproblem des Films* (Munich, 1930)

Schrott, Paul: *Leitfaden für Kinooperateure und Kinobesitzer* (Berlin, 1920, 5th edn.)

Schroubek, Richard: *Der Film: seine Herstellung, Verwendung und Bedeutung* (Prague, 1922)

Schultze, Ernst: *Der Kinematograph als Bildungsmittel* (Halle, 1911)

Schulze, A. R.: *Kinopraxis* (Berlin, 1929)

Schutz, Maurice: *Le maquillage* (in *L'art cinématographique,* VI, Paris)

Schwob, R.: *Une mélodie silencieuse* (Paris, 1929)

Scotland, John: *The Talkies* (London, 1930)

Scott-James, R. A.: Film Censorship (*Saturday Review,* cli, 1931, 8-9)

Seabury, William M.: *The Public and the Motion Picture Industry* (N. Y., 1926)

——: *Motion Picture Problems* (N. Y., 1929)

Seeber, G.: *Der Trickfilm* (Berlin, 1927)

Seeger, Ernst: *Die Prüf-Vorschriften für Lichtspiel-Vorführer* (Berlin, 1923)

Seldes, Gilbert: *The Seven Lively Arts* (N. Y., 1924)

——: The Movie Director (*New Republic,* xliii, 1925, 19-20)

——: Art in the Movies (*Nation,* cxxi, 1925, 148)

——: The Plot and the Picture (*New Republic,* xliv, 1925, 97-98)

——: Abstract Movies (*New Republic,* xlviii, 1926, 95-96)

——: Progress in the Movies (*New Republic,* li, 1927, 255-56)

——: *An Hour with the Movies and Talkies* (London, 1929)

——: The Mobile Camera (*New Republic,* lx, 1929, 298-99)

——: The Talkies' Progress (*Harper's Magazine,* clix, 1929, 454-61)

Seldes, Gilbert: The Other Side of it (*Century Magazine,* cxviii, 1929, 297-302)

——: The Movies in Peril (*Scribner's Magazine,* xcvii, 1935, 81-86)

——: Disney and others (*New Republic,* lxxi, 1932, 101-02)

Sellmann, Adolf: *Der Kinematograph als Volkserzieher?* (Berlin, 1912)

——: *Für und wider das Kino* (Schwelm, 1928)

Serrano, Alfredo: *Las películas españolas* (Barcelona, 1925)

Sewell, George H.: *Commercial Cinematography* (London, 1933)

Shaw, Bernard and Henderson, Archibald: Drama, the Theatre and the Films (*Fortnightly Review,* cxxii, 1924, 289-302)

Sherwood, H. F.: Democracy and the Movies (*Bookman,* London, xlvii, 1918, 235-39)

Sherwood, R. E.: The Renaissance in Hollywood (*American Mercury,* xvi, 1929, 431-37)

Shirman, A.: Библіотека, музей и кинематографъ какъ народно-образовательныя средства (St. Petersburg, 1914)

Shklovski, Victor: О законах кино (Русский современник, i, 1924, 245-52)

——: Чаплин (Berlin, 1933)

Shuttelworth, Frank K.: *The Social Conduct and Attitude of Movie Fans* (N. Y., 1933)

Siggins, A. J.: Will the Films wake up? (*Saturday Review,* cliii, 1932, 145)

Sitchev, Michael A. and Perlin, V. L.: Кино в Красной Армии (Moscow, 1929)

Skaupy, F.: *Die Grundlagen des Tonfilms* (Berlin, 1932)

Skinner, Otis: An Actor's View of the Movie Menace (*North American Review,* ccxii, 1920, 387-92)

Skinner, R. D.: More about Talkies (*Commonweal,* x, 1929, 104-05)

——: Provocative Thoughts (*Commonweal,* xii, 1930, 499)

Slevin, J.: *On Picture-play Writing* (Cedar Grove, N. J., 1912)

Sloane, T. O'C.: *Motion Picture Projection* (N. Y., 1922)

Slonim, Mark: Историко литературный кинематографъ и его задачи. , (Вѣстникъ воспитанія, i, 1917, 166-98)

Smith, H. M. K.: Mistakes that Directors make (*N. Y. Times,* Nov. 23, 1929)

Smith, Russell E.: *The Authors of the Photoplay* (Philadelphia, 1915)

Smith, S.: Camera Lies (*Collier's,* lxxvi, 1925, 14)

Smith, Samuel S.: *The Craft of the Critic* (N. Y., 1931)

Solito, G. and Randone, B.: *Guida film* (Rome, 1932)

Solskii, V.: Звучащее кино (Moscow, 1929)

Soulier, Alfred: *Le cinéma parlant* (Paris, 1932)

Soupault, Philippe: *The American Influence in France* (Seattle, 1930)

Spiridovskii, Nikolai I.: Гибель фильмы (Leningrad, 1929)

Spottiswoode, Raymond: *A Grammar of the Film* (London, 1935)

Stallings, L.: Celluloid Psychology (*New Republic,* xxxiii, 1923, 282-84)

Stearns, H.: Art in Moving Pictures (*New Republic,* iv, 1915, 207-08)

Stearns, M. M.: The Art of Suggested Motion (*Arts and Decoration,* xvii, 1922, 191)

———: Painting Beauty with the Camera (*Arts and Decoration,* xvii, 1922, 27)

———: *With the Movie Makers* (Boston, 1923)

Steer, Valentia ed.: *The Secrets of the Cinema* (London, 1920)

Stepun, F.: *Theater und Kino* (Berlin, 1932)

Sterzenbach, Ralph and Krieger, Ernst: *Das Schul- und Volksbildungskino* (Leipzig, 1922)

Stindt, G. O.: *Das Lichtspiel als Kunstform. Die Philosophie des Films: Regie, Dramaturgie und Schauspieltechnik* (Bremerhaven, 1924)

Strasser, Alexander: *Filmentwurf, Filmregie, Filmschnitt* (Halle, 1933)

Strauss, F. L.: A Synopsized View of Literature (*Bookman,* N. Y., lxiv, 1926, 454-56)

Stricker, Eberhard: *Wert und Unwert des Kinematographen* (Strassburg, 1913)

Strowski, F.: Le domaine du cinéma considéré comme un art (*Revue politique et littéraire,* lxx, 1932, 161-65)

Stuart, B. T.: The Movie Set-up (*Collier's,* xcii, 1933, 20)

Stüler, Alexander: *Filmtricks und Trickfilme* (Halle, 1933)

Sundborg, Åke: *Greta Garbos sagen* (Stockholm, 1929)

Surcoff, Maine: *Hollywood* (Paris, 1929)

Sutyrin, V.: Проблемы социалистической реконструкции советской кинопромышленности (Moscow, 1932)

Syrtzov, S. and Kurs, A., ed.: Советское кино на подеме (Moscow, 1926)

Tak, Max: *De groote kunstenaars van het witte doek* (Amsterdam, 1928)

Talbot, Frederick A.: *Moving Pictures: How they are made and worked* (Philadelphia, 1912; new edn., 1914; London, 1923)

———: *Practical Cinematography and its Applications* (Philadelphia, 1913)

Tallents, Sir Stephen: *The Projection of England* (London, 1932)

Tannenbaum, Herbert: *Kino und Theater* (Munich, 1912)

Tchaikovski, Vsevolod V.: Младенческие годы русского кино (Leningrad, 1928)

Thomas, Arthur W.: *How to Write a Photoplay* (Chicago, 1914)

———: *Photoplay Helps and Hints* (Chicago, 1914)

Thun, Rudolf: *Der Film in der Technik* (Berlin, 1924)

Thurstone, L. L. and Petersen, Ruth C.: *Motion Pictures and the Social Attitudes of Children* (N. Y., 1933)

Tilton, J. W. and Knowlton, Daniel C.: *Motion Pictures in History Teaching* (New Haven, Conn., 1929)

Tippy, Worth M.: *How to Select and Judge Motion Pictures* (N. Y., 1934)

Torbert, H.: Our Nickelodeon Athens (*North American Review,* ccxxix, 1930, 683-89)

Tourneur, M.: The Movies create Art (*Harper's Weekly,* lxii, 1916, 459)

Tousley, Victor H. and Horstmann, Henry C.: *Motion Picture Operation* (London, 1920)

Traub, Hans: *Zeitung, Film, Rundfunk* (Berlin, 1933)

———: *Als man anfing zu filmen* (Munich, 1934)

Troy, W.: An Academy of the Film (*Nation,* cxxxvii, 1933, 605)

———: Values once again (*Nation,* cxxxvi, 1933, 538-39)

———: Concerning narratage (*Nation,* cxxxvii, 1933, 308)

Trumbo, Dalton: Frankenstein in Hollywood (*Forum,* lxxxvii, 1932, 142-46)

———: Hollywood Pays (*Forum,* lxxxix, 1933, 113-19)

———: The Stepchild of the Muses (*North American Review,* ccxxxvi, 1933, 559-66)

———: The Fall of Hollywood (*North American Review,* ccxxxvi, 1933, 140-47)

Turkin, Valentin: Кино-актер (Moscow, 1929)

Tuttle, M.: The Magic of the Movies (*Saturday Evening Post,* cxcix, 1926, 12)

Tysell, Helen T.: The English of the Comic Cartoons (*American Speech,* x, 1935, 43-55)

Ude, J.: *Moralische Massenverseuchung durch Theater und Kino* (Gottingen, 1918)

Ugoletti, Ugo: *Stato e cinematografo* (Rome, 1932)

Ulrich, Hermann: *Film, Kitsch, Kunst, Propaganda* (Oldenburg, 1933)

Umbehr, H.: *Der Tonfilm* (Berlin, 1930)

Valentin, A.: *Introduction à la magie blanche et noir* (in *L'art cinématographique,* IV, Paris)

Van Zile, E. S.: *That Marvel—the Movie* (London and N. Y., 1923)

Variot, J.: La catastrophe du film parlant (*Revue politique et littéraire,* lxviii, 1930, 58-59)

Variot, J.: Où en est le cinéma parlant? (*Revue politique et littéraire*, lxx, 1932, 252-54)

Veale, F. J. P.: The Power of the Cinema (*Nineteenth Century*, cvi, 1929, 212-21)

Veisenberg, E.: Кино-техника сегодня (Moscow, 1929)

———: Конец немого кино (Moscow, 1929)

Vellard, R.: *Le cinéma sonore et sa technique* (Paris, 1933)

Veltman, S.: Задачи кино на Востоке (Moscow, 1927)

Vetter, Adolf and Schumann, Wolfgang: *Kinofragen der Zeit* (Munich, 1924)

Vieth, Hermann: *Der Film* (Euskirchen, 1926)

Vinogradskaia, K. A.: Киносценарий (Moscow, 1935)

Vuillermoz, E.: *La musique des images* (in *L'art cinématographique*, III, Paris)

Wagener-Pazzo, Siegfried: *Das Mustermanuskript* (Berlin, 1923)

Walkley, A. B.: *Pastiche and Prejudice* (London, 1921)

———: *Still More Prejudice* (London, 1925)

Walsh, J. J.: The Movies and History (*Commonweal*, xx, 1934, 299-300)

Walter, F. K.: *The Modern Drama: its Traits, Tendencies and Technique* (Boston, 1915)

Warburg, E.: Der sprechende Film (*Westermanns Monatshefte*, cxxxv, 1924, 491-92)

Warren, Low: *Journalism* (London, 1922)

Warstat, W. and Bergmann, Franz: *Kino und Gemeinde* (Munich, 1912)

Watts, Richard, Jr.: All Talking (*Theatre Arts Monthly*, xiii, 1929, 702-10)

———: The Movies are coming! (*Theatre Arts Monthly*, xvii, 1933, 795-800)

———: Films of a Moonstruck World (*Yale Review*, xxv, 1935, 311-20)

Waugh, A.: The Film and the Future (*Fortnightly Review*, cxxii, 1924, 524-31)

Weaver, R. T.: Prince Acmed, and other Animated Silhouettes (*Theatre Arts Monthly*, xv, 1931, 505-09)

Weigall, Arthur: The Influence of the Kinematograph upon National Life (*Nineteenth Century,* lxxxix, 1921, 661-72)

Welsh, R. E.: *The A B C of Motion Pictures* (N. Y., 1916)

Wesse, Curt: *Grossmacht Film* (Berlin, 1928)

Wessem, Constant van: *De komische film* (Rotterdam, 1931)

Weston, H.: *The Art of Photoplay Writing* (London, 1916)

White, Eric W.: *Parnassus to Let* (London, 1928)

——: *Walking Shadows* (N. Y. and London, 1931)

Williams, B. A.: Lets and Hindrances (*Saturday Evening Post,* ccii, 1930, 10)

Williams, D. P.: Cinema Technique and the Theatre (*Nineteenth Century,* cx, 1931, 602-12)

Williamson, Alice M.: *Alice in Movieland* (N. Y., 1928)

Willink, Luc: *Film* ('s-Gravenhage, 1928)

Wilson, E.: Eisenstein in Hollywood (*New Republic,* lxviii, 1931, 320-22)

Wimberly, C. F.: *The Moving Picture* (Louisville, Ky., 1917)

Wobson, D.: Cinema as a Fine Art (*New Statesman,* xx, 1923, 629-30)

Wolf-Czapek, K. W.: *Die Kinematographie* (Berlin, 1911)

Wolfe, H.: I look at the Theatre (*Theatre Arts Monthly,* xv, 1931, 49-52)

Wood, Benjamin DeK. and Freeman, F. N.: *Motion Pictures in the Classroom* (London and N. Y., 1929)

Woolf, V.: The Movies and Reality (*New Republic,* xlvii, 1926, 308-10)

——: The Cinema (*Arts,* ix, 1926, 314-16)

Wright, William L.: *The Motion Picture Story* (Fergus Falls, Minn., 1915)

——: *Photoplay Writing* (N. Y., 1922)

Wrigley, M. J.: *The Film; its Use in Popular Education* (London, 1921)

Wyatt, E. V.: The Stage and the Screen (*Catholic World,* cxxxv, 1932, 718-20)

Wyatt, E. V.: Before the Screen in Hollywood (*Catholic World*, cxxxix, 1934, 836-41)

Wylie, P.: Writing for the Movies (*Harper's Magazine*, clxvii, 1933, 715-26)

Young, Donald R.: *Motion Pictures: A Study in Social Legislation* (Philadelphia, 1922)

Young, S.: Screen Version (*New Republic*, lxxii, 1932, 259-61)

————: A Note: Moving Picture Acting (*New Republic*, lxxii, 1932, 150-51)

Young, W. H.: *Scenario Secrets* (Raleigh, N. C., 1925)

Zaddach, Gerhart: *Der literarische Film* (Berlin, 1929)

Zak, A. I.: Кинематографъ, книга и дѣти (Вѣстникъ Европѣ, № 9, 1914, 276-94)

Zehder, Hugo, ed.: *Der Film von Morgen* (Berlin, 1923)

Zelewski A. von: *Das Urheberrecht auf dem Gebiet der Filmkunst* (Emsdetten, 1935)

Zilboorg, G.: Art and the Cinema (*Drama*, xi, 1921, 352)

Zimmereimer, Kurt: *Die Filmzensur* (Breslau, 1934)

Zimmerscheid, Karl: *Die deutsche Filmindustrie* (Stuttgart, 1922)

Zschoche, Paul: *Bewegliche Anlagen für Tonfilmvorführung* (Halle, 1934)

Zukor, A. and O'Shea, P. F.: Looking Ahead a Decade or two (*Magazine of Business*, lv, 1929, 23-26)

Zwart, Piet: *Filmreclame* (Rotterdam, 1932)

Anonymous

L'activité cinématographique en France (*La Nature*, lxii, 1934, 418)

Anni tre di vita dell'istituto nazionale L. U. C. E. (Rome, 1928)

Appraising Films for Young People (*School Review*, xxxix, 1931, 329-30)

Aus den Werkstätten des Films (Berlin, 1925)

The Birth of a New Art (*Independent*, lxxviii, 1914, 8-9)

The British National Film Institute (*School and Society,*
xxxvii, 1933, 4-5)
Camera Tricks in the Talkies (*Popular Mechanics,* lvii,
1932, 227-28)
Celluloid Aesthetics (*Nation,* cxxx, 1930, 352)
Cenni sintetici di arte cinematografica (Rome, 1933, 2nd
edn.)
Charlie Chaplin and the Talkies (*Review of Reviews,*
lxxxvi, 1932, 49-50)
The Cinema: Its Present Position and Future Possibilities
(London, 1917; report of the National Council of
Public Morals)
Il cinematografo nella scuola (Rome, 1931)
La cinématographie moderne (Paris, 1921)
Does the Camera ever lie? (*Popular Mechanics,* lxi, 1934,
234)
Dreams and Visions in Moving Pictures (*Literary Digest,*
ciii, 1929, 35)
The Earliest Motion Pictures (*Scientific Monthly,* xxix,
1929, 90-93)
Enzyklopädie der Photographie und Kinematographie
(Halle)
Etchings for the Movies: Alexeiev's Living Etching (*Living Age,* cccxlvii, 1934, 174)
An Experiment in the Appreciation of Motion-picture
Plays (*School Review,* xli, 1933, 249-50)
Het Filmboek (Amsterdam, 1931)
Film Forum and Film Society (*Theatre Arts Monthly,*
xvii, 1933, 93)
The Film in National Life (London, 1932; report by Commission on Educational and Cultural Films)
Film Photos wie noch nie (Berlin, 1929)
Die Frau im Film (Zurich, 1919)
The Future of the Motion Picture (*Arts and Decoration,*
xvi, 1921, 168-69)
Galsworthy on the Talkies (*Living Age,* cccxxxviii, 1930,
349-50)
Das grosse Bilderbuch des Films (Berlin, 1925)

H. G. Wells predicts the Film of the Future (*Literary Digest*, ci, 1929, 24-25)

The Kinema (*Living Age*, cclxxii, 1912, 565-67)

Latest Movie Magic (*Popular Mechanics*, lix, 1933, 586-88)

Die Lichtbildkunst in Schule (Stuttgart, n. d.)

Лицо советского киноактера (Moscow, 1935)

Lost Illusion (*Literary Digest*, cix, 1931, 18)

The Motion Picture (*Theatre Arts Monthly*, xiii, 1929, 635-44)

Motion Pictures. Bulletin of the Russell Sage Foundation Library (N. Y., 1922)

Movie Magic in the Making (*Popular Mechanics*, lxii, 1935, 801 and lxiii, 1)

The Moving Pictures of Tomorrow (*Outlook*, cvii, 1914, 444-45)

Music on the Films (*Etude*, liii, 1935, 682)

The Psychology of the Movies (*Literary Digest*, li, 1915, 1279-80)

Pure Cinema (*Independent*, cxviii, 1927, 311-14)

René Clair indicts the Film Industry (*Literary Digest*, cxiv, 1932, 14-15)

School Children and the Cinema (London, 1932; report of the London County Council Education Committee)

A Selected Glossary for the Motion Picture Technician (Hollywood, 1930)

Speaking Up for the Silent Films (*Literary Digest*, ci, 1929, 22-23)

Театральный и музыкальный справочник (Moscow, 1929)

Theatre and Motion Pictures (London, 1933) (Collection of articles contributed to the *Encyclopoedia Britannica*)

What Shocked the Censors! (N. Y., 1933)

What's New in the Movies (*Popular Mechanics*, lxiv, 1935, 329)

PERIODICALS

(Only a few of the many periodicals devoted to the subject of the cinema are here listed. Several of those included, either because of their "popular" appeal or because of their specialized interests, do not, in general, contribute much to the study of the film as an art; in all, however, have appeared articles of value. Included in this list are both periodicals still in progress and periodicals which have ceased publication.)

THE UNITED STATES OF AMERICA

The American Cinematographer (Hollywood)
The American Motion Picture Directory (Chicago)
The American Projectionist (N. Y.)
The Best Moving Pictures of 1922-3 (Boston)
The Billboard (Cincinnati)
Box Office (Kansas City)
Bulletin of the Academy of Motion Picture Arts and Sciences (Hollywood)
Cinelandia (Hollywood; in Spanish)
Cinema (N. Y.)
Cinema Art (N. Y.)
Cinema Digest (Hollywood)
Cinema News (N. Y.)
The Cinematograph Annual (Hollywood)
Cinematography (N. Y.)
Cine-mundial (N. Y.; in Spanish)
Cue (N. Y.)
Educational Film Magazine (N. Y.)
The Educational Screen (Chicago)
The Exhibitor (Philadelphia)
Exhibitors' Forum (Pittsburg)

Exhibitors' Herald (Chicago)
Experimental Cinema (N. Y.)
Feature Movie Magazine (Chicago)
The Film Bulletin (N. Y.)
The Film Curb (N. Y.)
The Film Daily (N. Y.)
The Film Daily Year Book (N. Y.)
The Filmgoers' Annual (N. Y.)
The Film Index (N. Y.; merged in *The Moving Picture World*)
The Film-Lovers' Annual (N. Y.)
The Film Mercury (Hollywood)
Film News (Washington)
Film Progress (N. Y.)
The Film Spectator (Hollywood)
Harrison's Reports (N. Y.)
The Hollywood Filmograph (Hollywood)
The Hollywood Herald (Hollywood)
The Hollywood Magazine (Hollywood; later merged in *South*)
The Hollywood Reporter (Hollywood)
The Hollywood Screen World (Hollywood)
The Hollywood Spectator (Hollywood)
International Film Review (Hollywood)
International Photographer (Hollywood)
The International Projectionist (N. Y.)
The Modern Screen (N. Y.)
The Motion Picture (N. Y.)
The Motion Picture Almanac (Chicago)
The Motion Picture Classic (Brooklyn, N. Y.)
The Motion Picture Daily (N. Y.)
Motion Picture Enthusiasts (Los Angeles)
The Motion Picture Herald (N. Y.)
The Motion Picture Magazine (Brooklyn, N. Y.)
The Motion Picture News (N. Y.)
The Motion Picture Projectionist (N. Y.)
Motion Picture Record (Seattle)
Motion Picture Review Digest (N. Y.)

Motography (Chicago)
The Movie Album (Minneapolis)
The Movie Classic (Chicago)
The Movie Magazine (Los Angeles)
The Movie Mirror (N. Y.)
Movie Pictorial (Chicago)
Movies (N. Y.)
The Movie Weekly (N. Y.)
The Moving Picture Age (Chicago)
The Moving Picture Annual and Yearbook (N. Y.)
The Moving Picture Herald (N. Y.)
Moving Picture Stories (N. Y.)
The Moving Picture World (Brooklyn, N. Y.)
The National Board of Review Magazine (N. Y.)
The New Movie (N. Y.)
New Theatre (N. Y.)
The Photodramatist (Los Angeles)
The Photoplay (N. Y.)
The Picture Play (N. Y.)
Reel Life (N. Y.)
The Scenario Bulletin-Review (Hollywood)
The Screen Guild's Magazine (Hollywood)
Screenland (N. Y.)
The Screen Play (Hollywood)
The Silver Screen (N. Y.)
Sound Waves (Hollywood)
South (Hollywood)
The Stage (N. Y.)
The Story World (Hollywood)
Talking Picture Magazine (N. Y.)
Variety (N. Y.)
Visual Education (Chicago)

GREAT BRITAIN

The Bioscope (London)
The British Film Journal (London)
The Cinema (London)
The Cinema Handbook (London)

The Cinema Quarterly (Edinburgh)
The Cinematograph Times (London)
Close Up (Territet, London)
The Daily Film Renter and Moving Picture News (London)
The Era (London)
Film Art (London)
The Film Weekly (London)
The Ideal Kinema (London)
The International Review of Educational Cinematography (London)
The Kinematograph Weekly (London)
The Kinematograph Year Book (London)
Manchester Guardian Film Supplement 1931
Scenario (London)
Sight and Sound (London)
The Talking Screen (London)
The Times (London) Special Film Supplement 1929
To-day's Cinema (London)
Who's Who in Filmland (London; ed. L. Reed and H. Spiers)
Who's Who on the Screen (London)

CANADA

The Canadian Moving Picture Digest (Toronto)
The Film (Montreal)

INDIA

The Cinema (Lahore)
Filmland (Calcutta)
The Photoplay (Lahore)

FRANCE

Bulletin de la Société française de photographie et de cinématographie (Paris)
Ciné-Comoedia (Paris)
Le Ciné-Journal (Paris)
Le Cinéma (Paris)
Le cinéma d'Alsace et de Lorraine (Metz)

La Cinématographe française (Paris)
Le Cinéopse (Paris)
La critique cinématographique (Paris)
La Griffe Cinématographique (Paris)
Hebdo-Film (Paris)
La revue du cinéma (Paris)
Le Tout-Cinéma (Paris)

GERMANY AND AUSTRIA

Bildwart: Blätter für Volksbildung (Berlin)
Bühne und Film (Berlin)
Die deutsche Filmzeitung (Berlin)
Erste internationale Film-Zeitung (Berlin)
Der Film (Berlin)
Der Film Almanach (Berlin)
Filmburg (Berlin)
Der Filmfreund (Munich)
Der Filmhandel (Berlin)
Film-Hölle (Berlin)
Das Filmjournal (Hamburg)
Die Filmkunst (Berlin)
Der Film-Kurier (Berlin)
Filmland (Berlin)
Das Film-Magazin (Berlin)
Der Filmspiegel (Berlin)
Die Filmtechnik (Halle)
Die Film-Tribüne (Berlin)
Die Filmwoche (Berlin)
Film und Brettl (Berlin)
Film und Lichtbild (Stuttgart)
Film und Presse (Berlin)
Der Film von Heute (Berlin)
Die Flimmerkiste (Magdeburg)
Das Jahrbuch für Photographie, Kinematographie
   (Halle)
Der Kientopp (Berlin)
Der Kinematograph (Düsseldorf)
Kinematographische Monatshefte (Berlin)

Kinobriefe (Berlin)
Das Kinojahrbuch (Berlin)
Kino-Praktikus (Düsseldorf)
Die Kino-Rundschau (Vienna)
Die Kinotechnik (Berlin)
Kinotechnisches Jahrbuch (Berlin)
Kinotechnische Umschau (Berlin)
Komödie (Vienna)
Die Kunst im Film (Berlin)
Das lebende Bild (Charlottenburg)
Die Lichtbild Bühne (Berlin)
Die Lichtspiel-Zeitung (Munich)
Die Linse (Berlin)
Maske und Palette (Dresden)
Mein Film-Buch, ed. F. Porges (Vienna)
Der neue Film (Berlin)
Das Publikum (Charlottenburg)
Das Reichsfilmblatt (Berlin)
Die Süddeutsche Filmzeitung (Munich)
Der Welt-Film (Berlin)
Die Westdeutsche Filmzeitung (Düsseldorf)

ITALY

Cinegiornale (Rome)
Cinematografia (Turin)
Cino-convegno: supplemento mensile alla rivista Il Convegno (Milan)
Il Dilettante fotografo e cinegrafista (Milan)
Guida dei cinematografi d'Italia (Turin)
Intercine (Rome; journal of the Institute of Educational Cinematography, League of Nations)
La rivista cinematografica (Turin)
La Vita cinematografica (Turin)
Scenario (Rome)

SWITZERLAND

Le cinéma suisse (Montreux)
Kinema (Zurich)
Revue suisse du cinéma (Lausanne)

BELGIUM

   Cinema (Antwerp)
   La cinématographie belge (Brussels)
   Film (Antwerp)
   Filmgoer (Brussels)
   Film-revue (Antwerp)

HOLLAND

   Cinema-Kalender ('s-Gravenhage)
   Filmliga (Rotterdam)
   Hollywood-Kalender (Gouda)
   Kinotechnisch Zakboek (Amsterdam)
   Movie-Kalender (Hague)
   Nederlandse Film—en tooneelalmanak (Amsterdam)
   De nieuwe filmwereld (Hague)

CZECHO-SLOVAKIA

   Filmowý Kurýr (Prague)
   Die Internationale Filmschau (Prague)

SPAIN

   Arte y Cinematografía (Barcelona)
   Cine (Barcelona)

PORTUGAL

   Cinéfilo (Lisbon)

MEXICO

   La Revista de cinema (Merida)

BRAZIL

   Cinearte (Rio de Janeiro)

ARGENTINE

   Cinemundial (Buenos-Aires)

CHINA

   China Cinema Year Book (Shanghai)

RUSSIA

Экран, рабочий журнал (Moscow)
Кино-газета (Moscow)
Репертуарный бюллетень по кино (Moscow)

Советская кино-фотопромышленность (Moscow)
Советский экран (Moscow)
Советское кино (Moscow)
Театральная Москва: театр-музыка-кино (Moscow)

POLAND

Kino (Warsaw)

LATVIA

Daīles magazīna (Riga)
Objektivs (Riga)

SWEDEN

Biografbladet (Stockholm)
Svenska film—och biografmann asällskapet (Stockholm)
Tidskrift för svensk skolfilm och bildningsfilm (Stockholm)

INDEX

The Arno Press Cinema Program

THE LITERATURE OF CINEMA

Series I & II

American Academy of Political and Social Science. **The Motion Picture in Its Economic and Social Aspects,** edited by Clyde L. King. **The Motion Picture Industry,** edited by Gordon S. Watkins. *The Annals,* November, 1926/1927.

Agate, James. **Around Cinemas.** 1946.

Agate, James. **Around Cinemas.** (Second Series). 1948.

Balcon, Michael, Ernest Lindgren, Forsyth Hardy and Roger Manvell. **Twenty Years of British Film, 1925-1945.** 1947.

Bardèche, Maurice and Robert Brasillach. **The History of Motion Pictures,** edited by Iris Barry. 1938.

Benoit-Levy, Jean. **The Art of the Motion Picture.** 1946.

Blumer, Herbert. **Movies and Conduct.** 1933.

Blumer, Herbert and Philip M. Hauser. **Movies, Delinquency, and Crime.** 1933.

Buckle, Gerard Fort. **The Mind and the Film.** 1926.

Carter, Huntly. **The New Spirit in the Cinema.** 1930.

Carter, Huntly. **The New Spirit in the Russian Theatre, 1917-1928.** 1929.

Carter, Huntly. **The New Theatre and Cinema of Soviet Russia.** 1924.

Charters, W. W. **Motion Pictures and Youth.** 1933.

Cinema Commission of Inquiry. **The Cinema: Its Present Position and Future Possibilities.** 1917.

Dale, Edgar. **The Content of Motion Pictures.** 1935.

Dale, Edgar. **How to Appreciate Motion Pictures.** 1937.

Dale, Edgar. **Children's Attendance at Motion Pictures.** Dysinger, Wendell S. and Christian A. Ruckmick. **The Emotional Responses of Children to the Motion Picture Situation.** 1935.

Dale, Edgar, Fannie W. Dunn, Charles F. Hoban, Jr., and Etta Schneider. **Motion Pictures in Education: A Summary of the Literature.** 1938.

Davy, Charles. **Footnotes to the Film.** 1938.

Dickinson, Thorold and Catherine De la Roche. **Soviet Cinema.** 1948.

Dickson, W. K. L., and Antonia Dickson. **History of the Kinetograph, Kinetoscope and Kinetophonograph.** 1895.

Forman, Henry James. **Our Movie Made Children.** 1935.

Freeburg, Victor Oscar. **The Art of Photoplay Making.** 1918.

Freeburg, Victor Oscar. **Pictorial Beauty on the Screen.** 1923.

Hall, Hal, editor. **Cinematographic Annual,** 2 vols. 1930/1931.

Hampton, Benjamin B. **A History of the Movies.** 1931.

Hardy, Forsyth. **Scandinavian Film.** 1952.

Hepworth, Cecil M. **Animated Photography: The A B C of the Cinematograph.** 1900.

Hoban, Charles F., Jr., and Edward B. Van Ormer. **Instructional Film Research 1918-1950.** 1950.

Holaday, Perry W. and George D. Stoddard. **Getting Ideas from the Movies.** 1933.

Hopwood, Henry V. **Living Pictures.** 1899.

Hulfish, David S. **Motion-Picture Work.** 1915.

Hunter, William. **Scrutiny of Cinema.** 1932.

Huntley, John. **British Film Music.** 1948.

Irwin, Will. **The House That Shadows Built.** 1928.

Jarratt, Vernon. **The Italian Cinema.** 1951.

Jenkins, C. Francis. **Animated Pictures.** 1898.

Lang, Edith and George West. **Musical Accompaniment of Moving Pictures.** 1920.

L'Art Cinematographique, Nos. 1-8. 1926-1931.

London, Kurt. **Film Music.** 1936.

Lutz, E [dwin] G [eorge]. **The Motion-Picture Cameraman.** 1927.

Manvell, Roger. **Experiment in the Film.** 1949.

Marey, Etienne Jules. **Movement.** 1895.

Martin, Olga J. **Hollywood's Movie Commandments.** 1937.

Mayer, J. P. **Sociology of Film: Studies and Documents.** 1946. New Introduction by J. P. Mayer.

Münsterberg, Hugo. **The Photoplay: A Psychological Study.** 1916.

Nicoll, Allardyce. **Film and Theatre.** 1936.

Noble, Peter. **The Negro in Films.** 1949.

Peters, Charles C. **Motion Pictures and Standards of Morality.** 1933.

Peterson, Ruth C. and L. L. Thurstone. **Motion Pictures and the Social Attitudes of Children.** Shuttleworth, Frank K. and Mark A. May. **The Social Conduct and Attitudes of Movie Fans.** 1933.

Phillips, Henry Albert. **The Photodrama.** 1914.

Photoplay Research Society. **Opportunities in the Motion Picture Industry.** 1922.

Rapée, Erno. **Encyclopaedia of Music for Pictures.** 1925.

Rapée, Erno. **Motion Picture Moods for Pianists and Organists.** 1924.

Renshaw, Samuel, Vernon L. Miller and Dorothy P. Marquis. **Children's Sleep.** 1933.

Rosten, Leo C. **Hollywood: The Movie Colony, The Movie Makers.** 1941.

Sadoul, Georges. **French Film.** 1953.

Screen Monographs I, 1923-1937. 1970.

Screen Monographs II, 1915-1930. 1970.

Sinclair, Upton. **Upton Sinclair Presents William Fox.** 1933.

Talbot, Frederick A. **Moving Pictures.** 1912.

Thorp, Margaret Farrand. **America at the Movies.** 1939.

Wollenberg, H. H. **Fifty Years of German Film.** 1948.

RELATED BOOKS AND PERIODICALS

Allister, Ray. **Friese-Greene: Close-Up of an Inventor.** 1948.

Art in Cinema: A Symposium of the Avant-Garde Film, edited by Frank Stauffacher. 1947.

The Art of Cinema: Selected Essays. New Foreword by George Amberg. 1971.

Balázs, Béla. **Theory of the Film.** 1952.

Barry, Iris. **Let's Go to the Movies.** 1926.

de Beauvoir, Simone. **Brigitte Bardot and the Lolita Syndrome.** 1960.

Carrick, Edward. **Art and Design in the British Film.** 1948.

Close Up. Vols. 1-10, 1927-1933 (all published).

Cogley, John. Report on Blacklisting. Part I: The Movies. 1956.

Eisenstein, S. M. Que Viva Mexico! 1951.

Experimental Cinema. 1930-1934 (all published).

Feldman, Joseph and Harry. Dynamics of the Film. 1952.

Film Daily Yearbook of Motion Pictures. Microfilm, 18 reels, 35 mm. 1918-1969.

Film Daily Yearbook of Motion Pictures. 1970.

Film Daily Yearbook of Motion Pictures. (Wid's Year Book). 3 vols., 1918-1922.

The Film Index: A Bibliography. Vol. I: The Film as Art. 1941.

Film Society Programmes. 1925-1939 (all published).

Films: A Quarterly of Discussion and Analysis. Nos. 1-4, 1939-1940 (all published).

Flaherty, Frances Hubbard. The Odyssey of a Film-Maker: Robert Flaherty's Story. 1960.

General Bibliography of Motion Pictures, edited by Carl Vincent, Riccardo Redi, and Franco Venturini. 1953.

Hendricks, Gordon. Origins of the American Film. 1961-1966. New Introduction by Gordon Hendricks.

Hound and Horn: Essays on Cinema, 1928-1934. 1971.

Huff, Theodore. Charlie Chaplin. 1951.

Kahn, Gordon. Hollywood on Trial. 1948.

New York Times Film Reviews, 1913-1968. 1970.

Noble, Peter. Hollywood Scapegoat: The Biography of Erich von Stroheim. 1950.

Robson, E. W. and M. M. The Film Answers Back. 1939.

Weinberg, Herman G., editor. Greed. 1971.

Wollenberg, H. H. Anatomy of the Film. 1947.

Wright, Basil. The Use of the Film. 1948.

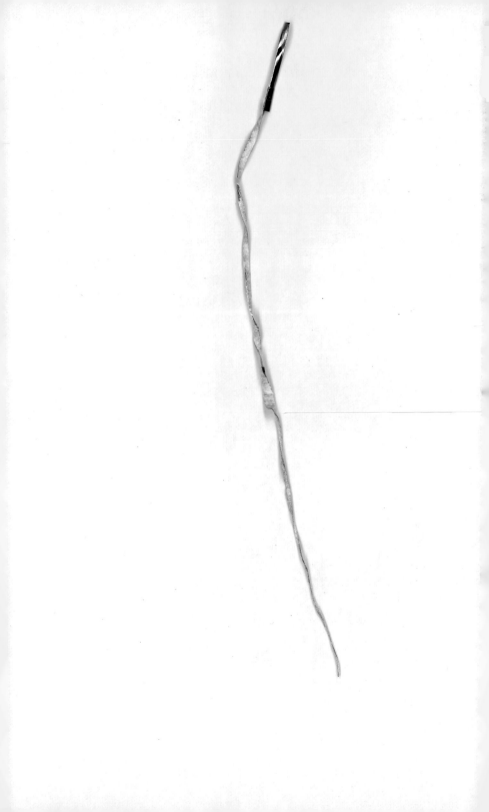